ACTION - RESEARCH AND THE NATURE OF SOCIAL INQUIRY

To the school-teachers
and other hard-pressed professional workers
whose creativity and care
within under-resourced institutions
inspires the optimism behind this study.

Action - Research and the Nature of Social Inquiry:

Professional Innovation and Educational Work

RICHARD WINTER

School of Education
Essex Institute of Higher Education

Avebury

Aldershot · Brookfield USA · Hong Kong · Singapore · Sydney

Published by

Avebury

Gower Publishing Company Limited,
Gower House, Croft Road, Aldershot,
Hants, GU11 3HR, England

Gower Publishing Company,
Old Post Road, Brookfield, Vermont 05036
USA

Winter, Richard, *1943-*
  Action-research and the nature of social
  inquiry : professional innovation and
  educational work.
  1. Social sciences——Research
  I. Title
  300'.72   H61

ISBN 0 566 05532 5

Printed and bound in Great Britain by
Biddles Limited, Guildford and King's Lynn

Contents

v

Preface

'Action-research': by now a widely used, but nevertheless a
somewhat awkward phrase. 'Action/Research': its use and
even its awkwardness serve to conjure forth that most
intractable of questions for social science: what is the
relationship between theoretical and practical knowledge?
The question concerns not only the nature of knowledge
itself, but the relationships between the various knowledge-
producing institutions, ranging from the university to the
workplace. The specific form of the question (distantly
echoing, perhaps, themes of social order or of class
antagonism) concerns <u>integration</u>: how can theory be more
closely integrated with practice (and vice-versa); how can
education be more closely integrated with work (and vice-
versa); how can research be more closely integrated with
action (and vice-versa)? Each call for integration assumes
that the separation referred to represents an impoverishment: the impoverishment of work and of research, of theory
and of practice. 'Action-research', then, is a phrase used
to invoke the desirability of closing these separations, of
enriching these impoverishments, and the following study is
an attempt to analyze the basis of such arguments.

At the centre of the study is a double argument; firstly
that the establishment of a proper basis for the practice of
action-research requires a reconsideration of long-standing
issues in the theory of social inquiry - concerning
reflexivity, rationality, validity and ideology; and
secondly that a proper resolution of these issues in the

theory of social inquiry will be found in the (reformulated) practices of action-research, since action-research addresses 'head on' social inquiry's fundamental problems - the relation between theory and practice, between the general and the particular, between common-sense and academic expertise, between mundane action and critical reflection, and hence - ultimately - between ideology and understanding.

There is, however, a further dimension to the work, namely its concern with 'professionalism', as a social role which specifically aims to bridge the theory / practice divide. 'Professionalism' points both to a form of practical work and to a form of relevant theoretical knowledge. The study therefore begins also to suggest a reformulation of the nature of the professional role, and in particular of professional workers' relationships with their clients and with their bureaucratic superiors, since these relationships also exemplify the theory-practice issue, as a problem concerning the hierarchical relation between different forms and sources of knowledge.

The professional context from which most of the examples of action-research are drawn is that of education, and this emphasis is not merely biographical: the concept of 'education' (again) is deeply involved with the resolution of the theory-practice issue. On the one hand 'education' refers always to a theoretically conceived ideal, which takes such forms as: The Good, Rationality, the Realization of Potential, Respect for Persons, or the Just Society. On the other hand, 'education' always requires some form of interpersonal effectiveness: 'education' has only taken place when 'teachers' have succeeded in helping 'learners' to develop towards some form of education's ideal. 'Education' is thus always both theoretical practice and practical theory. In this way, 'education' corresponds directly to action-research's aspiration to link the enlightenment of research with the effectiveness of action. And although some versions of social inquiry seem to say, 'Our business is merely to reveal the truth: whether others can or wish to learn from it, is not our concern', this is partly bravado: ultimately, social inquiry's aspiration is to discover truths which will 'inform' the practices of the culture in which it is situated. Deep down, social inquiry - like action-research - aspires to 'education'.

Here then is the combination of ideas at the heart of the study: the link between action-research, social inquiry, professional work, and education. Clearly, there is an ideal at work - a social and political ideal of a self-educating community, where 'work' is not so oppressive that it precludes the energy and the resources for critical analysis, and where inquiry is not a segregated and specialized prerogative. It is this ideal to which action-research aspires, based on an implicit claim that, where social affairs are concerned, hierarchies of expertise may always be questioned, since effective understanding is not the privilege of any special or 'qualified' status, but the generally and unpredictably distributed outcome of reflect- ive social experience. However, although it is clear that any society in which this contention had been fully accepted would indeed have been radically transformed, the argument is not 'idealist' - in the sense of holding up a general theoretical ideal as a future practical goal. Instead, the argument proceeds by analyzing the theoretical structure of certain current social relationships, in order to examine their possibilities, their scope for development.

Underlying all this, of course, there is also a biograph- ical basis for the study. For the past ten years I have been working with teachers on research projects relating to their professional practice, on courses ranging from informal intermittent meetings in teachers' centres to elaborately planned and theoretically prepared studies in the context of a Higher Degree course in educational research and evaluation. Even more importantly (perhaps) many of the ideas in the following study originated in my own experience of carrying out a research project, concerned with my own and my colleagues' work as teacher educators, and focussing particularly on the problems of 'teaching practice' (reported variously in Winter R, 1980a,b,c and 1982a,b). The theoretical discussions presented here started life then, as urgent practical difficulties as to 'what to do'.

Biographical contingencies not only posed the problems; they provided resources for addressing them, which it is a pleasure to acknowledge. The study arose out of the teaching practice research, and was originally undertaken as a Ph D thesis in the Sociology Department at Goldsmiths College, London University, under the rigorous guidance of Paul Filmer, Mike Phillipson, and Chris Jenks, whose sustained challenge and assistance were invaluable. I also owe a substantial and general debt to frequent discussions with Susan Hart, a support teacher with Newham Education Authority, whose grasp of educational theory and of educational practice, and of how they are (and can be) related, has been a continual source of inspiration. In a slightly different sense I am indebted to all my past and current colleagues in the world of educational action- research, whose work I may criticise, but only because their work has been so important for me, and continues to be so, I think, in the difficult struggle for the future of education, of social inquiry, and of professional autonomy. I am also extremely grateful to David Ball and Steve Decker at the Essex Institute School of Education, for their helpful suggestions and comments.

In a more general way, I am conscious of the influence of Michael Young, of the London University Institute of Education, whose original challenge to the basis of cognitive hierarchies continued to motivate and underpin this work, albeit in ways which he might well wish to disavow.

Finally, my thanks to Anne Jolly of Brentwood, Essex, who typed the manuscript ready for publication.

1 Introduction: action - research and the intelligibility of social inquiry

The interesting thing about action-research is that it
claims to reject <u>both</u> of the institutional traditions which
propose grounds for its activities: action-research rejects
the tradition of scientific research, by invoking as a
central principle the need for practical effectiveness at
the level of mundane activity; and it rejects the tradition
of mundane practice, by invoking as a central principle the
scrutiny of practical judgements by means of research.

It is highly significant therefore that action-research
has arisen in certain contexts of <u>professional</u> work, namely
social administration, management, and (in particular) in
education. 'Professional practice' in these contexts
conventionally exhibits a fundamental contradiction which
action-research seeks to address: professional expertise
representa a cognitive authority based in 'science', an
authoritative formulation of knowledge as <u>generally</u> valid,
such that clients' experiences can be conceived as
predictable specific instances of prior generalities, ie. as
'cases'. And yet the corpuses of knowledge appropriate to
these contexts where action-researchers have been active
(the 'theory of' administration, or management, or
education) are precisely not of that authoritative and
general form: the individual 'case' is acknowledged to
present a degree of 'uniqueness' which threatens the
relevance of experts' prior understanding and thus the

1

authority by which they are 'expert'. Action-research has not, therefore, arisen in such professions as engineering or agriculture, where 'science' seems to operate fairly successfully. Instead action-research seeks to re-cast the authority of the professional practitioner in 'people-processing' organisations, by means of a version of inquiry which aims to mediate between the prescriptive authority of science and the unique experience of the individual case, for which such prescription conspicuously cannot provide. The intelligibility of action-research's project depends, in other words, on the <u>problematic</u> nature of knowledge in the social sciences.

Action-research <u>questions</u> the basis of social inquiry, both by its challenges and by its claims: It <u>challenges</u> a scientific method of inquiry based on the authority of the 'outside' observer and the 'independent' experimenter, and it <u>claims</u> to reconstruct both practical expertise and theoretical insight on the different basis of its own inquiry procedures. Action-research thus plays both ends against the middle, with inevitable consequences: 'scientists' are scornful of action-research's claims to validity (action-research is dismissed as <u>muddled</u> science); and practitioners are scornful of action-research's claims to feasibility (action-research is dismissed as idealistic). The problem is that the 'middle', for which action-research wishes to speak, lacks theoretical definition, and is thus (with rare exceptions) defended by action-research only rhetorically or pragmatically. Such defences, lacking rigorous principles and theoretical grounds, are open to immediate rejection, as noted above. Thus it is in order to provide a theoretical elaboration of action-research's own mode of inquiry that this work is proposed. This will entail both a critique of the current state of writing on action-research, and the provision of theoretical resources for establishing <u>in principle</u> its intelligibility. (1)

In the remainder of this Introduction, I shall first of all introduce the parameters of the main discussion, in order to show how they constitute action-research's central issues, and how the central issues for action-research are also central issues for the general project of inquiry in the social sciences. Secondly, as a preliminary to the following chapters, I shall argue for a number of general epistemological and ontological positions, as theoretically necessary presuppositions, not only for action-research but for social inquiry in general.

TOWARDS A PROBLEMATIC FOR ACTION RESEARCH

<u>'Analytic Grounds'</u>

My argument can not begin by tracing a 'history' nor by reviewing 'the literature' of action-research, since that would be to presuppose a definition and a coherence for action-research whose absence, precisely, is the occasion for the work. Admittedly, my initial step was to consult the range of writing in which a mode of inquiry was described as 'action-research' (since I had no theoretical basis for rejecting any examples as cases where the label was either claimed or avoided 'illegitimately') but the 'legitimate' nature of action-research remains a crucial topic for the study and indeed this initial step merely raised the question as to what form of analysis could address 'legitimacy'; or in other words: how could 'action-research' be created as an object of theory?

Kant provides us with an indication of the requisite level of approach when he describes the 'transcendental exposition' of a concept as an exposition which shows the necessary assumptions for the concept to be 'possible' (Kant, 1933, p. 70). Hence his famous a priori categories of space and time as the conditions for the possibility of conceptualizing consciousness (pp. 72-8). However, Kant also draws attention to the limits (as well as the necessity and the possibility) of such transcendental knowledge: it is concerned 'not with objects but with the mode of our knowledge of objects in so far as this mode of knowledge is to be possible a priori'. (p. 59). Kant makes an important distinction between 'analytic' thought, whose 'highest principle' is that of non-contradiction (p. 189) since it is concerned with single concepts (p. 48), and 'synthetic' thought, which is concerned with the nature of the connections between concepts (p. 51), and whose highest principle is the unity necessary for the possibility of experience (p. 192).

Now, given the complexity and thus the conceptual multiplicity of lived experience - the starting point for a social science - the form of its unity must remain high problematic, and thus it is important to note that Kant's emphasis upon the provision of a priori grounds is qualified by his rejection of the 'sophistical' pretensions of prescriptive methods such as classical logic (p. 99) and by a reminder of the inevitability of the 'illusion' by which 'we take the subjective necessity of a connection in our concepts...for an objective necessity of a connection of things in themselves' (p. 299). In other words, my intention is not really to prescribe a priori grounds for identifying an object ('action-research'), but rather to provide grounds for identifying a mode of knowing such an object.

It is at this level and in this spirit, then, that I have sought to elaborate a general problematic for action-research. The work represents what certain sociologists have called (following Kant rather loosely) an 'analysis':

'Analysis is the concern not with anything said or written but with the grounds of whatever is said - the foundations that make what is said possible,

3

sensible, conceivable'. (McHugh et al., 1974, p. 2)

For action-research: what assumptions seem to underly its
claims and self-descriptions? What principles might unify
the concrete diversity of its experiences, as themselves,
in their diversity, nevertheless constituting that unity to
which the self-proclaimed label 'action-research' seems to
aspire? It is as answers to such questions that the four
main chapters of the work are presented: Chapter Two, on
action and research, articulates the central meaning of the
term itself and hence its implicit problematic, and
Chapter Three, on self-reflection, attempts to provide for
the theoretical possibility of this problematic. Chapters
Four and Five are concerned with criteria by which examples
may be judged to be adequate examples: Chapter Four
approaches this question concretely, from the starting-point
of a specific claim, and Chapter Five more generally and
comprehensively. These four chapters thus present four
constitutive themes for an analytical theory of action-
research, a set of conditions for its theoretic possibility.
The four themes are summarily introduced in the following
section.

Four Constitutive Themes

A)   Action and research

In proclaiming the intelligibility of a coupling between
'action' and 'research', action-research by its own self-
categorization challenges a conventional distinction
between one type of act ('action') whose rational properties
are necessarily taken for granted as culturally institutionalized glosses upon meaning, motive and communication; and
another type of act ('research') whose necessary claim is
that it 'brackets out' precisely such features in order to
question the nature of meaning, motive, etc. The question
therefore is: what form of unity could provide the site for
such a challenge? Does action-research propose that
research is necessarily a form of action (and thereby
question science's claim to be independent of its context)
or that action is a form of research (and thereby support
the claims of mundane social actors to create and possess
adequate understanding of their world)? If the distinction
action / research is to be transcended, what mediating
category or categories could provide grounds for such a
transcendence?

B)   Critical self-reflection

In order to realise the aspiration noted in Theme A,
action-research must reject the separate roles of an actor
who is merely the object of research and a researcher who
merely observes; instead, action-research proposes both
researchers who participate in the action under inquiry and
actors who inquire into the actions they engage in. For

such a proposal to be intelligible, it requires the
possibility of a potential theoretic competence among
social actors. This in turn requires the possibility of
formulating consciousness in terms of a specific
independence of both its cultural context and its psychic
history. Analytically, action-research's problematic may
be formulated as a search for a coherent mediation between
its necessary denial of determinism and its equally
necessary historical and cultural situatedness.

C) The improvement of professional practice

The concrete version of its unity which action-research
presents as reconciling its original disparity (see Theme A)
is that of professional practice. Professional practice is
that form of action which claims explicitly to be guided by
the discursive elaboration of theory, where actors invoke
as their auspices the findings of 'research', and thus
present a mundane rationality in the form of a scientific
expertise. In this way criteria for practice and for
knowledge can be made to coincide: the improvement of
professional practice becomes a criterion for research,
since for action-research this dichotomy is precisely what
has, supposedly, been removed. However, this 'professional'
knowledge derives its prescriptive authority over action
from the scientific auspices of positivism, which action-
research wishes to challenge: Action-research asserts the
cognitive authority of the individual case against the
authority of positivism's generalizing laws. Action-
research therefore finds itself simultaneously both
supporting and opposing the cognitive authority of
professional expertise. In order to resolve this contradiction it must seek a criterion whereby an analytically
justifiable formulation of validity may be distinguished
from the conventional authority of institutional roles and
from the conventional authority of 'science'.

D) The problem of validity

Following directly from the considerations raised in themes
A and C, it must be a condition for action-research's
intelligibility that it should address the possibility of
its own validity: by insisting on the association between
research and action, action-research claims to achieve
particularized relevance and effectiveness (ie. for
'practice'), but appears by the same token to forfeit the
possibility of generalizing any of its outcomes. In this
respect action-research reverses the familiar paradox
generated when a natural science model of inquiry is applied
to social situations: namely that the validity of a general
conclusion always lacks relevance for particular contexts -
to the extent that the 'significance' of the results of an
investigation becomes a pun between statistical and
interpretive meaning. Action-research's reverse paradox
converts the pun of positivist significance into an issue
whose analytically necessary form is: what formulation of

validity (of 'significance') could inquiry aspire to which might 'unify' the disparate notions of adequacy which inspire action (on the one hand) and science (on the other)?

Action-Research and the Nature of Inquiry in the Social Sciences

It must be clear from the above set of themes that the analytical requirements of a coherent theoretical basis for action research's problematic are of the deepest relevance for the social sciences. Each theme raises anew long-standing questions concerning the conditions under which social inquiry itself is possible as a theoretical enterprise (as opposed to its relatively clear-cut status as a sophisticated elaboration of mundane management). Thus, Theme A raises the issue of the relation between theory and practice, and Theme B poses the epistemological dilemma concerning the apparent interpretive freedom of consciousness, yet its (equally apparent) constitution within a specific biographical and cultural (ie. historical) matrix. Theme C poses the problematic relation between theoretic and institutional authority, and Theme D challenges once more the widespread acceptance of analogies between the natural and the social sciences.

In the main part of this work these four themes will be elaborated in relation to action-research. However the four themes themselves can be seen as exemplifying two further principles which are even more fundamental in providing grounds for the possibility of social inquiry in general, as well as action-research in particular, namely the epistemological and ontological principles of 1) reflexivity and 2) dialectics. Thus, it will be argued that the issues of theory and practice (Theme A) and freedom and determinism (Theme B) can only be grasped in terms of a set of dialectical relationships; and that only in terms of the reflexivity of inquiry can the issue of its theoretic as opposed to its institutional authority (Theme C) be satisfactorily addressed without recourse to spurious analogies with natural science's positivist auspices (Theme D).

These two principles (reflexivity and dialectics) will progressively unify the series of arguments concerning action-research, and it is in their terms (it will be argued) that action-research must seek to resolve its constitutive dilemmas. Both terms suggest their potential status as grounding principles for inquiry by their fundamental significance as principles for the understanding of both language and consciousness, which must indeed be presupposed as conditions for the possibility of social inquiry, if not for social life itself. Hence the remainder of this chapter will be concerned with the introduction of these two principles.

6

REFLEXIVITY, DIALECTICS, AND THE INTELLIGIBILITY OF INQUIRY

Reflexivity: Language, Theory, Self, and Other

Language is indexical: the sense of verbal expressions is
decided by a hearer (reader) in the light of his or her
elaborated understandings of the speaker's (writer's)
relevancies, the situation in which the expression is used,
and the verbal and cultural system of which the particular
expression forms an element. The 'indexicality' of
language is thus 'irremediable' except for the 'practical
purposes' of particular cases (Garfinkel, 1967, pp. 6-7).
Communication therefore is not merely the transmission of a
message. The words of a telegram may be 'transmitted'
between two pieces of electrical equipment, but its
properties as a communication of meanings are created by
the interpretive activities of the sender and the receiver
(at either end, as it were). (A single index is related to
a plurality of books in a library or to a plurality of
references in a single book in the same way as a single
signifier is related to a plurality of signifieds, ie.
concepts in the consciousnesses of the members of a
semiotic community (Saussure, 1974, p. 67). Hence the
intelligibility of language is a potentiality: language
users always have before them the task of realizing this
potential by means of their own interpretive procedures,
and a number of these practical interpretive procedures for
realizing the potential intelligibility of language have
been specified (Cicourel, 1973, pp. 52-6). What they all
share is a quality of reflexivity. (See Appendix).

   A reflexive action is one which is 'bent back' so that it
affects the doer: in doing the action to Another, I
necessarily do it to myself. This to be understood as
follows. Given the indexical quality of language, I can
only communicate by presupposing the intelligibility of my
speech for the Other, and I can only make this presupposition because I interpret its intelligibility for
myself by envisaging its intelligibility for the Other. In
other words, intelligibility resides in the presupposition
of the interchangeability of perspectives between speaker
and hearer, writer and reader. The shifting structure of
this intersubjectivity is handled by means of the
accomplishments of practical reasoning ('etc.', 'ad-hocing',
'retrospective-prospective sense creation' - see Cicourel:
loc. cit.) which remain unnoticed by members, as do many
other routinized cultural skills. Communication, then, is
always a formulation of the Self (Blum, 1971, p. 313) in
the light of the Self's mastery of the language, the
setting, and (above all) through the Self's awareness of its
own nature as the grounds for its assumptions about how this
speech or writing will be received by others, and hence what
this speech or writing should or might mean. This is why
educators and therapists think that people learn by talking
and writing: talking and writing (including this writing!)

are not descriptions of an already existing state of awareness, but a means for the self-reflective formation of
awareness.

Now these taken-for-granted reflexive competencies
required by mundane interaction may be 'uninteresting' to
lay members of a signifying community (Garfinkel, 1967,
p. 7), and indeed the repression of an awareness of such
reflexivity may well be a condition for the routine
accomplishment of social intercourse in a culture where
'knowledge' is taken to be a descriptive grasp of an
external object-world through the supposedly transparent
medium of a referential language. But for sociology to be
a 'science' it needs to theorize adequately both its objects
and its methods (see Husserl's critique of 'Naturalism' -
Husserl, 1965, pp. 80-3). (2) Thus, sociology must
formulate the relation between lay members' methods for
managing intelligibility and sociology's own methods for
managing lay members' management, and this relation must in
turn be formulated in relation to the culture, in which both
sociologist and lay members are engaged, where the
reflexivity of language and consciousness is energetically
denied by a positivist ideology of facts and labels. There
is, in other words, an inescapably sociological relationship
between sociologists and the social world they purport to
account for.

This is the sense in which reflexivity is an analytical
issue for sociology - a condition of sociology's
intelligibility as a general project, and a condition it
frequently ignores. For example, whereas Garfinkel reveals
lay members' reflexivity as a feature of their speech which
is uninteresting to them but interesting to a sociologist,
Garfinkel's own speech, like theirs, relies on reflexive
features which are tacitly used as an 'uninteresting'
resource for his revelation. For Garfinkel, the 'task' for
sociology is that members' reflexive procedures for
constructing mundane intelligibility may and should be
treated as 'data' for 'empirical research' (Garfinkel, 1967,
pp. 281-2), but Garfinkel has already argued at length that
the substitution of objective for indexical expressions
cannot be other than an 'unsatisfied programme' (p. 4)
except as a matter of practical social management in every
particular case' (p. 6), and thus his own 'data' and
'research' could be no more than yet another practical and
reflexive management of an indexical communication. In more
general terms, Garfinkel's own text glosses (in its writing)
the glosses of members which are its topic. His own text is
itself an example of 'practical social management' within
the highly interesting institutionalized speech community of
'sociology'. As Garfinkel himself says (quoted by Filmer,
1976, p. 80): sociologies are 'made to happen as events in
the same ordinary affairs that in organizing they describe'.

Filmer's article makes clear the general significance of
reflexivity as an analytical principle. Sociology's

8

conventional tradition is one in which the 'essential reflexivity' of sociology's 'authorship' of its own speech is denied by invoking instead 'the generalized and generalizable authority of science'. Whereas for 'science' the 'essential reflexivity of accounts...is uninteresting', a 'reflexive sociology' takes this essential reflexivity as its central interest. (Filmer, 1976, pp. 82-3). In other words, to be 'interested' in the reflexivity of accounts is an analytical requirement for social inquiry. To propose an 'objective' description of lay members' practices is to reproduce a process of mundane stratification, which denies the reflexive socio-linguistic processes of the social relation by which it is accomplished, in the same way as do lay members' practices themselves (see Phillipson, 1975, p. 165). The analytical requirement for sociology is to address the reflexive practices by which alone it is possible: a sociology which fails to do this is merely an instance of cultural stratification, an example within what Becker calls a 'hierarchy of credibility' (Becker, 1970, p. 126), a legitimizing agency within a functionally differentiated institutional order, such as a 'sociology of knowledge' (for example) would necessarily wish to investigate. Thus, only in taking its own essential reflexivity as its topic does sociology differentiate itself as an analytical, a theoretical enterprise, from the mundane practices which are its object.

The recognition of reflexivity is, generally, a basic mode of ordering and presenting communicative adequacy, a claim to grasp the symbolic process by which communication is accomplished. For sociology this is a central task, but in a different but analogous way it is also a substantial and widespread feature of other cultural forms which aim at a high degree of persuasiveness. Thus: novels are frequently written about writers, films about film-makers, and musicals about the staging of musicals; there are poems about language, plays which include dramatic representations and multiple disguise, and paintings of rooms hung with mirrors. In each case, the medium is turned back upon itself. At another level, jokes may be thought of as sudden reflexive turns, showing that the expectations on which mundane communication depends are indeed merely expectations, by suddenly thwarting them as expectations and revealing instead possibilities that had previously been concealed by their un-expectedness. (3)

In other words, mundane reflexivity embodies the fragility of communication: it is by addressing this very fragility, by noting explicitly the art-fulness, the art-ificiality of the signifying process whose fragility is currently in question, that fragility can be survived, and communicability reassured and achieved. As a move against the fragility of the sign, the recognition of reflexivity re-assures and disarms: by aligning the writer and the reader, the speaker and the hearer together, as it were, in complicity against the sign, it renews the very intersubjectivity on which the effectiveness of the sign depends. The recognition of reflexivity, then is a source of rhetorical power, and hence a dimension of persuasiveness, of both aesthetic and theoretical adequacy.

Now, as a requirement for sociological theorizing, this 'analytic' reflexivity has one important consequence which will be of great importance throughout the discussion of action-research: it denies the possibility that theory ('research') can achieve a final or a legislative relation to social action; rather, it presupposes a relationship between theorist and social actor which must be continuous and unending, because it is both irremediably particularized and endlessly problematic. This is because the theorist requires an Other, not as an object but, in some sense, as a 'collaborator' in that reflexive intersubjectivity where meaning itself resides.

The general point is made by McHugh et al. Their argument is that there can be no finality to speaking, since to speak is always to assume (and hence, at that moment at least, to forget) the grounds of that particular speaking. Writing can thus never be complete for the basic reason that it needs to be read:

'The papers in this book should be conceived of as displays which require alters. This is where readers come in. Readers are asked to treat our papers reflexively. They are asked to become our collaborators. That is our version of how to read'. (McHugh et al., 1974, p. 8).

This emphasis on the central theoretical importance of the creativity of the reader is found in the work of Barthes, as is the corollary that such a notion of creative reading must involve abjuring or abolishing the unchallengeable authority of the author as a source for meaning. (Barthes, 1977). Similarly Alan Blum (1974, p. 252) emphasizes that 'Speaking is controlled by its Rational relationship to hearing'.

Hence what McHugh et al. refer to as 'the exemplary character' of their work (McHugh et al. 1974, p. 12). The theorizer formulates an example not to provide an exhaustive description (impossible) nor to attempt a complete description which is regrettably doomed to incompleteness because of inadequate methods or funds (positivism): rather, the example stands as a provisional accomplishment and an invitation to the reader to continue theorizing. (What sort of an example is this? What would be a further or a contrasted example? How was it chosen?) Examples only exist as such insofar as they are elaborately embedded in the reflexive act of their presentation, and thus are only to be understood by an act of constructive responsiveness:

'Speech, except by example, would have to be perfect speech... Example is to say the speech is imperfect

because it does not speak its own auspices, but usable
because it allows alter (the reader) to formulate its
auspices'. (p.10)

Hence, speech can only proceed on the assumption that there
is Another, whose rational being can only be postulated by
analogy with, in reference to, the self-concept of the
speaker. Whilst the irremediable indexicality of speech
ensures that no speech can claim the finality of correctness
(as in 'logic' or 'science'), this is not a regrettable,
defeated lapse into solipsism; rather, the reflexivity of
speech, by anchoring the reality of the Other in the reality
of the Self, through the processes inherent in acts of
communication, allows (indeed requires) us to regard the
Other and the communicative process as equally real along
with the Self. (See McHugh, et al., 1974, final paragraph).
In other words, the reflexivity of language entails a
dialectical ontology of consciousness, a dialectic between
Self, Other, and Symbol, to which the argument now turns.

Dialectics: Self, Other, Language, Being, Time

The general project of theorizing proposes a relationship
between self and world such that the development of understanding is possible; the first question, then, is: what
conceptions of consciousness are compatible with knowledge
as a reflexive and developmental project? It follows from
the considerations in the previous section that we cannot
formulate a merely receptive subjectivity which simply
registers the existence of an external object, since this
would return us to a version of language as a system of
descriptive labels for their external referents. Sartre,
for example, rejects this simple dichotomization of
consciousness and its objects as an 'abstraction' (Sartre,
1969, p. 3) on the simple phenomenological grounds that 'all
consciousness is consciousness of something' (p. xxxvi).

   In this he follows Hegel, and Hegel's elaboration of the
point begins to display the sense of a dialectical (rather
than a dichotomous) relation between Subject and Object,
within which a knowledge-constitutive process may be
formulated. Hegel observes:

   'Consciousness knows SOMETHING; this object is the
   essence of the IN-ITSELF; but it is for consciousness
   the in-itself. This is where the ambiguity of this
   truth enters. We see that consciousness now has two
   objects: one is the first IN-ITSELF, the second is
   the being for consciousness of this in-itself ... The
   first object, is being known, is altered for
   consciousness'. (Hegel, 1977, p. 55).

This self-consciousness of the act of perception leads each
perceived quality to be surrounded by the awareness of its
potential variants, and hence to have a necessary dimension
of incipient self-transcendence, a sort of spontaneous

11

disunity. From this starting point (pp. 58-64) Hegel traces
an ontology of 'The Thing' as a 'manifold' of contradictions, experienced in almost instantaneous succession as
a single essence and a plurality of qualities, as universal
and specific, as self-defined and as defined-in-relation-to-
another' (pp. 67-71), in short as 'a whirling circle'
(p. 79).

Further dialectical complexities follow. Firstly, since
the consciousness which perceives the thing cannot
distinguish between the thing, consciousness itself, and the
act of perception, the constitution of the thing in
consciousness becomes an act of self- definition: the
complexity of the thing (the manifold of contradictions) is
reflected back into the structure of consciousness itself.
(Hegel, 1977, pp. 73-5). Secondly, this complex structure
of the process of experience can never be directly grasped
by language, since language can only utter the general: our
unique and fleeting experience of, for example, 'this tree
here' or 'that house now' is swept away in our uttering of
'tree' (referring to any tree), 'here' (referring to any
place), and 'this' (a reference from anywhere), and so on.
As Hegel says: 'It is just not possible for us ever to say,
or express in words, a sensuous being that we MEAN' (p. 60).

With a similar purpose, Heidegger criticizes the
equivocation which secretly undermines the pretension to
unity and integration of classical logic. Logic, he says,
is based on the distinction between subject and predicate,
so that rules concerning the compatibility of the two can be
devised, as a way of evaluating propositions (eg. the rule
of no self-contradiction - Heidegger, 1968, p. 155). But
since propositions contain these two elements - subject and
predicate - the main emphasis can be on one or the other, so
that meaning has an ambiguity, which cannot be
accommodated in a hierarchically unified rule system, and
thus, of necessity, 'Logic becomes dialectic' (p. 156).

The rejection of classical logic is a refrain throughout
Heidegger's book What is Called Thinking? and indeed, the
second series of lectures in that volume may be seen as an
elaborate struggle against the structures of conventional
syntax in order to rescue the freedom and creativity of
thought, ('Thinking') from the stultifying restrictions of
routinized linguistic usage: 'Every dialogue becomes
halting and fruitless if it confines itself obdurately to
nothing but what is directly said'. (Heidegger, 1968,
p. 178). In other words, Heidegger's argument is that
understanding cannot be accomplished simply by using
language itself as a set of tools, to be carefully honed and
skilfully manipulated as a descriptive ordering of reality
(p. 153).

Thus, since language cannot simply 'label' experience,
perception is never a uni-directional process but always
'a reciprocal interplay' (Hegel, 1977, p. 84) in which

successive stages of awareness 'are themselves self-
superceding aspects' (p. 81). It is interesting that Lenin
founds his notion of a dialectical cognition in a theory of
language which he explicitly derives from Hegel:

> 'Dialectics is general as a method since, as Hegel
> noted, every proposition itself contains the
> notion of the contradiction of the relation between
> universal and individual'. (Lenin, 1972, p. 361).

This 'contradiction' would, for Lenin, exemplify a 'unity
of opposites' which is 'the condition for the knowledge of
all processes in the world in their self-movement, in their
spontaneous development' (p. 360). In this way, we may
formulate a _dialectical_ knowledge-generating process, in
which Subject and Object, individual and universal, are
inseparably bound up in a process of reciprocity and self-
transcendence which constitutes the mode of being of human
consciousness itself. However, 'self transcendence' is a
rather elusive way of formulating this _active_ principle of
cognition. How might it be elucidated?

   The most famous version is Descartes', which may be
summarized as: 'I doubt the world; therefore I think;
therefore I (doubtless) exist'. Sartre explains in more
detail. When consciousness registers the _presence_ of an
object, the _acceptance_ of an idea, it is caught up by, and
causally determined by 'the positivity of Being' (Sartre,
1969, p. 23). This is consciousness without consciousness
of itself _as_ consciousness, and as such it is incomplete or
at least untypical (cf. the state of being 'lost in' contem-
plation). For Sartre, consciousness is always conscious of
itself as _not_ identical with its object, which he terms
consciousness's 'negative' aspect. For example: 'to believe
is to know that one believes, and to know that one believes
is no longer to believe'. (p. 69). Or, concerning objects:
'absence appears necessarily as a pre-condition of presence,'
(p. xxxvi), ie. objects are present to consciousness not as
ineluctable causes of their appearance, but as contingently
present, always potentially absent. The intelligibility of
the experience of being is thus _founded_ upon a sense of the
discontinuity between consciousness and its objects; otherwise, for example, 'my present state would be (determined as
- RW) a prolongation of my prior state' (p. 28) and thus
identity would lose its temporal dimension, which is a pre-
condition of the experience of identity (see Kant, 1933,
p. 79). Similarly, for the asking of a question to be
intelligible, the questioner must 'have the permanent
possibility of dissociating himself from the causal series
which constitutes being' (as unquestionable - RW) (Sartre,
1969, p. 23). And because of this 'impalpable fissure'
(p. 77) which constitutes the experience of self in relation
to world as one of possibility (it happens to seem thus now,
but it could, has been, and will be different) consciousness
cannot help but exist as a _questioning_ state: 'The being of
consciousness is a being such that in its being, its being
is in question' (p. 74). And this takes us back to

Descartes, with 'doubt' now established not as a technique or a choice, but as the very condition of being, as constitutive of consciousness itself. It also enables us to ground ontologically the competences whereby the reflexive procedures which render experience intelligible may be submitted to analytical questioning by the theoretic subject.

This last point suggests the structural parallel whereby 'reflexivity and 'dialectics' analytically require each other at the levels of both epistemology and ontology: the intelligibility of theorizing entails theorizing (reflexively) in collaboration with others (McHugh's point) and the intelligibility of Being entails Being-with-Others. Thus, Heidegger says: 'The world is always the one that I share with Others' (Heidegger, 1962, p. 155). And: 'Dasein's being is Being-with, its understanding of Being already implies the understanding of Others' (p. 161). Hegel's general argument also clearly links the two themes: it is through the dialectic between Self and Other that consciousness can develop towards 'self-consciousness', ie. the comprehension of its own reflexive nature. Hegel phrases it as follows: 'Self-consciousness...is the native realm of truth'. (Hegel, 1977, p. 104). It 'exists in and for itself when and by the fact that it so exists for another'. (p. 111). This is because 'being-for-itself' can only attain certainty of itself (ie. 'its truth') by 'confronting' itself, and this is only possible when, between two self-conscious beings, 'each is for the other what the other is for it' (p. 113). The true nature of one's own being is thus only achieved by confronting another (as the representative of oneself) in a 'struggle' whose prize is simultaneously freedom and truth (p. 114).

Although Hegel goes on to speak of the winners and losers of this ontological struggle in terms of 'the history of Spirit', it is clear that at another level he is formulating what might be called an 'interactive' dialectics of ('truthful') understanding, which he embodies in a sequence of 'ideal types' of increasing complexity:

a) the 'bondsman' conceives himself as an object; (pp. 117-8);

b) the 'lord' conceives the other as an object; (p. 118);

c) the 'stoic' achieves a fragile freedom through withdrawal from the other - unity at the cost of isolation (p. 122);

d) The 'Sceptic' transcends isolation at the cost of internal contradiction, <u>oscillating</u> between conceiving himself as free and as contingent: he experiences the dialectic of Self and Other as a struggle, but does not recognise its structure (pp. 123-6);

e) the 'unhappy consciousness', which suffers the sense of

its own contradictory and yet unified (ie., in the strictest sense, 'dialectical') structure. (pp. 126-32).

Without following through Hegel's evocation of the progressive history of 'Spirit', one can note the analytic value of a dialectic which thus concretely portrays the self-transcendental development of self-consciousness, and which progressively reveals the conditions of its own possibility to be its own dialectical structure. Following on from previous arguments, it is notable that Hegel's dialectic moves progressively from 'stratifying' forms of consciousness towards increasingly reflexive forms.

There is one further theme which is essential in a discussion of a dialectical formulation of consciousness and theorizing: that of their temporal dimension, within which both theorizing and consciousness must be situated for either to be intelligible, and which in particular seems to be implicit in action-research's coupling of research and action. If action is linked with research, then it must be more than an instantaneous - and thus a-temporal - response; and if research is linked with action, then it must be more than an instantaneous - and thus a-temporal - observation. Or, in other words: only if 'meaning' must always be negotiated within the temporality of experience before it is imputed, can the possibility of 'other meanings' conceivably be explored within a (temporal) process of inquiry.

Although Kant himself posits Time as a constituent category of experience, Heidegger is concerned to rescue understanding from the abstract instant of Kantian 'intuition' (Heidegger, 1962, p. 410), and to rescue truth from 'the superficial theory of propositions and judgements' (p. 401) by locating both understanding and truth within the temporality of Being:

> 'Only in terms of the temporality of discourse - that is of Dasein in general - can we clarify how "signification" "arises", and make the possibility of concept-formation ontologically intelligible'. (p. 401).

Time, here, is not the chronological sequence of discrete 'perceptions' by which a determinist model of cause and effect is erected, but the temporal dimension within which the Self is grounded in a structure of potential 'authenticity', ie. of 'Care' (p. 370) with respect to its past and its future (p. 390). This Care-ful sense of responsibility towards truthful understanding is differentiated from 'everyday interpretation' (p. 358) and from mere 'curiosity'. The latter, says Heidegger, seeks the future only in order to make it into the present (p. 397), and (by seeking to make discoveries which are both 'new' and final) aspires to convert the temporality of future possibilities into a time-less present of unchanging certainties. In contrast, Heideggerian 'Care' may be seen

as that overarching principle under whose aegis the process
of inquiry proceeds when it addresses the grounds of its
speech in the necessarily temporal structures of experience,
symbolization, and understanding, and thereby provides
grounds for its implicit commitment to an unending dialectic
of developmental and reflexive understanding.

COMMENTARY: GROUNDS, TEXTS, POSSIBILITIES, AND RESOURCES

In this Introduction I have tried to provide grounds for
this writing. It is important to stress that these
'grounds' are not intended as an origin, a set of principles
prescribing the remainder of the work as necessary. Rather
(since this is being written after the main text) it
attempts to show the possibility of the work, in the light
of the inevitable question: having written this, what made
it possible? More elaborately: what notions of
subjectivity, object-world, and language are consistent
with the activity by which the subjectivity currently
wielding this retractable pencil is assembling this text
now? Hence, a brief comment on 'texts' seems required.

Since my text seems to display a Subject re-viewing a
range of cultural resources (the published texts of McHugh,
Hegel, Lenin, and Kant, for example) in order to assemble
its own speech relating to a current concern (action-
research), it would be Quixotic (Another resource!) to
propose this text except as a resource whereby its readers
can review their concerns: texts do not prescribe meanings
for readers; they set meanings in 'play':

> 'Writing (does not) designate an operation of
> recording, notation, representation, 'depiction' ...
> (it) traces a field ... which, at least, has no
> other origin than language itself, language which
> ceaselessly calls into question all origins'.
> (Barthes, 1977, pp. 145-6)

Reflexivity predicates the intelligibility of writing upon
the reality of the reader, upon the inevitable question of
language's origin in the Other. In this sense, the
theoretic text can be seen in the light of Wolfgang Iser's
comment on the act of reading a literary text: 'Textual
repertoires and strategies simply offer a frame within
which the reader must construct for himself the aesthetic
object' (Iser, 1978, p. 107). The 'theoretical object'
also is constructed by writers and readers through the
repertoires and strategies of language, as organized
provisionally in a 'text'.

In that a text is predicated upon the reality of a reader,
as the necessary presumption of the intelligibility of the
act of writing, a text is essentially constituted not as a
legislative declaration, but as a horizon of possibilities.

It is this set of possibilities which is given by the 'play'
of the text: a ball 'in play' is open to the unpredictable,
skilful, improvisatory contingencies of the game-process
and its idiosyncratic players; only 'out of play' does it
become subject to a single prescriptive rule. 'Play', here,
is therefore used in the sense of creative exploration (cf.
theories of child development - see Jenks, C., 1982, p. 22).
'Play' is a metaphor for the creation of meaning, and thus
a metaphor for metaphoricity itself, that metaphoricity of
language which maintains the interpretive open-ness of
texts, and thus makes possible the creation of this text.
In contrast, a non-playful text, in which, say, a
prescriptive logic claims to organize correctly a system of
propositions, in which langage is supposed not to play but
to work within a framework of tautologically valid
definitions and objectively accurate references; such a
legislative text must propose to annihilate the legislations
of its predecessors and thus fears its readers as potential
executioners. Since it proposes its own finality, its own
existence as a text becomes an anomaly, a hopeful exception
to the very rule whereby it supercedes its predecessors.

But the 'possibilities' referred to above are presented
here only as preliminaries, as providing an intelligibility
for theorizing as a project: 'possibilities' do not remain
'an open horizon'; they are culturally located as a set of
limits and resources. As Alan Blum says (1971, pp. 301-2):
'Theorizing ... constitutes a particular method for treating
and reconstructing one's biography as a practically
conceived corpus of knowledge'. Or, as John O'Neill quotes
from Merleau-Ponty: 'Expression is always an act of self-
improvisation in which we borrow from the world, from
others, and from our own past efforts' (O'Neill, 1972,
p. 95). Now, my resources and thus my limits for theorizing
are inevitably i) my membership of a societal community and
of a number of epistemic 'sub-communities' - professional,
academic, political, domestic, etc., and ii) my conception
of theorizing itself as my most complete and most fully
grounded and articulated response to i). For me to theorize
must involve me in seeking to integrate, transform, and
transcend my actual resources, and similarly for others.
Hence, in a sense, knowledge and cultural tradition are
biographically contingent and thus mutually 'limiting'.

However, this is merely to say that self and cultural
tradition define each other: the self as a creative and
changing 'improvisation' constitutes and is constituted by
culture, as membership in a plurality of possibilities.
Hence, theoretical resources and limits may be conceived
without exclusivity or legislation, and not merely in an
academic dimension: in that theorizing is above all an
engagement with the reflexive processes of language and its
relation to truth and experience, its resources are not just
those of 'sociology' and 'philosophy'; rather, its
resources are potentially as wide as the social world which
is so overwhelmingly constituted by linguistic practices.

The linguistic practices of the social world include not
only the 'mundanely reflexive' talk whereby members
accomplish practical interaction (Garfinkel's topic), but
also the playful, creative practices of joking, word-games,
crosswords, satire, and parody - practices which implicitly
but with varying degrees of elaboration begin to take
mundane intelligibility as their topic. More elaborately,
the social world includes widespread aesthetic practices,
such as song, theatre, and narrative fiction (in print,
in films and on radio and TV), where again the mundane world
is re-framed, re-structured, and thus - in varying degrees -
made available for re-formulation. Hence, just as
'possibilities' do not mean that <u>any</u> formulation is
possible, 'limits' do not mean that cultural tradition
<u>imposes</u> itself as a final closure, since culture and
tradition have their own constitutive and playful open-ness.

   This relationship between possibilities and limits applies
to the ensuing work in two ways. Firstly, it evokes the
sense in which the present text consults (and yet is
constituted in) a series of resources for the conducting of
its argument: its process is not the construction of an
authoritative corpus which might then be evoked as a
legislation, since this would be to deny the essentially
interpretive status of the meanings these textual resources
must have for my argument. Resources are consulted to set
meanings 'in play', as the only rigorous and self-consistent
sense for a reflexive and dialectical theorizing.
Secondly, and consequently, the following attempts to
provide theoretic grounds for action-research do not seek a
site outside the culture in which action-research operates
from which to impose upon action-research a legislative
framework. Rather, each chapter begins with the set of
possibilities and limits which action-research itself
invokes, and proceeds to assemble and explore the further
resources which action-research's self-proclaimed
aspirations seem to require. This introduction has sought
to delineate the analytic limits within which such resources
may be conceived to be on the one hand required and on the
other hand available.

NOTES

(1) Even Carr and Kemmis (1986) (the most elaborate
     published account action-research) significantly
     approach the provision of a 'theoretical rationale'
     (p.1) for action-research in educational contexts
     through a lengthy analysis of what is distinctively
     <u>educational</u> about educational research, and through a
     discussion of positivism, phenomenology, and critical
     theory in the recent history of social science. Their
     account of action-research per se takes for granted the
     processes of language, consciousness, and theorizing
     which are the starting point for this study.

(2)   Otherwise, as Rutherford is supposed to have put it:
        'There is only Physics - everything else is stamp-
        collecting'.

(3)   The aesthetic power of music is often attributed to
        the way in which its 'abstract' signifiers allow
        evocative reference to a realm of signifieds which is
        universal because it is completely individualized -
        the 'emotions' of Everyman. But perhaps the lack of a
        specific referent for the musical sign allows scope
        not so much for universal evocation but for unimpeded
        self-reference. Music is in this sense always 'about'
        itself. Development sections in sonata form,
        variations on a theme, fugues, key modulations, shifts
        in orchestration (often, in Haydn, for example, quite
        consciously <u>jokes</u>): these all represent explicit
        demonstrations of the transformative power, the
        effectful <u>work</u> of the musical art itself. And perhaps
        it is this expressiveness of its own reflexivity which
        makes the musical text such a powerful and inexhaust-
        ibly repeatable utterance.

2 Action - research, action and research

'ACTION-RESEARCH'

The fundamental problematic of 'action-research' is the
attempt to question what is taken to be a conventional
differentiation between 'action' and 'research'. Thus: 'A
realistic view of both action and research reduces the
difference between them' (Halsey, 1972, p. 178). Alfred
Clarke makes the point in slightly different terms:
'Action-research ... follows Popper's idea ... that all
social administration should be conducted as experimentation' (Clarke A, 1976, p. 1) and thereby 'combine discovery
and implementation in one process' (p. 2). By formulating
discovery ('research') and implementation ('action') as one
process rather than as two distinct processes, Clarke
argues, action-research will be able to ensure that the
'findings' of research will be 'applied' to action, and
thereby also ensure that the research efforts of 'social
science' will be able to claim relevance (p. 2). Thus
'action-research' poses for social science the challenge of
relevance. Jon Nixon, for example, begins:

> 'What is educational research? Disputation on
> irrelevant issues in impossibly esoteric journals ...?'

before going on to formulate 'action-research' as 'research
... initiated, conducted and disseminated from the inside'
(Nixon, 1981a, p. 5) - ie. from a vantage point where
'relevance' could seem to be unquestionable.

20

Clarke's version of action-research's question takes the
form of a paradoxical juxtaposition: 'social administration' evokes a form of life in which bureaucratic procedures
require a specific emphasis on the predictability of rule-
guided actions, where knowledge of general rules is invoked
(deductively) as the authority for particular actions;
'experimentation', in contrast, conventionally suggests an
attempt to derive the authority for general rules
(inductively) from the knowledge of particular actions - ie.
action-guided rules. Action-research asserts the unity
underlying this distinction in order to assert the ambiguity
underlying such a simple polarization, an ambiguity which
must be faced at the level of epistemology, in theorizing
the cognitive practices which relate the rules of knowledge
and action. Hence Clark's rejection of the dichotomy
between discovery and implementation: action-research
desires an epistemology which will in principle transcend
the terminology of journeys of discovery (where 'truth' is
'somewhere else') and of implements (which exist in themselves and may or may not be utilized) - cf. Heidegger's
various arguments against language as a 'tool' (Heidegger,
1971). The nature of this proposed epistemology, the
nature of the principles which underly the invocation of the
'one process', is the theme of this work.

But in spite of its bold speaking for a problematic unity
against established separations, action-research also
recognizes its fragility: as Halsey observes: 'Bringing
together what is normally conceived as separate has caused
the confusion over the nature of action-research' (Halsey,
1972, p. 178), a confusion created in part by the attempt to
integrate procedures and professional roles with different
traditions, methods, styles, and interests (p. 165). The
challenge of action-research is thus not only epistemological but political. In institutional terms also action-
research wishes to recover unity, the unity which a
'division of labour' in the production of knowledge has
fragmented and thereby lost. Action-research speaks for the
possibility of a set of social relations in which 'Theory'
and 'Practice' are no longer institutionally segregated in a
dichotomy which fractures the coherence and rationality of
social inquiry and creates 'the problem of relevance'.
Hence it is central to Clark's assertion that in order for
action-research to avoid the problem of 'relevance' the
researcher must act 'in collaboration' with the subjects of
the research, so that his problems are also their problems.
In this way, he claims, the experimental 'additions' to the
situation do not need 'partialling out or controlling'
(p. 1). In other words, a consensual politics of inquiry
is proposed as a resolution of a methodological dilemma.

This theme of a collaborative relationship underlies many
formulations of action-research's ideal. For example, Cory
(1953) observes:

    '(Action-research is) a cooperative activity:

21

interested parties to the action proposed need to be
collaborators ...' (p.18).

Similarly, Eric Midwinter (1972) explains:

'So we had to join in dialogue with the schools ...
By these means we endeavoured to relate real and
ideal, or, to put it another way, theory and
practice'. (p. 56).

And Brown, Henry et al. (1982):

'Action-research is distinguished by its adherence
to a collaborative ethic'. (p. 4).

In putting forward this 'collaborative' principle, action-
research explicitly adopts from Habermas a problematic of
consensus formation as a basis for truth (see chapter three)
and thereby opposes what Brian Fay (1975) describes as the
'control' problematic of positivist social science. The
quotation from Clarke (above) uses 'control' in a methodological context, but Fay himself makes clear that he sees
the political sense of 'control' as a significant metaphor,
even a systematic isomorphism between a conception of
inquiry and a conception of political order (Fay, 1975,
p. 58). A similar line of argument is implicit when action-
research denies the claims to cognitive privilege made by
institutionalized 'science', ranging from Midwinter's
characterization of 'univeristy research' as 'wishing to
stop life in order to measure static, that is, unreal
situations' (Midwinter, 1972, p. 50) to Jon Nixon's
presentation of his book <u>A Teachers' Guide to Action-
Research</u> as 'a radical alternative to the paternalism of
traditional research' (Nixon 1981a, p. 9).

In order to provide a theoretical basis for action-
research, therefore, the nature of the relation between
research and action must also be analyzed as a social
relation: how can the theoretical <u>authority</u> of a research
stance be distinguished (in its relation to action) from the
institutionalized <u>power</u> of research initiatives, in terms of
political, economic, and ideological influences? What forms
of interpersonal collaboration could possibly address 'the
division of labour' between action and research as a
<u>problem</u>? And there is a further question: Nixon's 'radical
alternative' is exemplified largely by cases where
practitioners' research efforts take the form of <u>self</u>-
evaluation; and so we must ask: what version of
subjectivity could enable research and action to be carried
out as a dialectic of self-transcendence by one person?

Underlying all these questions is one question: how could
'action' and 'research' possibly be separate, and,
conversely, how could they possibly NOT be separate? In
asking the question, one is not seeking to arbitrate between
two potential <u>answers</u> ('action and research ARE separate'

versus 'action and research ARE NOT separate'): rather the
asking is an attempt to recover the complexities implicit in
the possibility of the question itself. (See Heidegger,
1968, p. 159).

To note action and research as a difference is to note
that action proceeds on a basis which must always fall short
of a theoretically conceivable certainty. The knowledge
which guides action can always provisionally be deemed to be
sufficient for that course of action at that time, but it
can also always be deemed insufficient, in the light of a
notion of 'greater understanding', which not-action-but-
research could possibly create. The separation of action
and research is thus one articulation of a faith in the
possibility of change: action is conceived as meshed (however loosely) into a social system, whereas research is the
process whereby the self-perpetuating processes of that
system might be interrupted. However, although the
possibility of change is grounded in the distinction between
action and research, it requires equally an intimate and
principled linkage between the two, in order that the
'findings' of research can be translatable back into the
world of action: indeed the intelligibility of the metaphor
of translation requires both difference and similarity. In
this way action-research's original question is revealed as
an insight into a complexity: a conception of the rational
development of the social world (and of the possibility of
inquiry into the nature of that rationality) suggests that
action and research must be both distinct and mutually
required. This mutual relationship between the two, as
elements in a dialectical progression, is what is glimpsed
in the action-research literature, but what is not
recognized is the theoretical necessity of a reflexive
conception of research's relation to action, so that their
relationship may be theorized in ways which (as action-
research also urges) preserves the authenticity of both, ie.
which preserves research's capacity for achieving a critical
distance from action AND preserves action's intelligibility,
as a creative, rather than a causally determined response to
interpretive meaning. (1)

Action-research thus renews a long-standing debate in
sociology concerning the proper relationship between the
'common-sense rationality' of mundane social action, and the
'scientific rationality' of social investigation; and it
renews its question in the light of a commitment to the
possibility of rational procedures both for valid critique
and for justifiable change.

ACTION AND RESEARCH - THE EVALUATIVE RELATION

One of action-research's central formulations of the unity
and intelligibility of its project is that research can be
the evaluation of action: 'Action-research is ... the study
of a social situation with a view to improving the quality

23

of action within it' (John Elliott: 1981, p. 1). In this
respect, action-research is not different from other
attempts by sociologists to formulate the link between
research and action, for example Wilkins (1967, p. 109):
'Social action ... should be evaluated and this means
research'. Thus a central question becomes: from which
site might research be carried out from which it could
claim to judge the 'quality' of action? Many action-
research theorists have been content to follow sociologists
such as Wilkins and to answer: the objectivity of
scientific method. Thus Alfred Clarke (1976) begins: 'At
the centre of action-research lies the traditional
scientific paradigm of experimental manipulation and observation of effects', (p. 1). For this to be possible it must
be assumed that the researcher is able to be both present to
the action (in order to manipulate a phenomenon which really
is the action under investigation) and absent from the
action (in order to observe the action without affecting
it). (The importance of the complexity underlying this
proposal is brought in Phillipson: 'Sociological Practice
and Language', 1981).

This complexity is focussed by Clarke when he goes on to
suggest that action-researchers and their subjects should
'collaborate' in the formulation of 'problems' (op. cit.,
p. 1). In this way, for Clarke and others, research's
distance from action does not take the form of a different
set of questions, and thus action-research appears to
abandon one plausible way of formulating the site from which
evaluation could be carried out; namely, that research has
its own specific interests - a formula which underpins much
writing on social science. Norman Denzin for example
defines 'the research act' as 'those endeavours of the
sociologist that take him or her from theory to the
empirical world and back again' and he elaborates: 'I
assume that the only justification for an empirical observation is the refinements, development, or refocussing of
social theory' (Denzin, 1978, p. ix). In contrast, the
'action-research act' would wish to be an endeavour leading
from the empirical world to theory and back again: 'The
research needed for social practice can best be characterized as research for social management or social engineering. It is a type of action-research, a comparative
research on the conditions and effects of various forms of
social action, and research leading to social action'.
(Lewin, 1946, p. 35).

If, then, for action-research, research shares with action
a cognitive interest in managing or constructing that same
social world which is the arena of action, could it be that
research's independence from that world rests in its methods
of understanding, and if so, in what respect? Cory (1953)
suggests that 'the most important characteristic that
differentiates action-research from more casual inquiry is
that evidence is systematically sought, recorded, and
interpreted' (p. 26). But if action research is 'systematic',

in what sense could action be thought of as based on 'casual' evidence? Not, surely, that action is careless about its outcomes or its grounds. On the contrary, as Garfinkel's work has shown (Garfinkel, 1967) action is always most care-ful to construct its rational basis. Garfinkel's theme is precisely that social actors seek, record, and interpret evidence in ways which are elaborated, flexible, and interrelated. In what sense could these procedures be identified as not 'systematic'? Could it perhaps be suggested that action is systematic in its improvisation of methods in a <u>particular</u> case, whereas perhaps research (for Cory: action-research) wishes to specify the system of relations between evidence and action separately from and in advance of any particular case?

But the impossibility of achieving this uncontexted version of 'being systematic' has been argued at length by Cicourel (1964). For example:

> 'The logic of everyday activities in which the social object under study is embedded must be related to the logic of the observer's theory (but) the transformations which relate one system to another and the language which describes each system taken separately and both systems taken together will never be perfect. There can be general congruence but not perfect correspondence'. (p. 186).

In other words, language's attempts to be 'systematic' would become enmeshed in the inextricable embeddedness of its processes in the reflexive interpretive procedures by which alone it 'means': even the modest sufficiency of 'a general congruence' would have to be decided upon in each situation as 'sufficiently congruent' for this here-and-now purpose. The theoretical impossibility of ever 'being systematic' in an absolute sense only serves therefore to raise yet more sharply the question: why might research wish to <u>claim</u> such a possibility? And thus one returns to the basic concern of research to subject action to a form of judgement which, research claims, action itself avoids.

We have already seen that Lewin characterizes the aim of action-research as 'social management': later in that paper he says that the evaluation of action programmes will occur as a result of 'fact finding' (Lewin, 1946, p. 58) Elsewhere he states: 'the aims of action research are to bring about certain changes under sufficiently controlled conditions in order to understand the laws which govern the nature of the phenomenon under study' (quoted in Foster, 1971, p. 3). In other words, the <u>method</u> of 'controlling' variables will achieve the <u>aim</u> of creating the 'factual' basis on which the effectiveness or otherwise of 'social management' may be evaluated. In this way Lewin takes over, for action-research, the evaluative site of natural science: research can treat actions as <u>behaviour</u>, as phenomena which

are governed by laws-of-nature, and these may be managed by
being understood. The unacknowledged complexity of Lewin's
version of the research / action relation is that which is
noted by Brian Fay: the metaphor of 'control' evokes a
critical stance towards the evidential basis of social
action but an acquiescent stance towards the purposes of
social action. Analytically the problem is that Lewin does
not address the ambiguous mingling of presence and absence,
critique and acquiescence in the relationship between action
and research as he himself formulates it. So we must ask:
whose aims? which changes? and consequently: what will
count as 'sufficient' control or as adequate understanding?
And we must ask: how does research take action's purpose of
social management as an unquestioned resource rather than as
a topic for critical inquiry? We can only answer: by
failing to notice the reflexive relationship between its own
activities and those same social purposes. Further: on
what basis may research treat the actions of members as
observable behaviour ('facts'), while not addressing the
apparent consequence that (in order to be consistent)
research's own activities would need to be treated in the
same way - as behavioural data obeying as yet undiscovered
laws? On this basis research's own claim to have good
grounds for distinguishing itself from other actions would
seem to be annihilated by the very form of the claim.

In this way, Lewin's version of the research / action
relation seems to embrace an ambiguity without analyzing its
terms, and in this respect his analysis seems, if anything,
weaker than the conventional 'applied social science' that
action-research wishes to oppose. Wilkins (op. cit.) for
example addresses in more detail both the unity and the
difference of purpose which relate action and research. On
the one hand, the unity of purpose which enables collaboration:

> 'Those who wish to evaluate social action and
> test the effectiveness of social agencies want to
> do so for the very same reasons as those who plan
> the work of such agencies ... wish to do the
> action part. The work of social rehabilitation,
> reconstruction, preservation, and preventive action
> is a joint enterprise for action and research'
> (pp. 9-10).

On the other hand, the difference which requires collaboration: the world of social action is in principle conserv-
ative, muddled, and defensively obscure (pp. 26-7) so that
'scientific method' can operate as a 'court of appeal'
(p. 27), using 'measurement' as its tool (p. 10), enabling
knowledge to be tested, ignorance to be admitted, and
'meaningful' questions to be asked (p. 27). Wilkins has two
striking metaphors for the principled difference between
action and research. The first is concrete: research is a
'raiding operation' upon the world of action ('enemy
territory') (pp. 108 ff.), which adds a dramatic dimension

to Brian Fay's image of science as control, and casts an ironic light on the 'joint enterprise' in which both raiders and raided are said to be engaged. The second is highly abstract: research and action, like ends and means, science and ethics, are related as 'possibly orthogonal dimensions' (p. 25), suggesting a principle of unlimited independent variation between them. Nevertheless:

> 'the scientist should be integrated into the
> system (ie. of action, of social administration - R.W.).
> Both social research and social action are concerned,
> for essentially the same reasons, with the same
> objectives ... If we believe in democracy, then we
> should not seek to apply autocratic of dictatorship
> methods in the sub-world of social action, social
> policy, or social research' (p. 34).

Here we can see once more the political metaphor underlying the epistemology: the liberal 'separation of powers' in opposition to the 'monolithic' social unity of dictatorship: only through its independence ('orthogonality'), even to the point of a principled hostility to its environment ('raid-ing'), can research act as an incorruptible court of appeal for action, and thereby guarantee not (as Brian Fay would have us believe) an effectively controlled society, but a democratically open, progressive society, based on the possibility of effective evaluation, ie. the asking of 'meaningful' questions in order to subject action's prag-matic assumptions to research's objective testing.

We may agree with Wilkins in wishing to establish the possibility that research should have a site from which to subject action to critique, and criteria for rationality which are distinguishable from those of action; and that on such a possibility (amongst other things) depends the democratic conduct of social affairs. What must be placed at issue, however, is whether Wilkins, and other sociolog-ists invoking the quantifying rigour of 'scientific method' have formulated adequately the basis for such a site and such criteria. The following objections start from Wilkins's own formulations, but implicitly refer to the general stance, of which, in this respect he may be taken to be representative.

First, in constructing 'science' as a source of prescript-ive social authority, Wilkins does not explain why science itself might not become yet another social institution characterized by the defensive conservatism which - he says - is typical of other institutions. (2) Secondly, Wilkins constructs the authority of science as a prescription precisely by ignoring the ambiguities implicit in the metaphorical basis of his formulation, metaphors whose inevitable ambiguity renders problematic the very authority Wilkins claims they assert. How can the difference between action and research, science and ethics, be presented in terms of the geometric construction of a perpendicular

('orthogonal')? Only by prior assumption of mathematics as
a realm of simple essences which may be invoked to order the
complexities of the social world. This is the myth of
geometry, the aspiration of man towards a divine abstraction, the aspiration of knowledge to move from Garfinkel's
obscure jury-room to Plato's sunlit hillside; a poetic
image which enacts the actual complexity, the hubristic
risk, of analysis, while describing its apparent simplicity
as a manageable technical accomplishment. (The nature of
such contradictions as the underlying structure of myth is
of course Levi-Strauss's theme - See Chapter Four). Again:
Wilkins elaborates the imagery of wartime operations against
an enemy in order to evoke the contribution of research to
a consensually agreed project of 'social rehabilitation,
reconstruction', etc: the metaphor both affirms and denies
the taken-for-grantedness of the social values at stake - it
affirms the necessity for prior commitment, but denies that
the shared commitment is shared: the researcher is both
enemy and partner. Wilkins affirms science's independence
and clarity of analysis while exemplifying the dependence of
his own analysis of that clarity on complex ambiguities
which he treats as not requiring analysis.

Third, in the same way as he treats language as merely
'conceptual' by denying its metaphoricity, he asserts the
possibility of treating measurement as mere quantification,
by denying its indexicality - its reliance on those interpretive judgements by which phenomena are chosen to be
counted - or not, as the case may be. Again, this ignores
Cicourel's well-known critique of measurement's claims to
mechanical replicability, claims which Wilkins rehearses
fully, by means of a 'philosophy of measurement' derived
from a model of language as the transmission of messages
between coders and decoders (pp. 183-4). Again we have a
highly evocative metaphor, which imposes the intelligibility
of quantification upon language, as the myth of science's
authoritative method, a metaphor which would need to be
explicated through an analysis of the relation in language
between acts of numerical awareness and acts of metaphorical
generalization.

Such versions of the possibility of research as the
authoritative evaluation of action thus rest on a number of
crucial simplifications and impositions concerning the
research / action relationship, which result in a
prescriptiveness of method and a restrictiveness of truth
criteria which action-research wishes precisely to avoid:

> 'Action-research is nothing if not eclectic.
> This eclecticism may prove to be a stumbling
> block to the reader who has too narrow a view
> of educational research. A conscious effort
> should be made to bracket any preconceived
> ideas concerning the correctness or otherwise of
> a particular research model. What matters is
> the extent to which the model is appropriate;

appropriate to the skills of the teacher, the constraints of the classroom, and the nature of the problem to be explored'. (Nixon, 1981a, p. 7).

However, mere eclecticism opens up a whole range of crucial issues concerning criteria for validity (see Chapter Five), and is thus no remedy for the inadequacy of Lewin's attempt to preserve the framework of a positivist epistemology while minimizing the distinction between research and action on which such an epistemology depends. And we have also seen that, for example, Wilkins's more coherently positivist account of research's claim to possess evaluative authority over action fails to address analytically the basis of that claim. My argument therefore turns to consider in detail those exponents of action-research who have attempted to free action-research from its involvement with positivist versions of the evaluative relation between research and action.

ACTION-RESEARCH: BEYOND EVALUATION?

Both Halsey and Midwinter claim that positivist forms of evaluation necessitate the subjection of the creativity of action to research's authoritative constraint. Midwinter says, 'University research wishes to stop life in order to measure static ... situations' (Midwinter, 1972, p. 50). Halsey suggests that researchers' desire for 'clear variables' tends to influence the naturally 'exploratory' tendencies of administrators, and results in greater 'conservatism' in the design of investigative strategies (Halsey, 1972, pp. 173, 177). Halsey implicitly agrees with Midwinter's claim that the notion of studying static situations is 'unreal' (Midwinter, 1972, p. 50) when he recognizes that research itself will have an impact on the action it researches (p. 175-6). More explicitly and elaborately, G. Smith (1975) admits that his action-research project had actually begun with a model of 'discrete and self-contained ... programmes of action' (p. 191), evaluated by researchers whose authority was guaranteed by their invisibility (p. 194), but that this hope had foundered in the 'turbulence' (p. 193) of social arenas characterized by conflicting social interests (p. 195), in which action programmes had no clear boundaries and were thus always vulnerable to invasion by the 'sudden effects' of massive social forces (p. 193), and where evaluation could thus be neither final nor non-controversial. As an action-researcher Smith thus accuses positivist evaluation of being 'unrealistic' in its characterization of the social world and therefore inevitably ineffective: 'the conventional weapons of research are cumbersome; heavy field-pieces dragged slowly into position - hardly suitable for the swift-moving, rapidly changing targets of an action programme' (p. 194).

Hence, rather than attempting to capture the swift-moving

target of action in order to subject it to controlled experimentation, action-research proposes to observe action's complex movements in its habitat: it will be through the analysis of the occurrence of change that action will be understood. Thus, whereas Smith sees the absence of boundaries to action as a problem for action-research, Halsey claims, optimistically, that action-research can resolve the longstanding disputes concerning holistic OR piecemeal approaches to reform by 'adopting an open-minded approach to scale' (Halsey, 1972, pp. 4-5), and can thereby treat conventional institutional boundaries (such as that which separates the school from its community) as a starting point for innovative action whose ramifications will be both a topic and a resource for research. Using a metaphor from economic theory, he explains: 'Unlike the planning model, (action-research) seeks to use the social context of the project to increase its own effects ... The function of the research here will be largely a search for likely 'multiplier' effects and an attempt to identify the outcomes that occur' (p. 167). It is significant that here again the theoretic basis for social research is grounded in a metaphor (the 'multiplier effect') which evokes authority - the cognitive authority of a conceptually bounded system of assumptions concerning the motives of 'economic man', a system in which variables are derived (almost literally) from a 'model' and given a mathematical value so that its outcomes can be calculated from its presuppositions. Halsey thus implies above all the ambiguity of action-research's ostensible willingness to follow action down the ramifications of a process of open-ended change: his metaphor suggests an action context whose parameters are defined in advance and which is therefore in principle predictable, even though his intention is to evoke the un-predictability resulting from the number of variables at work.

This ambiguity is indeed required by Halsey, since he also notes that the action project is from the outset conceived in 'theoretical terms' (p. 172), which would suggest that research leads rather than follows action, although his list of 'theoretical terms' ('disadvantage', 'power', 'context-bound operations') in fact raises once more the question as to whether such terms arise from action, from research, or from both, and thus reveals that the nature of the research / action relationship still remains unaddressed.

Halsey's 'multiplier' is a modification of a broadly experimental approach to action-research (see Halsey, 1972, pp. 165-7); it does not address the problem of how to conceive of research's procedures when action is varying in accordance with other criteria than those of research's requirement, ie. when the principle for research is no longer a positivist epistemology relating to evaluation by experiment. The characteristic response of action-research exponents to this challenge is to assert that action-research cannot determine its methods in advance, since it cannot know which direction action will take: thus Cory

says: 'the very nature of action-research makes it highly
improbable that the investigator or investigators will know
definitely and in advance the exact pattern of the inquiry
that will develop' (p. 13) and Elliott (1981) invokes a
procedure of cyclical 'shift' of the project as the
successive phases of action are evaluated. Midwinter
describes the process as follows:

>'Action-research for us differed from research
>alone chiefly in its avoidance of the static,
>controlled, and contrived model and its emphasis
>on a fluent, on-going approach, one not afraid
>to attempt properly guarded assessments in
>unpropitious circumstances. Action-research
>differed from action alone mainly in the constant
>feeding back of evaluation and the effect this had
>on crucial shifts of direction in the action'.
>(Midwinter, 1972, p. 52).

This account immediately suggests a problem. If research is
'assessing' action while action is still 'on-going', this is
indeed 'unpropitious': it will not be clear what criteria
might be appropriate, since in principle there are neither
origins nor outcomes to be compared, and, unlike 'social
science research' (which has its own 'theoretical problems'-
see Denzin, quoted above) we have not yet found action-
research making explicit any criteria of its own (beyond
attempting to borrow the notion of 'fact finding'). How
therefore could action-research know that the evaluation it
was 'feeding back' to action was any different from action's
own evaluations (of its effectiveness and appropriateness)
which are action's perennial taken-for-granted resources?
How, then, can we attempt to provide an epistemology for the
process in which action and research are united by being
modified through their reciprocal relation?

Lawrence Stenhouse (often cited as an authority in this
respect by other writers) argues for 'a particular kind of
professionalism ... research-based teaching' (Stenhouse,
1975, p. 14) whereby research and action are both the
province of the practitioner, ensuring the relevance of
research to action and the improvement of action by means of
research. The theoretical framework invoked to support his
wish to abandon 'the separation of developer and evaluator
... in favour of integrated curriculum research' (p. 121) is
Popper's model of scientific rationality. Against the
positivist argument that the evaluator needs to be 'independent', Stenhouse proposes:

>'a more scientific procedure which builds action
>and criticism into an integrated whole. The dialectic
>between proposition and critique which is personified
>in the relation between artist and critic (3) is
>integrated in the scientific method. Conjectures and
>refutations (Popper, 1963) are woven into one logic'.
>(Stenhouse, 1975, p. 124).

Hence the need for what Stenhouse calls 'a Popperian view
of policy' which means 'treating current policies as only
tentatively established, always open to change, admittedly
imperfect, and thus necessarily in an important sense
"experimental"' (p. 125). Stenhouse is not alone in
invoking Popper as a theoretic authority: Clarke (1976,
p. 1) says: 'Action-research ... follows Popper's idea
(Open Society and its Enemies) ... that all social
administration should be conducted as experimentation'.

However, the recurrence of the term 'experiment' must
alert us to the weaknesses in the claim that Popper's work
could be the basis for a non-positivist version of science
as dialectic and critique. Popper does indeed assert the
primacy of 'critical discussion' in defining the nature of
'science' (Popper, 1963, p. 127); he opposes the positivist
claim that knowledge can be 'positively' established (p. 29)
and aligns himself instead with the Presocratic philosophers' stance that knowledge cannot arise from observation and
must remain irremediably uncertain (p. 153). And yet, as
Habermas observes (Habermas, 1974, p. 201), Popper suggests
that conjectures are 'refuted' by being shown to be 'in
contradiction with facts' (Popper 1963, p. 327) and thus
knowledge appears after all to be not conjectural but
positive. Consider also the implications of Popper's statement, 'Only the falsity of a theory can be inferred from
empirical evidence, and this inference is a purely deductive
one' (p. 55): this would leave Popper (and action-research)
with a weak model indeed of critique, since validity would
remain unaddressed, and falsity could not be shown either,
since refutation would depend upon 'deductive' inferences
which, as suggested by Cicourel's arguments (see above),
must themselves depend on interpretive judgements which are,
once more, in Popper's terms 'conjectures'. Hence, by not
addressing the reflexivity by which alone the imputation of
meaning is accomplished, Popper cannot prevent his
'dialectic' lapsing into a circle: 'refutations' become
indistinguishable from the conjectures for which they are
supposed to legislate. Furthermore, while placing all his
analytical emphasis on the 'testing' phase of his cyclical
process of scientific method, Popper is content to formulate
the nature of conjectures in whimsical, non-rational terms
such as 'jumping to conclusions' (p. 53) or 'trial and
error' (p. 323), in total contrast to the deductive rigour
of 'refutation'. Action-research's hope that Popper could
provide a unified logic for inquiry is thus misplaced:
Popper either returns action-research to the dualist terms
of a planning/evaluation cycle, or he provides no basis for
the authoritative, 'experimental' form of evaluation which
Stenhouse and Clarke are seeking.

The key to Stenhouse's misplaced hope lies in his use of
the term 'dialectic' to characterize the unified logic of
action-research. Dialectic does indeed provide a mode of
theorizing both unity and complexity, change without
randomness, but this is precisely what Popper's epistemology

lacks. For Popper, contradiction is a symptom (indeed the
symptom) of error; for dialectics it is a condition of
understanding: 'The condition for the knowledge of all
processes of the world in their 'self-movement', in their
spontaneous development, in their real life, is the
knowledge of them as a unity of opposites' (Lenin: 'On the
question of Dialectics', 1972, p. 360). Although Stenhouse
recommended the study of Mao Tse Tung's works for their
illumination of action-research (personal communication) and
although Midwinter deemed Lenin to be 'perhaps the master
action-research officer of all time' (Midwinter, 1972,
p. 57), action-research has invoked the rhetoric of
dialectics' complex unity, but has - on the whole - not
sought to base its activities on an epistemology actually
derived from dialectics. (4)

However, the reason why Popper dismisses dialectics and
uses contradiction as a simple procedure for diagnosing
error returns us finally to the problem of evaluation and
the relationship between the rationalities of action and
those of research.

ACTION AND RESEARCH: TOWARDS A REFLEXIVE DIALECTIC

For Popper the notion of contradiction is not a complexity
in phenomena but a rule for the construction of valid
propositions according to a canon of logic (Popper, 1963,
p. 320). Contradiction offends against the rule of
scientific method, and it is the subjection of social life
to the rule of science which is the defence against tyranny
(p. 52). In other words, the technical method of science
(social phenomena converted to empirical propositions and
testable within a deductive system of logic) can be, indeed
must be, politically, the evaluative criterion for social
action. But Garfinkel observes ('The Rational Properties of
Scientific and Common Sense Activities' - in Garfinkel,
1967) that for science to treat its own rationalities as
direct criteria for the evaluation of social action is to
prevent an understanding of the complex rationality which
action itself actually displays, and also to prevent an
understanding of the specificity of science's own procedures
and assumptions; instead such arguments merely generate
'ironic comparisons' between the ideal of science and the
'distortions' and 'inefficiency' of action processes, which
are presumed to be understandable as defective realizations
of that same ideal (Garfinkel, 1967, p. 280).

For action-research operating with a problematic of
'evaluation' this is a crucial problem. As we have already
noted in this chapter, action-research wishes to install
practitioners as researchers; it wishes to install the
improvement of professional practice as a possible ideal for
research, and scientific experimentation as a possible ideal
for institutionalized action. Action-research thus would
seem wholly undermined by Garfinkel's suggestion that the
attempt to subject action to evaluation by science's ideal

will lead to an irremediable irony. Nevertheless I wish to argue that Garfinkel's argument does not disable action-research's project but rather - at last - clarifies it. The 'scientism' criticized by Garfinkel denies the authenticity of action by treating it as a deficient version of research, and thereby legitimates the hierarchical authority of research over action which action-research would wish specifically to oppose. But without a clear assertion of the difference between research and action, which Garfinkel enunciates, action-research cannot prevent research and action defining each other in an ironic circle: action will be judged by the canons of 'experiment' and will thus always be judged 'unrigorous'; and research will be judged by the canons of 'improving practice' and will thus always be judged as 'impractical'. If action-research continues to unite action and research under one rule (the rule of 'science') while dismantling the institutional and strategic separation between action and research which alone gives authority to the rule of science (the rule of experimental methodology), then action-research will merely be the disablement of both research and action: action may become absorbed into research (whereby action-research becomes merely 'applied research' of dubious 'validity') or research may become absorbed into action (whereby action-research becomes merely a portentous rhetoric for management's planning procedures or the common-sense thoughtfulness of practitioners' decision-making). In contrast it would be by following Garfinkel (in asserting clearly the difference between research and action) that action-research could then formulate the collaboration of action and research in the terms of that unified and constructive dialectic which action-research seeks, could abandon the model of the relation between research and action given by the scientific model of evaluation inherited from conventional social science, and could begin, finally, to formulate action-research's own ideal.

We may start this task by noting Garfinkel's list of the 'rationalities' (Garfinkel, 1967, p. 263) which guide the actions of 'daily life'.

1) Categorizing and Comparing - the successful and frequent practice of and concern for seeing matters as 'an instance of a type';

2) Tolerable Error - close attention to the varying degrees of precision required between observations and types of account, the attention which sometimes provides for a 'literary allusion' and sometimes for 'a mathematical model' as appropriate;

3) Search for Means - the ability or inclination to review past actions in order to transfer successful procedures to current actions;

4) Analysis of Alternatives and Consequences - care and attention paid to 'rehearsing in imagination'

the alternatives which different possible actions might produce;

5) **Strategy** - the awareness that a number of alternative circumstances are hypothetically possible and that actions must be prepared 'in case of' these hypothetical variations;

6) **Concern for Timing** - a definite sense of the restricted possibilities for the scheduling of future events;

7) **Predictability** - concern to restrict the unpredictability of events;

8) **Rules of Precedure** - recognition that rules should be followed 'without respect for persons' rather than in order to 'respect ... certain interpersonal solidarities';

9) **Choice** - recognition that choices are actually possible;

10) **Grounds of Choice** - are rational to the extent that they:

    a)   involve inferences from a scientific corpus of knowledge;

    b)   involve references from empirical laws;

    c)   involve the strategies of 5) above;

    d)   involve constructing an account of a past action in order to render it coherent or publicly acceptable.

(In this summary of Garfinkel, 1967, pp. 263-7, I have made clear the element in Garfinkel's own account which stresses that 'rationality' is a **normative judgement** (see, in particular the rather anomalous statement at 10a) even though later (p. 270) Garfinkel is concerned to distinguish between rationality as 'a stable property' and as 'a sanctionable ideal'.) Garfinkel then goes on to give an account of 'the scientific rationalities' (pp. 267-8) as a further set of norms which govern the practices of 'science' but specifically do **not** govern the practices of 'daily life'.

11) Compatibility of ends-means relationships with principles of formal logic;

12) Semantic clarity and distinctness - as a criterion for practical judgements;

13) Clarity and distinctness 'for its own sake' (as well as for the purpose which 'clarity' is intended to serve);

14) Compatibility of the definition of a situation with scientific knowledge.

The first point about these two lists to which I wish to draw attention is that 'daily life' (or 'action' in the terms of the present discussion) possesses its own elaborate series (1 - 10) of <u>norms</u> for rationality, norms which are always, for action <u>itself</u> 'sanctionable ideals', such that whether or not they are 'stable properties' will be a matter of interest to actors themselves, as well as to 'scientists'. Garfinkel has here provided a resource for the formulation of action's own grounds.

Secondly, even though Garfinkel's argument stresses the <u>separation</u> of the two lists, such that the norms for daily life may <u>not</u> be assimilated to those of science, there is nevertheless an intimate relation between them as follows: each of the norms for scientific rationality (11 - 14) is constructed by taking one or more of the norms for the rationality of daily life and converting it into a topic. ie. by subjecting it to a further elaboration according to science's own norm. For example, Strategy (norm 5) and Search for Means (norm 3) would be scrutinized under the aegis of 'formal logic' (norm 11); Tolerable Error in the management of the appropriate precision of accounts (norm 2) becomes subject to an abstract notion of 'semantic clarity' (norm 12), and so on. This relation between the two lists appears at first sight to recreate (in spite of Garfinkel's declared purpose to the contrary) the subjection of common-sense to the rules of an algorithmic version of rationality (unmotivated clarity, formal logic, a corpus of findings, etc., pp. 267-8). But this is to forget that Garfinkel is here listing <u>norms</u>: the thrust of Garfinkel's work is that norms are <u>related</u> to specific instances by means of procedures for the construction of intelligibility ('the interchangeability of standpoints', 'ad hoc', 'etc.', etc.) which again common-sense takes as an available resource but 'science' must treat as its topic. And <u>this</u> is where science must cease to be the authoritative <u>revelation</u> of 'the truth' about common-sense. For in the same moment it <u>topicalizes</u> the interpretive procedures by which common-sense invokes its norms of rationality, science <u>utilizes</u> those same interpretive procedures, in order to <u>invoke its</u> own norms of rationality and thus to accomplish that topicalization; science itself is charged by its own insights with addressing its own irremediable reliance (in its own activity AS science) upon the interpretive procedures it makes explicit as features of common-sense intelligibility. (It is Garfinkel's failure to follow through this argument that Filmer notes in his article on Garfinkel) (Filmer, 1976, - see Chapter One).

At the end of his paper, Garfinkel poses two helpful and radical questions concerning the relation between action and theory (even though his tacit desire to exclude science from the rule of reflexivity which otherwise governs the

practices of communication leads him to characterize the
questions as 'empirical'):

> 'Why are the rationalities of scientific theorizing
> disruptive of the continuities of action governed
> by the attitude of daily life? What is there about
> social arrangements that makes it impossible to
> transform the two 'attitudes' into each other·
> without severe disruption of the continuous activity
> governed by each'? (Garfinkel, 1967, p. 282)

Research, we can answer Garfinkel in analytical terms,
<u>disrupts</u> action's taken-for-granted reflexivity; and action
<u>disrupts</u> research's endless seeking for the grounds of that
reflexivity. Action-research's ideal and its challenge are
that it seeks (and needs) to formulate the nature of the
mutual 'disruption' of research and action, so that this
'disruptive' relation can be creatively transformative of
both action AND research, as conventionally conceived.

How could this relation be formulated? We can make a
preliminary statement as follows. The possibility of action
being managed depends on its taking for granted the
interpretive basis on which, without remedy, its
intelligibility depends. In other words, mundane action is
<u>always</u> (at one level) reflexive, but only tacitly so:
mundane action (for its practical purposes) ignores, takes
for granted, its (reflexive) basis, and to this extent may
be termed '<u>unreflexive</u>'. Hence, 'research' is always
possible - as providing an <u>explicitly</u> reflexive account of
action's basis - a showing of the conditions of its being
produced as intelligible. <u>But</u> research must then address
its own possibility - its own production as intelligible
action. Action and research thus <u>confront</u> one another, but
never finally. Whereas positivist evaluation suggests that
action CAN in principle become experimental (only to lament
action's continual failure to be sufficiently rigorous in
this respect, leading to the clashes of principle and
personnel described by Halsey, Midwinter, and others),
research as reflexive analysis does not suggest that action
can <u>become</u> analytically reflexive, but that the moment of
analytical reflexivity can clarify action's ultimately and
necessarily '<u>unreflexive</u>' process and research's intimate
but ultimately and necessarily non-directive involvement
with the understanding of that process. Research as
analytical reflexivity cannot <u>prescribe</u> analytical
reflexivity for action, since it knows that its own attempts
at showing how action ignores its reflexive basis must
themselves finally lapse into taking their own reflexivity
for granted. The analysis of reflexivity and taken-for-
granted '<u>non-reflexivity</u>' are moments in the dialectic of
analysis, a form of analysis which allows action and
research to be moments in the dialectic of investigation.

But how might one specify the content of such a dialectic,
so that it would be a 'clarification' and a creative

transformation, as well as disruption? One approach would
be to formulate action-research as a 'questioning dialectic'.
This would be to see Garfinkel's work in terms of the ideas
of Sartre and Hegel concerning the dialectics of consciousness and the 'negativity' of thought and language, as noted
in Chapter One. For example:

> 'The being of consciousness is a being such that
> in its being, its being is in question'. (Sartre,
> 1969, p. 74)

And it would link such arguments with Heidegger's
'disruption' of literal syntax and propositional meaning in
What Is Called Thinking?':

> 'To understand a thinker is to take up his quest
> and pursue to it the core of his thought's
> problematic ... a way of questioning in which
> the problematic alone is accepted as the unique
> habitat and locus of thinking'. (Heidegger, 1968,
> p. 185)

However, for action-research (and following Garfinkel)
both actors and researchers are thinkers. So the argument
is as follows. Research questions action: research's
concern is the irremediably question-able basis of action's
intelligibility; research will never cease questioning
action, for its rule is the question which is always begged
by action. But action also questions research: action
questions the possibility, the intelligibility, and the need
for questioning; for action's rule is: for all practical
purposes, this (here and now) MUST go un-questioned. And
since research knows it must question reflexively, it will
indeed support the questioning of the question: action will
thus find in research both an ally and an interrogator.

This is the fundamental significance of Garfinkel's list
of the rational norms of 'daily life' and of the
'interpretive procedures' by which they are applied. They
constitute action's own ideal, being both theoretical and
always located in a particular action context. 'Reflexive
research' is not a reminder to action that action's
rationalities must be seen in the light of science's other
rationalities; it does not question (for example) action's
pragmatic assembly of strategies by asking (for example) how
far they 'measured up' to the canons of 'formal logic'.
Rather, 'research' would disrupt the assembling and operating of strategies by posing the question: what are the
reflexive judgements by which these strategies (and not
others) are being assembled and operated as intelligible and
normative decisions? 'Questioning', here, is calling upon
actors to recover their grounds for action - the
'sanctionable ideals' for the rationality of actions and the
interpretive judgements whereby those ideals are invoked.
Thus, although the ideal of research would indeed be theory-
not-action, this would not be the 'external' ideal of

scientific-theory-in-the-light-of-which-action-seems-to-be-non-rational, which Garfinkel rejects and which provokes the critical stance of action-research writers towards 'academic' research. Instead, the moment of research would be the moment when action is summoned to recall its own ideal, ie. when action's essential reflexivity is made explicit, as a delicate set of judgemental procedures which constitute an 'acceptable' and situationally located relation between subjectivity, consciousness of the Other, and symbolized meaning. Research is the theoretical moment when action reviews its resources for meaning construction, and thereby recollects its unending question-ability, and in doing so recognizes that surrounding action's here-and-now choices are an array of possibilities, which so far have <u>all</u> been glossed but <u>some</u> of which could, now, be formulated as indeed possibilities.

This presents us with research's moment as the theoretic formulation of action's possibilities:

'Theorizing consists of the methods for producing a possible society. A possible society is the theorist's methods for re-forming his knowledge of society. Since the theorist is engaged in re-forming <u>his knowledge</u> of society, he can be seen as re-forming his knowledge. One who is re-forming his knowledge is re-forming his self: theorizing is then best described ... as a self-transforming operation, where what one operates upon is one's knowledge of the society as part of one's history, biography, and form of life'. (Blum, 1971, p. 313).

But for the present argument, theorizing is formulated as a moment in a dialectic between theory <u>and action</u>: Blum's weakness is that he formulates possibilities without formulating their analytically necessary <u>limits</u>. The cultural context for theorizing is not merely an initiating <u>occasion</u> for theorizing, but an ever-present set of practical influences and symbolic resources, which will always stand in an interesting sociological relationship with theorizing's attempts to re-formulate those influences and to re-order those resources. Hence, although Blum's notion of 're-forming' suggests how 'research' questions action, we now need to consider the <u>other</u> moment in the dialectic, which Blum ignores: how action can question research.

Firstly, it must be stressed that the notion of a dialectic between action and research is not intended in principle to characterize a relationship between personnel (as described by Halsey) but the necessary process of social inquiry. Hence we are not making an 'optimistic' assumption about the 'open-mindedness' of individuals when we emphasize that the moment of research, as outlined above, <u>anticipates</u> its counter-moment. Rather: this is analytically required, since the posing for action of the question of reflexive grounds may not, without a disabling self-contradiction, forget that, in turn, reflexive grounds will also have to be given for the posing of the question, as itself an interesting action. This is why theory here is no longer prescriptive: analytically reflexive theory is in principle formulated as that form of thinking which makes explicit its own transience and limit, as a moment (only) in a trajectory between two points at which reflexivity must be taken for granted and meaning glossed as 'sufficient'. In providing for its own always unfinished status, theory provides for the recurrence of the moment of action, since theory itself once more becomes question-able concerning the point at which theory chooses to finish, and in that choice has to rely once more on the pragmatic rationalities which theory shares with action.

For example, when action has been challenged by theory to ground a set of here-and-now strategies and meanings in a set of possibilities, and thus to re-formulate the knowledge on which the initial strategies and meanings were selected, action thereby acquires resources for conducting a practical review of the decisions on which the strategies and meanings were based. Such a review, in the light of reformulated knowledge, may lead to amendment, but this again will be a practical, here-and-now decision - though of course both 'here' and 'now' are changed. Such practical decisions could not conceivably be a direct carrying out of theory's injunction (as an 'implementation'), nor is it condemned to be an ignoring of theory's request (as though it were 'irrelevant'). Rather, action's response to the moment of theory will be its own (practical) counter-question: which of these possibilities is a here-and-now-feasibility? Which of these reflexively elaborated rationalities and intersubjectively constituted meanings must once more be glossed and treated as 'adequate-for-the-purpose-at-hand). Action, after all, must 'go on'. But, of course, as soon as it does so, theory's reflexive questioning (now concerning 'amended' strategies and meanings) will once more become possible and necessary.

This, then, would be the form which inquiry would take as a questioning dialectic between action and research. It is a dialectic in a strict sense. Both terms ('action' and 'research') are enabled to interact by their own internal contradictions and inherent instability (see the quotation from Lenin above). The complexity of the process is embodied in the image of the dialectical 'moment': in physics there is a moment of counteracting forces which constitutes for a given structure its temporary equilibrium, and the analytic necessity that this equilibrium is temporary and thus will change is given by the inevitability with which each 'moment-in-time' will be succeeded by the next. Thus, on the one hand action is formulated as, of course, pragmatic, but also as constituted by its own elaborate set of normative rational ideals and interpretive procedures, and thus as anticipating its own researchability; on the other hand research is formulated as, of course, theoretic, but also as constituted by its location in the procedural rules for mundane intelligibility, and thus as anticipating its own inevitable incompleteness, its reliance upon the recurrence of action for its own continuation.

Such a dialectical formulation provides for action-research's requirements of an intimate connection between action and research. It locates research in action's process and problematic, and it formulates a mode in which action could respond to research without that response being one of action's subjection to research's prescription, a subjection which of course could never be 'sufficient' for action to gain recognition as 'having put theory into practice'. In this way, by reformulating (as a dialectic) action-research's proposal to 'unite' action and research, we can formulate the intelligibility of that aspiration, by enabling action-research to cast aside a model of 'evaluation-by-experimentation' which presupposes precisely the methodological and hierarchical separation of research and action to which the very idea of 'action-research' is opposed.

NOTES

1) For example, R. Lees (1975) writes, concerning 'The Action-Research relationship':

'The Community Development Project anticipates an intimate and productive working relationship between administrators, field workers, research-orientated social scientists and local residents ... The aim of promoting participation is in itself seen as a desirable goal ... The research problem in this situation is to define participation ...' (pp. 59 and 61).

2) This is indeed the point urgently at issue between Kuhn and Popper in their contributions to Musgrave and Lakatos's volume: Criticism and the Growth of Knowledge (1970).

3) See Chapter Five.

4) An exception is the author's own article on 'Dilemma Analysis' (Winter R. 1982). See Chapter Four for a discussion of its limitations. See also Carr and Kemmis, 1986, pp. 184-7, where (however) 'dialectics' is treated as implying 'historical embeddedness', without reference to the structure of contradictions which characterizes this 'embeddedness'.

3 Action - research and critical reflection: theorizing and the self

'CRITICAL REFLECTION'

In the previous chapter it was argued that action-research is founded upon an implicit challenge to positivism's version of the relation between theory and practice, and theoretic resources were presented for making that challenge explicit. The argument now necessarily turns to an analysis of the ways in which action-research's challenge to positivism rests upon a conception of the theoretic competence of the social actor, which most action-research writers present unproblematically as a process of 'critical reflection':

> 'Action-research is simply a form of self-reflective enquiry undertaken by participants in social situations in order to improve the rationality and justice of their practices ...' (Carr and Kemmis, 1986, p. 162).

This chapter begins by collecting the questions raised by action-research writers' attempts to evoke the possibility of 'critical reflection', and then presents theoretic resources for addressing these questions within an analytically rigorous conception of the relation between theorizing, cultural authority, and the self.

It is the hubristic claim of positivist science that it possesses a methodology for inducing Nature 'itself' to

speak. In one version Nature's data are 'collected' to
provide grounds for the scientist's interpretation; in
Popper's more sophisticated version Nature either refutes
the scientist's conjectures, or - by not offering a
refutation when called upon to do so - provides a quasi-
corroboration, of typical, Delphic ambiguity. In both
cases Nature is summoned by the power of methodical logic.
Action-research, in contrast, has no such firmly articulated
logic: its invocations of the logic of positivism are
always ambivalent, and this is both a strength and a weakness. Its strength is that its ambiguity implies the
spuriousness of claims to speak with the voice of Nature;
ie. there is an ambiguous recognition that investigators can
only speak for themselves: their speech is not 'findings'
from Nature but 'reflection upon' Nature, and indeed
'critical reflection'. However, action-research's weakness
is that, still haunted by an illusion of Nature's own speech
and thus of Nature's authority for speech, investigators
note the need to speak independently of Nature but do not
analyze their grounds for doing so, so that conditions for
the possibility of 'critical reflection' are ignored by
being presupposed.

For example, Brown et al. propose that the sequence of
action-research is as follows:
Strategic planning ⎯⎯→ Action ⎯⎯→ Observation ⎯⎯→ Reflection
(Brown, et al, 1982, p. 2) together with the suggestion
that 'reflection' will lead back cyclically to further
strategic planning. Similarly Elliott, (1981) presents the
process as:
Review ⎯⎯→ Diagnosis ⎯⎯→ Planning ⎯⎯→ Implementation ⎯⎯→
Monitoring effects (p. ii) and also goes on later to suggest
a continuous 'spiral' (p. 2). But what is not addressed is
how, in either version, the process manages to be developmental rather than merely repetitive. How does a 'view'
become a 're-view', such that 'diagnosis' becomes more than
a prelude to a repeat prescription? What sort of reflection
upon observation will be, as Brown et al. go on to suggest,
a 'critique' leading to 'self-renewal' (p. 3)? Similarly,
Carr and Kemmis take Lewin's version of this spiral to be a
formulation of a 'dialectic' which can lead to
'transformation' (Carr and Kemmis, 1986, p. 184). But the
unanswered question remains: how may the Self be envisaged
such that its 'renewal' is a process of self-transcendence
rather than of self-reproduction? In both sequences of
terms given above, the possibility for an _increase_ in understanding is silently inscribed in the _space_ between
observation and reflection, between the investigator and the
world investigated.

Ultimately, such formulations are merely a faint but
hopeful echo of positivism's formulations of _its_ methods.
As such, they fail to enforce the prescriptivism of
positivism and they do not of course provide an alternative:
if Nature itself can not be the origin of action-research's
innovative insights, we are left with a mere question-mark
as to how insight occurs. Clearly, more is required than a

space. Rather, what is required is a formulation of the
Self which can provide for the possibility of self-
transcendent theorizing, and a formulation of culture which
will provide for the limits of theorizing without falling
into determinism; a formulation, in other words, of
'critical reflection' - which is neither determined by the
world nor grounded in an assumption of freedom (from the
world) which seems 'spacious' only because it is empty.

ACTION-RESEARCH'S ATTEMPTS TO FORMULATE CRITICAL
REFLECTION:

Action-Research and Individual Self-reflection

At its simplest, action-research seems to suggest that
individual consciousness has a spontaneous and un-
problematic capacity for self-transcendence. Thus, Jon
Nixon, in his introduction to A Teachers Guide to Action
Research, says that the action-research practitioners whose
work he is presenting 'have started from their own skills
and inclinations and from their own enthusiasms ... from a
simple desire to learn, and progressed, sometimes by hints
and guesses, towards the development of a research style
which suited their own particular needs and circumstances...
The single most important point to be taken from this book
is the necessity of developing one's own unique way of
looking' (Nixon, 1981a, p. 7). However, the word
'necessity' suggests that the development of 'uniqueness'
may encounter resistances, and these resistances are what
Nixon ignores. Similarly, elsewhere (Nixon J. 1981b) Nixon
cites Foucault as presenting an 'optimistic' view of the
possibilities for 'specific intellectuals' working
theoretically at their own professional contexts (p. 31),
whereas the article which Nixon invokes (Foucault, 1977)
emphasizes the political struggle of the intellectual
against 'the forms of hegemony (social, economic, and
cultural) within which it operates' (p. 14).

Admittedly, most formulations of the action-research
process recognize the contribution of an Other to the
subject's capacity for theorizing, and this will be the
topic of a later section. But the nature of this
contribution is often left open. Thus, Brown et al. suggest
that 'practitioners ... may be emancipated from ...
institutional assumptions and habitual ways of thinking ...
through the processes of collaborative effort, rigorous
critique, and self-reflection' (Brown et al, 1982, p. 3).
The point to be made here is simply that the list seems to
identify separable processes, and thus the implication is
that critique and self-reflection are conceivably not
dependent on any form of self-other dialectic. Similarly,
the conference report 'Action-research in schools - some
guidelines' (Elliott, 1978), suggests that 'teacher /
researchers' might 'deepen' their understanding by 'adopting
a critical, questioning stance' (p. 2), as though such a

44

'stance' might be the result of an individual decision. And it is significant that Elliott entitles one of his papers: 'Action-research, a framework for <u>self-evaluation</u> in schools' (Elliott, 1981 - my emphasis).

Hence the question arises: what would be meant by a 'critical' stance? Also: what would differentiate 'self-reflection' and 'self-evaluation' (as processes of creative cognition) from the complex yet routine 'practical reasoning' by which consciousness achieves its mundane purposes? Action-research certainly <u>intends</u> to address such questions, since much of the writing considered here aims at creating a 'practical' methodology for individual innovation. However, the concreteness of the practical suggestions presented seems to conceal the question of how particular activities could achieve the transcendental effect to which they aspire. The central quality of innovative thought, by which the whole project of practitioner action-research stands or falls, remains merely a presupposition, without being grounded in a theoretical analysis of its possibility.

Elliott's influential work shows the nature and scope of the problem. He lists a number of 'practical' procedures which an action-researcher may undertake:- making lists (of potential issues and methods) (1977, p. 8), keeping a diary, producing a 'profile' (eg. of a lesson), conducting a 'shadow study', making a 'running commentary' or a 'document analysis' (1981, pp. 16-17). In each case the outcome is described in terms of creating 'information' or 'facts', but no explanation is given of how this process of constructing a factuality might make available <u>new</u> conceptions, as opposed to merely documenting (and thus reinforcing) the basis of previously held interpretations. Elliott himself shows the need for such an explanation when he describes the procedure of writing 'analytic memos' as follows:

> 'Analytic memos contain one's systematic thinking about the evidence one has collected ... These memos may record such things as new ways of conceptualizing the situation under investigation which have emerged; hypotheses which have emerged ... statements about emerging problems and issues'.
> (1981, p. 10)

The recurrent metaphor of 'emergence' here encapsulates the central feature of innovative thought during the process of investigation: what was originally 'hidden' gradually 'comes out' and finally stands revealed. 'Emergence' presents the difference between the beginning and the end of inquiry as a difference between ignorance and knowledge, between the dark cavern of illusion and the sunlit vista of truth. But the metaphor itself suggests the crucial questions which Elliott ignores: what was the nature of the concealment, and what induced the emergence from conceal-ment? What are the differences which create the intelligib-ility of the metaphor, and what process of thinking, acting,

and writing are being referred to, which would enable
'profiles', 'shadow studies', 'memos' and the rest to
address analytically that difference which is embodied in
the purpose of inducing knowledge to 'emerge'?

At one level such issues are perhaps implied. Each of the
listed procedures suggests the possibility of constituting
differently the central relation between experience and
language in the processes of 'reflection' and 'interpretation' (Elliott 1981, p. 16) whereby experience is
routinely assimilated into current practices: documents
once 'analyzed' may be compared across the contexts which
produced them; even lists and diaries make explicit and
review-able what is normally implicit and irrecoverably
transient. Indeed a strong argument could be made that it
is the process of writing itself which in each of these
procedures 'interrupts' mundane intersubjectivity (cf.
Silverman and Torode, 1980) and thus constitutes that
differentiation which theorizing requires. Yet Elliott does
not argue that the process of undertaking these procedures
will be a process of theorizing, but that the product of the
procedures will be 'evidence'. In this way Elliott shows
how action-research remains haunted by the voice of Nature
as the auspices of inquiry.

There is one interesting exception. Elliott observes that
it is the transcription of tape-recorded interaction which
'enables (the researcher) to move backwards and forwards
through an episode' (Elliott, 1981, p. 14), ie. to
deconstruct the temporal dimension of language and
experience, so that (to complete Elliott's argument) their
elements and relationships can be explored and reordered.
This is an important point, which can be generalized as
follows: action-research's proposal that inquiry could
differentiate itself from mundane practical reasoning as a
process of 'individual self-reflection' requires a theory
which would permit multiple relationships between experience
and language, relationships (in other words) which would
allow for exploration, play, ambiguity, and transformation.
More concretely, as suggested by Elliott's listing of
practical procedures, one might conceive of action-research
as needing a theory of writing, as the central process in a
self-transcendental relationship between thought and experience.

Meanwhile it is clear that, without any explicit theory of
language's inevitable distance from experience, investigation along the lines such as Elliott puts forward cannot
articulate that theoretical space which it must presuppose;
in the end it appears to articulate a subjectivity
determined by the 'facts' of experience, and thereby seems
to deny the possibility of that self-transformative
innovation which it nevertheless wishes to urge as a
practical programme.

Action-Research's Notion of the Subject

A subjectivity thus determined by its cognition of a factualized experience is a subject in a 'rationalistic' relation to its context, ie. a subject with no complex internal processes but only externally oriented relationships of perception and instrumentality (See Weber, 1971, pp. 130-1) and indeed much action-research writing does seem to treat the subjectivity of the investigator in this way, as a taken-for-granted, instrumental rationality. (See Chapter 4). Underlying Elliott's emphasis on investigation as 'information gathering' (Elliott 1981, p. ii) is Nixon's confidence that a research style can be grounded in practitioners' 'unique way of looking', their 'simple desire to learn', their 'needs and circumstances' (Nixon 1981a, p. 7).

However, questions concerning the limitations of this view of subjectivity are raised by other writers on action-research. For example, Lippett (1948) suggests that one of the problems for 'action-research' (p. 6) is that 'the backlog of knowledge about more effective skills of living and working' has not been 'communicated into action' (p. 7) because of the specific resistance to change derived from our 'ego-investments in the present way of doing things' (p. 8). One of Lippett's co-workers on the Connecticut training programme he describes was Kurt Lewin, and although Lewin's best known article on action-research (Lewin, 1946) presents investigation as based upon 'fact-finding' (p. 37), he presents a radically more problematic version in a slightly earlier article (Lewin and Grabbe, 1945), a version which casts doubt on the efficacy of fact-finding by suggesting that changes in belief 'cannot be merely a rational process' (p. 56). The authors continue: 'As a rule the possessing of correct knowledge does not suffice to rectify false perception' (p. 57). Rather, what is required is a change in the 'culture' (p. 55) of the individual, which is variously formulated as 'a change in social perception, namely the position in which we perceive ourselves and others within the total social setting' (p. 57), as a 'change of (the individual's) superego' (p. 59), and as a change in the individual's 'system of values' (p. 60).

Clearly, Lippett, Lewin, and Grabbe wish to draw attention to cultural and unconscious structures which pose the rationality of the subject as a problem. But how could one understand the problematic which leads them to align so crudely and without explanation the notions of values, perceptions, culture, and Freudian categories of the psyche? A suggestive starting point is the contradiction encapsulated in Lewin and Grabbe's use of the notion of 'change'. On the one hand they emphasize that individual change is difficult because individuals are determined by their culture/social perceptions/systems of values/superego; on the other hand they formulate as though it were un-problematic their intention (as action-researchers) to

change just that - the individual's culture/social
perceptions/systems of values/superego. In other words it
seems that their account of the non-rational determination
of the subject is not intended epistemologically as a
general theory, since such a theory would necessarily apply
to the investigators as well as to the investigated.
Rather, their account draws attention to the technical
problems in changing the subjectivity of others, ie. the
'trainees' enrolled in their 'training programmes', whose
imperviousness to the presentation of 'correct knowledge'
requires the manipulation of group pressures (p. 62) by
those whose own possible determination by group pressures is
ignored. The curious list of cultural and unconscious
determinations is thus not a theory of the subject but a
pragmatic model of the manipulation process. In this
respect is is likely that neither Lippett's reference to
'ego-involvement' nor Lewin and Grabbe's reference to
'superego' is intended to invoke the Freudian notion of the
unconscious, but are merely grandiose terms for 'emotions'
and 'beliefs'.

But Pandora's box is not so easily closed. Lippett, Lewin,
and Grabbe have, for their own purposes, noted that the
subject is constituted in a matrix of cultural and psychic
forces, so that consciousness cannot be conceived simply as
a retina upon which data impinge, nor as a container in
which facts are gathered. To take this point seriously is
to raise important questions concerning the investigative
process as a biographically located exploration of cultural
resources, and as a necessarily reflexive analysis of the
investigator's relationship to those resources. And not all
action-research writers are unaware of the seriousness of
the issue of reflexivity. Nevitt Sanford ('Whatever happened to action-research?') (in Clarke A, 1976) provides a
fitting comment on the pretensions of Lewin and Grabbe: as
sociologists, we should, rather than 'disseminating a
monstrous image of researchable man ... demonstrate our
willingness to study ourselves, which in turn would help to
restore trust in our competence to study others' (pp. 29,
31).

But if this complex theme, of the relation between
determination, rationality, and reflexivity, and between
subjectivity and culture, is indeed a central issue for
action-research, it is essential that action-research
should face the challenge posed by institutionalized
authority systems to the possibility of individual critical
reflection, and thus the next section examines how far
action-research writers have been aware of the scope of this
challenge.

Action-Research, Reflection, and Institutionalized
Authority Systems

At the end of his article 'Action-research and minority
problems' (Lewin, 1946), Lewin notes the significance of

'the relation between the local, the national, and the
international scenes' and he goes on to state: 'Intergroup
relations in this country (ie. the USA) will be formed to a
large degree by events on the international scene and
particularly by the fate of the colonial peoples' (p. 45).
But how would 'relations' between local groups be 'formed'
by international 'events'? Lewin's theme of course is
racial prejudice, and his phrasing at this point seems to
plead for a coherent formulation in terms of a linkage
between societal authority and individual experience, ie. a
theory of culture as the resource for the self-representation of the subject. And yet other passages demonstrate the
incoherence of Lewin's approach to this issue: on the one
hand he elaborates 'the international scene' of race
relations at the most general level of historical forces
('the policy of exploitation which has made colonial
imperialism the most hated institution the world over' -
p. 46); on the other hand he elaborates the 'local' problem
of race in terms of a rationalized individual consciousness,
namely the creation of 'the same level' of 'self-esteem' and
'group loyalty' for members of different racial groups
(p. 45). Thus Lewin's presentation of the need to relate
history and biography, institutionalized authority and
subjective experience, is made in terms which render such a
relationship un-thinkable: historical and political racism
is constituted solely as a 'macro-structure', while the
interpersonal experience of racism is constituted solely as
an individualized phenomenon, presumably so that 'levels'
may be measured as collections of 'facts'. What is missing
is an awareness of the embodiment of history and politics at
the level of intersubjective relationships, either among the
social actors whom Lewin wishes to study, or between such
actors and Lewin himself, as a necessary reflexive dimension
of the process of the study.

Both of these dimensions are implicitly present in John
Collier's study of the US Indian Administration (Collier,
1945), invoked by Lewin himself at the end of his 1946
article. Collier criticises 'the dead hand of an absolutist
and unlearning bureaucracy' (p. 272) whose desire for
control 'atomized' the Indian by 'destroying the tribal and
community organizations' (p. 272). As a result the U.S.
Indian Administration failed to understand Navajo culture,
and Navajo culture has 'no mechanism for translating ...
insights and impulses into tribal decisions and actions'
(pp. 288-9). Thus Collier's theme is precisely the relation
between knowledge and social authority, and the problematic
for 'action-research' (p. 294) is how understanding may
transcend the effects of such authority relationships. In
contrast to many writers on action-research, Collier's
account of this is admirably complex. He articulates
clearly action-research's central tenet that 'research'
requires the transformation of institutional relationships,
ie. by substituting 'participation' for super-ordination
(pp. 276, 294). But he does not argue that understanding
is determined by its social relationships, and he thereby

preserves the possibility of action-research's transformative effect. For example, he does not claim that the
Indian's subordination to colonial power results in the
destruction of the Indian's capacity for insight, only of
the means for translating such insight into practice. He
goes on to suggest that if only the 'unlearning' bureaucrat
is 'faithful to the spirit of science, to the spirit of that
knowledge which he has not yet mastered' (p. 298), he will
recognize that 'what (the Indians) are must be known in
relation to what they must become' (p. 297) and thus be able
to 'encounter (the Indian's) ample capacity to think' and
their specific 'sentiment of responsibility' (p. 289). Thus
the bureaucrat may transcend his readiness to appropriate
'thinking' and 'responsibility' as his own prerogative, and
come, finally, to 'learn'.

What Collier presents here is a formulation of knowledge
as inherently reflexive, of understanding as grounded in a
sense of its own incompleteness and of its developmental
ideal, and thus in the possibility of critical reflection
upon the status quo. He is clear that institutional
authority relations leave intact the possibility for such
critical reflection; but he is less clear about the specific
inhibition of this possibility created by the hierarchical
relationships he describes, and thus he does not address in
detail the procedures by which such inhibitions might be
removed. Hence his implication that the capacity for insight on the part of the dominated simply survives intact
seems over-optimistic, if by 'insight' more than 'some
interpretation or other' is meant.

And equally optimistic is his suggestion that the
'bureaucrat' can achieve a reflexive understanding if he
merely 'goes quietly there, to the homes and little
neighbourhoods (of the Navajo) and stays a while ...'
(p. 289) as though the state of truthful understanding were
available as a sort of pastoral refuge away from the 'noise'
of institutionalized authority. But pastoral versions of
truth are profoundly ambivalent, presenting a way of life as
valid because of the apparent absence of the very
sophistication through which that absence is celebrated.
This disables Collier's ethnography. He emphasizes that the
relationships and the possibilities for understanding
between the bureaucrat and the Navajo are constituted within
an authority relation: he cannot then propose that valid
understanding could take the form of a pastoral absence, ie.
a simple rejection or denial of the effect of the authority
relationship by one or both of the parties to that relationship. What is needed, rather, is an account of the specific
resources for meaning as these are constituted dialectically
and reflexively within the authority relationship - as
symbols and myths, as ambiguities and contradictions.

Analogous with Collier's optimism concerning action-
research's capacity simply to 'reject' institutionalized
authority is that of Nixon. He presents action-research by

teachers as an attempt 'to reject the paternalism of
traditional research', to reject (in other words) the
subjection of practitioners' creative analytical potential
to the prescriptiveness of 'academic' methodologies (Nixon,
1981a, p. 9). We have already seen that Nixon's view of
action-research rests precisely upon a libertarian
principle. But this of course immediately undermines
itself. If teachers are 'free' to choose a research style
in accordance with their 'needs' or enthusiasms, they are
quite likely to choose ('freely'?) to adopt a style derived
from that 'paternalist' tradition which influences the
awareness within which they make such a choice. And indeed
a number of writers in Nixon's book proclaim their reliance
on the theoretical perspectives and methods of conventional
positivist social science (see for example pp. 17, 92, 155).

This ambivalence in Nixon's work raises directly the
question which so far has only been hinted at: how far
forms of understanding themselves may be recognized as
adequate (or inadequate) only within a cultural order which
is structured by institutionalized authority relations.
Nixon's argument is presented more elaborately by Elliott
(1982a). He begins by claiming that teachers do not see
themselves as potentially competent theorists because of a
'doctrine' which separates theory and practice, and makes
truth a matter of having access to an 'objective' reality
'external to (people's) minds' (p. 3). This (widespread)
epistemological position, whose conventional status is
conveyed by the word 'doctrine', leads to a set of
perspectives on the part of teachers which Elliott sums up
as professional practitioners' 'assumption of intellectual
dependence' on the personnel and practices of 'the kind of
higher education institutions which qualified them' (as
professional practitioners) (pp. 2-3). In other words,
Elliott continues, positivist epistemology is institutionally
embodied in a division of labour which segregates the
clarification of ideals by 'philosophers', the clarification
of means-ends relationships by 'scientists', and the
'application' of the results of such work by practitioners
who thus see themselves as 'technologists' (pp. 4-5). (The
hierarchical relationship here is dramatized and
biographically located in the process of 'qualification'.)
This general argument is derived, of course, from Habermas's
criticism of the notions of science and technology as
'ideology' (Habermas, 1971), as legitimated forms of
knowledge expressing a political oppression, which requires,
as a response, 'the determination to take up the struggle
against the stabilization of a nature-like social system
over the heads of its citizens ...' (the closing sentence of
Legitimation Crisis, Habermas, 1976). For Elliott, action-
research is this struggle, a struggle to reunite theory and
practice, action and research, which the cultural and
occupational order of industrial society systematically
strives to put asunder.

However, there is a general irony surrounding the notion

of 'epistemological' ideology. If a way of conceptualizing knowledge is ideological in a <u>determinist</u> sense, then indeed one has an urgent sense of the cultural constraints upon understanding, but one then needs analytical grounds for differentiating an alternative form of cognition, in order that theorizing itself may be intelligible. Otherwise the theory of ideology is self-engulfing: <u>all</u> knowledge would become the outcome of an authority system, including of course the assertions of a theory of ideology; in this way theorizing would simultaneously say that theorizing is impossible and also say that it has no grounds for saying so. It would have grounds neither for speech nor for silence.

Now Elliott's theory of positivism as an ideology is certainly phrased <u>non</u>-deterministically - as a 'doctrine' (which therefore one might reject) and as an 'assumption' (which therefore one might renounce) - and thus Elliott could go on to claim, in response to criticisms of action-research by structuralist Marxism, that action-research 'did not assume that the process of schooling was not constrained by its political and economic context, but did assume that teachers could become aware of such constraints, and in doing so increase their capacity to devise strategies for overcoming them' (Elliott, 1982a, p. 28). But notice that at this point Elliott is no longer considering the epistemological level: having now posed the question in terms of the ideological separation of theory and practice, means and values, a question which indeed radically threatens the cognitive capacity of the individual, his answer is merely in terms of the determination of <u>role</u> relationships. A <u>consistent</u> theory of ideology, concerning the relation between social authority and the investigative process, challenges action-research <u>not</u> by suggesting that (for example) the process of <u>schooling</u> is constrained by its cultural context, but that the process of <u>understanding</u> schooling is thus constrained. Hence, although Elliott is right to reject a determinist social theory, his formulation of the individual's response to institutionalized authority as merely 'becoming aware' is apparently incompatible with his previous account of how that awareness is itself institutionally constructed and biographically effective. In order to avoid this dichotomy Elliott's theory requires a formulation both of consciousness and of social structure in terms of their mutually constitutive dialectical contra-dictions.

In contrast to Elliott's argument, Moser (1978) formulates the issue of action-research's relation to the authority structures of its context by specifically denying that there can be any question of the <u>practitioner</u>-as-researcher. The researcher and the researched are defined in terms of 'different life-situations', which in turn means that the former has a theoretical competence which the latter lacks (p. 141). Consequently problems are derived by the researcher, and he has the task of 'convincing'

participatory groups of 'relevance' (p. 148). It is thus
the researcher's special capacity for analysis which enables
him or her to show, 'in concrete social situations ... that
gap between claim and reality, between formulated democratic
principles and real domination, in which we are constituted
by late capitalism' (p. 78). (1) It is the researcher's
analysis which explores contradictions, reveals
mystifications, and leads first to 'enlightenment'
('Aufklärung') and thence to 'Praxis' (p. 78). But what
Moser does not address is the grounds for the researcher's
understanding, given the reality of 'domination'.
Conversely, given the researcher's understanding, what are
the grounds for the social actor's ignorance? Hence his own
final formulation of the possible achievement of action-
research is highly ambiguous. On the one hand he envisages
the creation of a form of consciousness 'which can
differentiate between being and appearance, essence and
phenomenon, is and ought ... which transcends the merely
given situation and includes in discussion the overarching
set of relationships which determine that situation'
(p. 169). (2) (In other words we are given a determined
context within which individuals can transcend those
determinations only insofar as they can note and discuss
them.) On the other hand, in the next (and final)
paragraph he suggests that action-research will enable
'those concerned to take their destinies into their own
'hands' (p. 169), (3) except that by this he explicitly
means merely that social members ('Feldpersonen') who have
been involved in an action-research project will be able to
pursue the aims of the project even after the 'scientists'
('Wissenschaftler') have eventually withdrawn. Thus, in
complete contrast to Elliott and Habermas, Moser envisages
that the citizen will be freed from the internalization of
societally enforced norms only at the price of internalizing
the norms of the action-researcher. Whereas for Elliott the
intellectual dependency of the practitioner upon the
researcher was the problem, for Moser it is the beginnings
of a solution - a necessary prologue to liberation. Theory
is envisaged in a prescriptive, rather than a dialectical
relation to action, and thus critical reflection is
constituted 'unreflexively', as an intellectual procedure
which tacitly removes itself from the institutionalized
relationships which are its object. Although this is a
conventional position for critical theory, it denies the
aims and the specific contribution of action-research, which
Moser elsewhere urges as a necessary intervention in order
to remedy critical theory's own inability to relate theory
and practice (Moser, 1978, p. 40).

The question thus becomes: how can the relationship
between the intellectual authority of theory be formulated
as analytically different from the legitimating relationships of an institutional order, without falling back into
that academic prescriptiveness which action-research wishes
particularly to avoid? What is required is the formulation
of an analytical relation between ideology and reflexivity,

such that a recognition of the challenge of ideology to
valid understanding can be assimilated to action-research's
dialectical relation between theory and practice. (This is
the topic of a later section.) Meanwhile, Moser has raised
in an urgent form the question of the nature of the social
relationships, between those involved in action-research
investigation, which might facilitate the development of
critical reflection.

Action-Research, Critical Reflection, and the Social Relationships of the Research Process

We have seen that for Moser the citizens' understanding can
only be emancipated from its subjection to institutionalized
authority on condition that the citizens apprentice themselves to the theorist: the theorist hopes in the end to be
able to withdraw from the scene, his/her work completed, but
the theorist's authority is presented as the necessary
condition for the achievement by others of autonomy. This
tension, between authority and liberation from authority,
constituted in action-research's double aspiration that
action may be both informed by 'research' and yet remain
free from determination by 'theory', is central to the
action-research problematic. It is perfectly expressed, for
example, in the following passage from D. Krech and
R. Crutchfield (1948, p. 524) articulating Lippett's notion
'the community or organizational self-survey' (Lippett,
1948, p. 2):

> 'A community self-survey can be described as
> action research in which the members of the community
> themselves, under the expert guidance of applied
> social psychologists, are responsible for the
> collection and analysis of community data'.
> (emphases in the original).

Notice the specific stress on the responsibility of 'the
members of the community themselves' in contrast to the
tacit ambiguity with which their responsibility is undercut
by the 'expertise' of the scientist, and hence the crucial
need for an explication of the contradictions within
'guidance' as the mediating category. Krech and
Crutchfield, however, avoid such issues. For them the
principles of their approach are as follows: 1) 'the facts'
must be 'obtained'; 2) 'facts thus uncovered by the
citizens of the community will be more readily accepted by
the community'; and 3) the process of carrying out the
survey will 'have a powerful motivating effect' upon the
citizen-surveyors. (pp. 524-5). In other words, the 'expert
social psychologists' are engaged in what the authors term
'the educational process', which they define as 'any measure
designed to change the motivational structure or perception
of an individual (through) manipulation of the person's
environment for specific ends' (p. 519). There is a double
authority here. Firstly, experts have 'specific ends' in
mind for the community, and 'design' manipulative means to
achieve them; secondly, community situations are

constituted as 'facts' which communities must be induced to 'accept'. The two bases for authority are linked: the unquestioned authority of the expert scientists may be presumed to rest on their unquestioned access to the authoritative facts of Nature. Once more, by failing to question a positivist epistemology, action-research presents theory as an unreflexive authority borrowed from the same scientific practices it wishes to oppose, and lapses into the manipulative devices of managerialism. And yet the original passage italicized the members of the community themselves, and wished to make them 'responsible' ...

A similar tension is expressed in the work of Cory (1953). Cory stresses that studies of educational practice 'must be undertaken by those who may have to change the way they do things as a result of the studies ... Teachers, pupils, supervisors, administrators and school patrons (must) continuously examine what they are doing ... use their imaginations creatively and constructively ... etc. This is the process I call action-research'. (p. viii) And yet on p. 18 we read that the reason why action-research must be a co-operative' activity is that, unless 'interested' parties to the action become collaborators, they may well become an opposition. Thus action-research gives autonomy to practitioners-as-researchers but only as a manipulative strategy, in order to subject them to the authority of the action-research process, which creates auspices not only for cooperators but also ('unfortunately', as it were) for opponents.

But it is precisely these auspices which need to be theorized, even (for example) when the social relations of the research process are formulated in accordance with the Habermasian 'ideal speech community', in which, alone, the integration of consensus and emancipation enables freedom to be inscribed within authority itself.

It is the Habermasian ideal of a speech situation in which possibilities for initiative and critique are 'symmetrically' distributed (Habermas J. 1970, p. 143) which underlies the work of Elliott, and thus enables him to present the social relations of action-research as in principle those of an anti-hierarchical collective. The ideal of 'dialogue' in which 'participants must have equal freedom' for interpretation and criticism explicates 'a procedure for determining the objectivity of practical judgements' (Elliott: 1982a, p. 19) and this constitutes 'Habermas's reconstruction of the interpretative model' for social science. Elliott continues: 'In my view ... educational action-research constitutes the concrete expression of a reconstructed interpretative paradigm with respect to the study of schooling'. (p. 22). The ideal of a 'symmetrical' discourse leads Elliott to describe the interaction between the participants of an action-research project very differently from the rhetoric of manipulative management discussed above. For example 'interviewing' is presented as 'a good way of finding out what the situation looks like from other points of view' (Elliott, 1981, p. 15); researchers are told to 'use the experience of other teachers/researchers' and to seek 'access to varying interpretations' (Elliott, 1978, p. 8). The symmetry of the interactional process is embodied in the idea of 'triangulation', namely the comparing of different accounts in order to 'mount discussions on points of disagreement between the various parties involved, preferably under the chairmanship of a 'neutral' party' (Elliott, 1981, p. 19). And in order to protect the symmetrical interaction of the investigative process from the hierarchical interactional norms of its institutional setting, it is necessary to negotiate an 'ethical framework' concerning 'confidentiality', in which participants retain 'control' over information concerning their activities and opinions: 'they have the final say' (Elliott, 1981, p. 9).

For Elliott, then, action-research's possibilities for the development of understanding seem to rest upon an analytical difference between mundane interaction, beset by institutionalized role norms, and the symmetrical interaction of the investigative process, in which the Self-Other relationship is freed to become an explorative dialectic. 'Theory' then would implicitly reside in such a difference. From this point of view the notion of a need for a 'neutral' chairman and for a defensive framework of confidentiality embodies an awareness of the inevitable fragility of the Habermasian ideal.

But there is a crucial problem here. Elliott does not say that action-research requires the implementation of a non-authoritarian dialogue. The article from which most of the above quotations are taken is subtitled 'A Framework for Self-evaluation ...' And the other article cited, ('Action-research in schools, some guidelines') begins as follows:

> 'Basically classroom action-research relates to
> any teacher who is concerned with his own teaching;
> the teacher who is prepared to question his own
> approach in order to improve its quality.
> Therefore the teacher is involved in looking at
> what is actually going on in the classroom ...
> This research may be extended to include other
> individuals'. (Elliott, 1978, p. 1) (my emphasis).

The formulation of theorizing in terms of a symmetrical dialogue thus seems to be only an option, depending on 'the scope of the research'. In the absence of such dialogic possibilities, action-research can still, apparently, rely on the individual's solitary capacity to 'question' and to find access to a Natural world of facts - 'what is actually going on'. The central question of the analytical relation between the authority of theorizing and the authority of Nature remains unaddressed by this tacit juxtaposition, which reduces a principle to an option. Until it has been addressed, one can have no confidence that Elliott's 'neutral' chairman will not burst out of his inverted commas and begin to adjudicate between interpretative differences in the name of Nature, rather than calling upon all interpretations to recollect their irremediable reflexivity.

Whereas Elliott's use of Habermas is undermined by a residual empiricism, the work of Brown et al. seeks to assimilate Habermas to an activist epistemology. Thus, they invoke Habermas's notion of a 'critical social science which is conditioned by the explicitly political emancipatory knowledge-constitutive interest' (Brown et al, 1982, p. 14) and continue immediately to describe it as 'a science specifically oriented to the development of improvement and understanding through the strategic action of participants in social situations through action-research'. This contrasts strongly with Habermas's own statements that 'the emancipatory cognitive interest aims at the pursuit of reflection as such' (Habermas, 1978, p. 314) and that there is an inevitable disjuncture between self-reflection and strategy (Habermas, 1974, p. 39). Perhaps it is this attempt by Brown et al. to short-circuit Habermas's highly complex formulation of the theory-practice relation which leads them into an interesting ambiguity, reminiscent of the problems in Heinz Moser's work. Firstly, Brown and his co-authors present a notion of 'collaboration' among action-research participants which seems distantly to evoke the Habermasian ideal of self-reflection through symmetrical dialogue:

> 'Action-research is distinguished by its adherence to a collaborative ethic. Action-research is a collaborative endeavour in which groups of practitioners work together to understand better their own practice, to increase their awareness of the effects of their practice, and of their control over the situation in which they work'. (Brown et al., 1982, p. 4).

But in practice, they go on to say, action-research by practitioners requires the 'assistance' of 'a facilitator from outside the immediate situation being studied' and it is towards the explication of the nature of this role, rather than the possibility of collaboration among practitioners themselves that they devote the remainder of their article.

Their account of the role of the facilitator embodies many of the tensions which are the topic of this section. On the one hand, the facilitator is 'a supportive friend ... providing a sympathetic ear in times of doubt' (p. 6), and a 'group recorder', who, by circulating notes on meetings generates 'a sense of group identity and history' (p. 6). In contrast, the facilitator provides 'an outsider perspective', providing criticism and the challenge of 'alternative' viewpoints, or acts as a 'Devils advocate'

(pp. 5-6). The tension between challenge and support
embodies the facilitator's commitment _both_ to the
possibilities for transcendence _and_ to those activities on
the part of practitioners in which such possibilities must
(for action-research) be grounded. This is focussed in a
complex notion of _discourse_: the arrival of the facilitator
requires practitioners to 'articulate their respective
points of view', ie. to _explain_ what has previously been
'taken for granted', and thus to challenge the 'history' of
communication within the social situation (p. 4). This
seems to suggest a notion of the facilitator as the Other
of discourse, who precipitates a realization of the space
between language and action and thus enables critical self-
reflection (in Habermasian terms) to extricate itself as a
moment of consciousness _distinct_ from consciousness's otherwise inevitable commitment to mundane action. This, again,
might be taken as a starting point for the formulation of
the 'authority' of theory as residing in its analytic
difference from action, and as such to be enacted in a
reflexive discourse between a practitioner and one-who-is-
not-a-practitioner:

> 'By their own openness, sharing questions and
> doubts, facilitators seek to engender an environment
> where obstacles to progress can be frankly
> examined' (Brown et al., 1982, p. 4)

But Brown et al. are not content to present such a model of
authority: they also present the facilitator as 'a teacher
of action-research' (p. 5). As a _teacher_, the facilitator
'frames the principles' of the work and 'clarifies the
process'. _But_, for strategic reasons, he does _not_ 'explain
the entire rationale for each practical step' (p. 5). The
facilitator now is no longer the Other of self-reflective
discourse but the one who _tells_, who prescribes principles
and defines clarity, who possesses (and decides when to
provide) 'a rationale'. Rather than the _analytic_ authority
of theorizing as a moment in the dialectic between action
and language, which must be action-research's underlying
aspiration, we have here, once more, the _social_ authority of
the expert, whose procedure once more, seems to be a form of
manipulation which profoundly contradicts the ideal of
collaborative, reflexive discourse. Another familiar
problem re-surfaces here, when we are told that the
facilitator-as-teacher should possess expert knowledge
concerning 'data-gathering techniques', so that authority
for inquiry is once more reinforced by the supposition of a
methodological access to Nature on the part of a rationalized consciousness constituted by the factuality of its
context.

But Brown and his colleagues do hint at the limits of such
a version of rationality when they refer to the
facilitator's reliance upon and need to generate 'an atmos-
phere of trust ... (among) a sympathetic audience' (p. 5)
and indeed by the general suggestion that the facilitator

should be 'supportive'. Such mundane comments in themselves
of course hardly add to the coherence of their account of
the social relations of facilitation; however, they do
serve as reminders of an awareness among writers on action-
research that the rationality of the subject is constituted
within a complex psychic structure, and hence of the
inherent fragility of self-reflection.

Within this perspective, Brown et al.'s brief references
to 'trust' and 'support' may be seen in the light of Michael
Foster's statement, in his article 'An introduction to the
theory and practice of action-research in work organizations' (1971):

> 'This brief review of early action-research
> thinking could not be complete without reference
> to the development of 'T-groups', which are often
> part of the repertoire of the change agent' (p. 7)

Foster then goes on to quote various 'streams of development' which have characterized action-research, including
'an integrative psycho-analytical ... approach' and a
'group dynamics approach' (p. 8), and admits that there is
a necessary debate concerning the relationship within
research between 'interchange at the cognitive level'
(p. 29) and 'interpersonal feeling' (p. 30). Similarly
Lippett (1948, p. 254 ff) works towards a triangular framework consisting of 'action, research, and training', and
Moser (p. 53) cites with approval Lewin's comparable
association. By references such as these, action-research
writers begin to acknowledge a possible contribution from
psycho-analysis in formulating the possibility of developing
self-reflection through the dialectic of action and theory.
And thus, in formulating the social relationship through
which this might be achieved, an adequate theory for action-
research's problematic would need to consider not only the
nature of 'collaboration' and of 'facilitation', but also of
'therapy'.

The notion of therapy makes explicit and central the ideas
which action-research writers like those I have discussed
present merely as peripheral hints: that inquiry faces a
challenge from the resistances created by its own interactional process; that rationality's problem is that it
seems to be both an outcome and a presupposed resource for
inquiry; that the authority for interpretation is
precariously balanced between the investigator and the
object of investigation, and that (indeed) perhaps this very
distinction is itself questionable; that inquiry must enact
its problematic in order to grasp its object; that the
understanding of specific situations can only be grasped as
inter-sections of symbolic structures which ramify afar,
both in time and place, both in culture and biography. It
is interesting to note that Habermas, who inspires action-
research's ideal of 'collaboration', and who is invoked as
an authority for 'facilitation', explicitly raises the

possibility of psycho-analysis as a formulation of the
relation between authority, rationality, and discourse
(Habermas, 1970, p. 116 ff.) and equally interesting that
action-research writers who cite Habermas either ignore this
apsect of his work or treat it as of secondary importance
(while also citing other action-research writers whose pages
refer to 'changing people's superego's'!). Hence, even
though the work of Freud is significantly ignored by action-
research, it will figure quite substantially in the following pages, in which I shall outline the theoretical
resources necessitated by action-research's failure to
articulate coherently its self-proclaimed problematic of
'critical self-reflection'.

THEORETICAL RESOURCES FOR THE FORMULATION OF CRITICAL
SELF-REFLECTION

Critical Self-reflection and Theories of the Self

A version of the inquiring subject simply as a 'rational'
consciousness leaves action-research open to a charge of
naive idealism, which would disable action-research's
fundamental commitment to theorizing above all the links
between theory and practice. On the other hand, a determinist version of the subject as a product of its action
context would undermine action-research's need to formulate
an innovative, theorizing subject which (through action-
research) can transcend its context. How can this polarity
be reformulated into a coherent complexity?

   Freud's work is often seen as exemplifying a crude
determinism, at the level of biological drives ('the Id'),
neurological process (eg. the theory of memory in The
Interpretation of Dreams, Freud, 1976a, p. 687), and the
'universal' Oedipus complex. However, in many ways Freud's
work is ambiguous with respect to determinism. Certainly,
he tends throughout his work to seek an 'instinctual'
explanation of mental acts, which Habermas criticizes
(Habermas, 1978, pp. 253-4): for example, Freud's analysis
of jokes explains that the comic' builds up 'a surplus of
psychic energy' which then needs to be 'discharged' (Jokes
and their Relation to the Unconscious, Freud, 1976b,
pp. 254-6) (4). On the other hand he often presents
accounts of mental life in terms of a cultural system
structured like a language: a vocabulary of images, derived
from 'folklore, popular myths, legends, linguistic idioms,
proverbial wisdom, and current jokes' (1976a, p. 468), and
a syntactical process of condensation and displacement,
which constitutes mental productions in a form which is
representative in function, metaphorical in texture, and
mythic in structure. (Even at the biological level Freud
moved towards a dialectical model, based on the 'dualistic'
principle of mutually opposed instincts - Freud, 1961,
p. 47). And Freud's 'linguistic' model of subjectivity does
not have at its centre the determinism and fixity of a

dictionary (with defined meanings) but the open horizon of
words themselves, 'which, since they are nodal points of
numerous ideas, may be regarded as predestined to ambiguity'
(1976a, p. 465).

From this point of view, the Freudian unconscious with its
web of symbolic metaphor and ambiguity is not so much an
obstacle to rationality but rather rationality's own
resource. Conventional 'philosophy of science' is
embarrassed to admit that the instrumental model of rationality can explain only how theoretical insights may be
checked; the process of theoretical insight itself remains
anecdotal and sentimentally mysterious - dreams or
accidents, contingencies without principle, except as Fate's
reward for 'genius'. Hence the importance for my argument
of works such as Koestler's The Act of Creation (Koestler,
1969) which argue systematically for the metaphorical
processes of unconscious mentality as the resources for
theoretical work. In this way the opposition between Self
and Rationality is mediated by the complexity of the symbol,
as constitutive of both Self and Rationality. This, then,
is the significance of Freud for the present argument: the
unconscious not simply as a limitation upon the subject's
capacity to respond 'rationally' to its context (ie. as the
origin of 'neurosis'), but as the resource for the subject's
capacity to respond 'creatively', ie. not merely to respond,
but to transform its context from an experiential given into
a range of symbolic possibilities. The unconscious, in this
view, adds to the logical constituents of mind, posited by
Kant, both desire and metaphor, and thereby formulates for
creative consciousness both motives and pathways.

Jung formulates this view of the unconscious as a resource
quite directly:

> 'The same psychic material which is the stuff of
> psychosis is the fund of unconscious images,
> which fatally confuse the mental patient but ...
> is also the matrix of a mythopoeic imagination
> which has vanished from our rational age'.
> (Jung, 1967, p. 213 - my emphases)

The mythopoeic imagination has vanished because reason has
abandoned the resources of the unconscious - the
'archetypes' in favour of various reductionist versions of
thought, such as 'concepts of averages' (Jung, 1967, p. 17)
or 'systems of concepts' (p. 154). The notion of
'archetype' attempts to formulate thought as structured by
forces external to the individual consciousness, but not
determined by them. Thus, when Jung makes a parallel
between the 'mythological motif (of) the hostile brothers'
for the human psyche and the 'instinct' of nest-building in
birds (Jung, 1977, p. 228) one can hear this as a riposte to
Freud's reduction of psychic phenomena to 'instincts':
Freud is, as it were, implicitly accused of making a
'category error': for man the instinctual is the mythic.

In other words, archetypes are an extension of arguments concerning the constitutive categories of thought. Kant presents <u>consciousness</u> as structured by the constitutive categories of <u>perception</u> (Space, Time, Subject, Object); Piaget makes a similar argument at a more specific level when he presents <u>instrumental rationality</u> as structured by the constitutive categories of <u>purposeful action</u> (relations of part/whole, cause/effect) (see for example Piaget, 1977, p. 727); and Jung presents <u>subjectivity</u> in general as structured by constitutive categories of experience, structured, that is, at that level where the apparently physical ('hunger, disease, old-age, death') is mediated as the cultural ('war, the hero'), and thus structured above all in ambivalence (Jung, 1977, pp. 238, 443):

> 'Symbols, by their very nature, can so unite
> the opposites that these no longer diverge or
> clash, but mutually supplement one another and
> give meaningful shape to life'. (Jung, 1967, p. 370)

In a curious way, then, the Jungian notion of archetype seems to take Levi-Strauss's mythic structures of metaphor and contradiction and install them alongside Garfinkel's procedures for 'practical reasoning' - as the unnoticed conditions for intelligibility, communication, and inter-pretation. To follow through this suggestion would be to show what a 'mythopoeic imagination' might achieve as a current theoretic practice (rather than as an exotic reference). It would be tempting to 'de-mythologize', as Barthes does (see Barthes, 1976) and to forget the require-ment that such 'mythopoeic' theorizing must, like any form of analysis, be reflexive: Garfinkel forgets that his own writings exemplify the procedures for 'etc.' and 'ad hoc' (see Filmer, 1976); does Jung forget that 'archetype' is an archetype?

This is an important question. There is a real danger that one might attempt to <u>collect</u> archetypes as a 'fund' or dictionary of 'real' meanings prescribed with the authority of a universal unconscious. But Jung's emphasis is <u>both</u> on an archaic and universal inheritance (Jung, 1977, p. 228) and on the irremediable uniqueness of the personal:

> 'Interpretation cannot be a method based on
> rules: it requires a study of the wholeness of
> the symbol-producing individual' (ibid., p. 250)

The Self is not merely a repository of resources nor a product of their combination, but is 'the principle and archetype of orientation and meaning ... a personal myth' (Jung, 1967, p. 224). The individual Self can grasp the universal because it is not a simple component of a complex totality, but rather a complex microcosm of that totality. The reflexive self is thus inevitably a theorist of meaning in general, which again suggests that 'meaning' is made possible not by the symbol as a clarified label for an

element in an external reality, but by the inherent
metaphoricity of the symbol itself. The strength with which
the Jungian version of myth holds both to the universal and
to the personal can be related to Hegel's view of this
aspect of symbolism in general (Hegel, 1977, p. 62). It is
also profoundly significant for action-research's problem
concerning how the individual instance can 'achieve'
generality. The question for theoretical adequacy ceases
to be: how can the individual phenomenon be related to an
external pattern in which it can take its place as an
element in a system (of quasi-objects), but rather: how can
the individual phenomenon be 'grasped' in its own inherent
complexity (as a symbolic structure)?

At one level, this problem is engaged by 'ego-analysts'
who preserve the complex dynamics of the Freudian psychic
structure but remove the Freudian theme of a determining
and relatively inaccessible unconscious. Such procedures
as 'self-analysis' (Horney, 1962), 'self-discovery'
(Rogers, 1983), and 'transactional analysis' (Berne, 1967,
Harris, 1973) are presented as feasible (if lengthy and
difficult) processes whereby the subject can achieve self-
understanding, ie. achieve a measure of autonomy with
regard to its own complexities. But in order to be fully
intelligible, these accounts would themselves need to be
grounded in a general theory of the relationship between a
self-reflective subjectivity and the symbolic order in
which it is constituted as potentially self-reflective,
rather than as a determined outcome of prior causes.

This indeed is Lacan's problematic. The self-representations of the subject may not be understood by tracing them
to an experiential origin (which would of-course formulate
consciousness as determined by its antecedents). Rather,
the 'signifying chain' pursued by an interpreter of the
'meaning' of the subject is a sequence of symbolic
substitutions (metaphor) and combinations (metonymy) (Lacan,
1977, p. 258). Hence (for example) Lacan re-formulates the
Freudian phallus not as an objective feature of a traumatic
experience, but as a 'signifier' (p. 285). In emphasizing
that the subject is constituted as a structure of symbols,
rather than a structure of motives, Lacan's major theme
becomes the 'alienation' of the Self, following, in many
ways, Sartre's view of language as 'negativity', and
attempting to provide developmental grounds for this view.
Thus, from the moment at which the infant finds a problematic image with which to unify its experience of its own
body (a phase necessitated by the relative 'prematurity' of
the human neonate - Lacan, 1977, p. 4), consciousness of
self is mediated by the symbol, which embodies the
dependence of the subject on the Other (p. 5) and thus
converts primary narcissism into a sense of perennial
threat, and hence into aggression (pp. 5-6), reconstituting
all objects (including the self) in a 'paranoid mode'
(p. 17). Hence the game which the infant plays with its own
identity, his baffling presence AND absence in its image

and its name (Freud's 'Fort ... da' game - see Freud, 1961, p. 9) - the game which is the 'point of insertion of a symbolic order that pre-exists the infantile subject, and in accordance with which he will have to structure himself' - (Lacan, 1977, p. 234)-is fraught with an inescapable danger: the symbolic order is one in which 'the Other is the locus of the deployment of speech' (p. 264), and thus the Self-Other dialectic of reflexive speech which constitutes consciousness (p. 86) is structured as the Hegelian struggle between Master and Slave (Lacan, 1977, pp. 80, 305). In this way, through its original constitution in the symbolic, the subject is from the outset in a perpetual state of 'discord with its own reality' (p. 2). And it is through this 'primordial' discord and self-alienation that metaphor and metonymy, displacement and fictionalization are subjectivity's constitutive modes of being.

In this way, Lacan argues for the 'intellectual' potential of the self (p. 171) while maintaining a sense of its tragic limitations: its very creativity resides in a specific and irremediable fragility. Thus Lacan's theme can be added to those of Kant, Piaget, and Jung noted above: he gives us language as a further constitutive structure of subjectivity, but language neither as a determining system of concepts and rules, nor as an available mechanism for independent external reference: 'language' here is the 'parole' which Saussure neglected, that discursive reality in which the self is located, biographically and with Others (Lacan, 1977, p. 86), in which meaning is continuously created, and yet (condemned to reflexivity by the instability of the Self-Other dialectic) continuously transformed.

But there seems to be a discrepancy in Lacan's work precisely between versions of the self as constituted in the structures of reflexive discourse, and of the self as structured in developmental phases, eg. the 'mirror phase', and the 'Oedipal stage' (p. 282). In one we have a matrix of metaphoricity (as a theory of speech) and in the other we have a causal sequence (as a theory of biography). Lacan does not address this tension as possibly inevitable, but rather attempts a radical fusion, for example in his theory of the phallus as the 'signifier' of the Self-Other dialectic in general (p. 289) and of 'the Name-of-the-father' as 'the law of the signifier' (p. 217), of which the very least that can be said is that it suggests a reductionist and determined version of discourse, and one which would undermine Lacan's own emphasis on its ramifying metaphoricity.

The question raised by this aspect of Lacan's work is crucial: if the self is indeed and inevitably structured in time as well as in language, how can these two be related so that a determining causal chronology does not threaten the explorative, innovative quality of self-reflection? The nature of the problem can be seen if we once more consider

the ambiguities of Freud's work. On the one hand Freud
seems to propose a causal relationship between symbol and
origin: the structure of the individual is a set of
repressions which conceal infantile traumas by preserving
instead a symbolic 'memory trace' (Freud, 1976a, p. 687).
Hence to understand is a process of re-tracing a linear
chronology of cause and effect. And in the therapeutic
process, re-tracing is made possible by re-enactment. But
're-enactment' suggests a one-to-one relationship between
symbol and experience - otherwise re-enactment could not be
known to be a 'genuine' re-enactment, as distinct from, say,
a distortion, a variation, or even an antithesis; and hence
therapy could not be a re-tracing. But, as we have seen,
Freud is at pains to <u>deny</u> that symbols are unified labels
that can be simply <u>attached</u> to experiences: symbols, for
Freud, as for Jung and for Levi-Strauss, are inherently
ambiguous, and it is precisely their ambiguity (in their
relation to experience and to each other) that constitutes
their effect <u>as</u> symbols.

How, then, can the structure of symbolization be related
to the structure of experience, such that the subject may,
without self-contradiction or self-reduction, engage in
theoretic reflection upon experience? This must be a
central concern, since the subject's theorizing must be
reflexive, ie. grounded in the processes of its experience,
and (particularly) in the processes whereby experience is
conceived as available to interpretation. For example:
theorizing may not 'make use of' symbolic structures as
though they were 'equipment' with which an external reality
might be (accurately) 'described' (see Heidegger, 1968).

It is Derrida's work which is helpful at this point.
Derrida observes:

> 'There are two interpretations of interpretation,
> of structure, of sign, of play. The one seeks to
> decipher, dreams of deciphering a truth or an
> origin which escapes play and the order of the
> sign, and which lives the necessity of interpretat-
> ion as an exile ... (and thus) throughout (its)
> entire history has dreamed of full presence, the
> reassuring foundations, the origin and the end of
> play ... The other ... no longer turned towards
> the origin, affirms play ...' (Derrida, 1978,
> p. 292)

'History' here is the history of western culture, which has
constructed for itself 'linear' self-representations (in
terms of 'origins' and 'foundations') as 'enigmatic models',
in such various forms as 'scientific economy ... technics,
and ... ideology ... hierarchy ... graphic phoneticism (in
writing) ... and the mundane concept of temporality', each
of which depends in different ways on 'the repression of
pluri-dimensional symbolic thought' (Derrida, 1976, p. 86).

The link between these two passages from Derrida is as
follows: it is the linear model of thought which creates
the notion of truth as a re-tracable origin, and the mundane
model of temporality as a linear chronology which suggests
that investigation can, by 'reversing' chronology, re-enter
the presence of a past cause of a current effect. But
linear thought knows that it is only a model, that it
operates by denying the pluri-dimensionality (the
metaphoricity) of the symbols it claims to reduce to its own
linearity, and hence that the 'full presence' of truth is
always only a dream: linear thought is thus condemned to
approximate interpretations which it cannot theorize except
as always lamentable failures (in 'exile'). In terms of the
original question, then: linear thought (the ideal of logic,
of positivism) cannot be reflexive, since it does not
correspond to the structure of experience nor to the structure of reflective thought.

It is within this general orientation that Derrida wishes
to liberate Freud from the linear model of the symbol as a
translation from an original experience, by quoting Freud's
own awareness of the 'pluri-dimensionality' of the symbol:
symbols 'frequently have more than one or even several
meanings, and, as with Chinese script, the correct interpretation can only be arrived at on each occasion from the
context' (Derrida, 1978, p. 209, quoting Freud). In
Derrida's revision of Freud there is no 'origin', only a
plurality of symbolic structures: 'The unconscious text is
already a weave of pure traces, everything begins with
reproduction' (Derrida, 1978, p. 211). Hence the process of
repression is no longer (as with Freud) the 'forgetting' of
an experience, but the creation of the meaning of experience
through the 'deferral' of its interpretation. Indeed, only
'deferral' makes interpretation possible. 'Différance (ie.
deferral) is originary and indeed it is the essence of life'
(p. 203).

This argument is thus not merely a revision of Freud but a
general theory of meaning. How might its generality be
grasped? If metaphoricity is the essence of the symbol,
then it must be conceived in terms of an essential Difference. (Without Difference a symbol lapses into the
simplistic unity of a label). But the symbols in which the
subject represents experience to itself partake of the
temporal dimension of experience and of subjectivity, since
the subject is analytically formulated (for Lacan quite
explicitly) as discursively constituted in the Self-Other
dialectic of its biography - rather than in the a-temporal
moment, of individual perception or intuition. (See
Heidegger's critique of Kant in Being and Time - Heidegger,
1962, p. 410.) Derrida's 'Différance/Différence' thus
evokes the dialectical structure of consciousness as
temporal as well as analytical; indeed his double
formulation is intended to cancel precisely such a distinction (by reminding us of an earlier etymological unity) in
order to express the conditions, the possibility, and the

effectivity of consciousness as a symbolic process. Without
Difference ('différence') the symbol loses its metaphoricity
and thus its interpretive effect. Without Deferral
('différance') experience loses its biographical structure
of references and thus its capacity for meaning. Hence we
can remedy Lacan's failure (noted above): difference and
deferral together make up the dialectical conditions for the
possibility of discourse - both the discursive consciousness
in which subjective experience is constituted as
intelligible, and the discourse of theorizing by means of
which subjects can formulate their Being and re-formulate
reflexively the possibility of their so doing.

For Derrida this is particularly the case with <u>writing</u>.
(See Derrida, 1976, p. 9). Through the pluridimensionality
of writing, and through the playful, critical interpretation
of writing's pluridimensional text, the 'ideologies' of
linear expression, linear thought, and linear time may be
deconstructed' and hence transcended. Such arguments have
important analogies with dialectics. Lenin indeed observed
that 'rectilinearity' of thought was a feature of
'obscurantism' (Lenin, 1972, p. 363). From this point of
view, dialectical thought is characterized by not having an
origin or a final truth 'at the end of the line' - but
rather the endless 'play' of contradiction, the ceaseless
deferral of differences, by which each synthesis becomes the
thesis for further antithetical questioning. 'Writing bears
within itself the necessity of its own critique' (Derrida,
1978, p. 284). The 'play' of dialectic allows for the
possibility of the temporal and symbolic development of a
discursive subjectivity, and of the theoretical, critical
comprehension of that development.

With such considerations we may formulate intelligibility
for action-research's desire to disrupt the linearity of
positivism. Action-research requires the possibility of a
self-transcendent subject and the possibility of inquiry
founded in interaction and in a <u>non-determined</u> dialectic
between action and interpretation, ie. a form of inquiry
located in biographical experience and hence in <u>time</u>, but
<u>not</u> based on a determinist chronology in which a naturalized
factuality provides a warrant for observation as 'having-
been accurate'. It was earlier pointed out (in the
introduction to this chapter) that action-research, finding
no coherent alternative to such a chronology, lodged its
hopes in its 'spaces', which we may now interpret as action-
research's awareness of positivism's 'exiled' status. This
section has tried to provide theoretic grounds for action-
research (in this respect) through a notion of dialectical
play, which constitutes both Self and Theory as well as
Action and Research, and thus can articulate their possible
mutuality as well as their difference.

However, although the rejection of determinism is a
necessary beginning to the formulation of a competent
theoretic subject, there are other important stages in the

argument. It is disquieting to read: 'The domain of play
... of signification henceforth has no limit' (Derrida,
1978, p. 281), since such a lack of 'limit' seems to imply
a theoretic subject without a context and thus without
cultural resources: a symbolic order is indeed an 'arena'
for 'play', but an arena is defined by its limits - hence
the value of the contributions of Freud and Jung to the
foregoing discussion. Indeed action-research is particularly concerned to theorize contextually, and thus part of
its central problematic is the relation between the
possibility of theory and the institutional context (and
above all the professional practices) to which theory
addresses its possibilities as possibilities. Action-
research could have no interest in a form of theorizing in
which 'play' is taken not merely as the openness of the
dialectic but, concretely, as 'a positive affirmation of a
world without fault, without truth, without origin'
(Derrida, 1979, p. 292) since action-research is defined by
its need to address the limits of its institutional
possibilities. In this, action-research is wiser than
Derrida, whose playfulness fails to be reflexive when it
ignores its relationship with the linear culture whose
resources it is forced to use at one level even while
opposing it at another. Derridean 'play' risks being either
intimidated, when it transgresses limits whose existence it
denies, or being issued with a license to affirm the
faultlessness of a world whose reasons for issuing such a
license are of the deepest sociological interest. In other
words, theorizing as a social practice must, in order to be
reflexive, address the relation between the authority of
theory itself and the distribution of institutionalized
authority among different social practices. We need, then,
a theory of 'ideology'.

Reflexivity and Theories of Ideology

The problem with the notion of ideology is that it
articulates theory within the contingencies of cultural
authority, but that in order to accomplish this the theory
of ideology must articulate itself as not subject to such
contingencies. In other words, the theory of ideology
demands from itself an account of its own possibility, as
non-ideological. This is the general problem of reflexivity.
There is a further issue, however: how can a theory of
ideology differentiate itself in principle from its cultural
contingencies without recourse to the notion of an absolute
and thus a prescriptive science of human action, especially
since action-research bases its claim for a necessarily
unending dialectic of action and research upon the
impossibility of such a prescriptive science? Hence the aim
of this section will be firstly to question the claims of
'science' to prescribe remedies for 'ideology', and secondly
to consider how theorizing might recognize its institutional
context in ways which are both reflexive and self-
consistent.

Self-consistency is an issue which Althusser explicitly raises for himself. Having presented as his 'central thesis' that 'ideology constitutes individuals as subjects' ('Ideology and Ideological State Apparatuses', in Althusser, 1971, p. 160), he then admits:

> 'Both he who is writing these lines and the reader who reads them are ... ideological subjects' (p. 160)

and also that:

> 'The author, insofar as he writes the lines of discourse which claims to be scientific is completely absent as a 'subject' from 'his' scientific discourse (for all scientific discourse is by definition a subject-less discourse)...' (p. 160)

Another irony is added when he says: '(this) is a different question which I shall leave on one side for the moment' (p. 160), without specifying whether the 'I' who does the leaving on one side is the ideological subject who is writing the text, or whether the phrase 'I leave on one side' could claim to be part of a scientific discourse and thus 'subject-less'. If so, then what theoretic status can be attributed to a decision to leave aside the question of whether a text concerning the relation between ideology and science itself exemplifies ideology or science? The questions could be multiplied at this point: they would all focus on the issue of Althusser's reflexive awareness as a theorist; on the unaddressed issue of the relation between what the text asserts ('subjectless-ness') and what the possibility of writing the text requires (an 'I').

There is a further irony. Two years later Althusser wrote his Eléments d'autocritique (Althusser, 1974), in which he confesses as an error (not as a superceded moment in a dialectical development) his 'theoreticist tendency' (5) (p. 50) and withdrew important propositions, including his treatment of the notion of error (p. 42) and his 'theory of the difference between science and ideology in general' (6) (p. 50-1), original emphasis).

How is this to be understood? One starting point would be to consider Althusser as writing within a problematic of functionalism, such that all elements are explained by their necessary contribution to a material totality. Hence, for Althusser, ideology is a set of 'practices' and not a set of ideas (Althusser, 1971, p. 159-60), and the framework within which these ideological practices are presented is the 'reproduction of the relations of production' (p. 141) through the medium of 'ideological state apparatuses'. Now: 'there is no ideology except by the subject and for subjects' (p. 159). Indeed there is a 'double constitution' where by 'the category of the subject is ... constitutive of all ideology' and at the same time 'all ideology has the function (which defines it) of 'constituting' concrete individuals as subjects' (p. 160). Hence 'there is no practice except by and in ideology' and the various cultural formations become 'apparatuses' whereby the state determines subjectivity. The general argument is thus one in which Parson's monolithic integration of institutions and role expectations is extended to the level of consciousness itself. This argument, according to Ernesto Laclau (1979, p. 100) stems from Althusser's reading of Lacan's formulation of the 'Mirror phase' in the development of the subject's self-representation.

Now, functionalism integrates all social actors by installing Society-in-general in each one, and Althusser is no exception: every subject is 'interpellated' by a Subject ('Unique, Absolute' - Althusser, 1971, p. 166) and this Subject is (in various 'ideological' guises) the state. Althusser's problem then is clear: he cannot be a subject, because all subjects are <u>determined</u> by the state, whereas in Althusser's writing the state, precisely, is his object. And yet he cannot <u>not</u> be a subject, because <u>all</u> subjects are determined by the state! Only through the 'scientificity' of his writing could he be free of ideology (and hence of this dilemma) since 'scientific writing' is the only practice which is not ideological. He must thus insist on his authorship (which is indeed continuously asserted by a marked professorial tone) while denying the subjectivity of his authorship, thereby illustrating perfectly the contradictions of 'logo-centric' language as noted by Derrida (1976, p. 4, p. 12). (Clearly action-research's purposes are in no way served by a professorial, prescriptive science, nor by a reproductionist theory of consciousness: indeed it is precisely against such notions that much of Elliott's writing is directed, see Elliott, 1982a, p. 1, p. 25 ff.)

But Althusser himself, in his <u>Eléments d'autocritique</u>, analyzes the instability of the functionalist argument in ways which are relevant to action-research's needs. First of all he admits and regrets 'the absence of contradiction' in his theory of ideology (pp. 81-2), which had led him into a regrettable 'entanglement' with structuralism (7) (p. 53), which he rejects as 'mechanistic' (p. 61):

> 'Marxism is not a form of structuralism, not
> because it affirms the primacy of process over
> structure, but because it affirms the primacy
> of contradiction over process'. (p. 64) (8)

Indeed, Althusser elsewhere presents a theory of 'the materialist dialectic' in terms of 'overdetermined contradiction' (Althusser, 1977, p. 113) derived from his reading of Freud and Lacan on the nature of symbolization as a process of 'displacement and condensation' (Althusser 1971, p. 191). And at both the psycho-analytic level and the historical level Althusser is arguing <u>against</u> a simplistic notion of determinism, either by 'the economic

level' or by 'the unconscious'. Althusser wishes to speak
on behalf of the 'metonymy and metaphor of language'
(p. 191) and the 'dislocation of discourse' (p. 192), and
on behalf of philosophical thought as the play of
difference between metaphors (Althusser, 1973, pp. 18-19
footnote). Each point here, however, would undermine his
own attempt at the literal description of a reproductive
apparatus for consciousness in his theory of ideology, and
thus weaken the challenge that such a theory would pose for
action-research.

Althusser is also concerned to remedy his former 'theoret-
icism' (1974. p. 13), by arguing that the practice of
philosophy is 'class struggle at the level of theory'
(p. 86) (9), and thus he asserts 'the primacy of the
practical function over the theoretical function in
philosophy itself' (p. 88).(10) Hence 'the particular
dialectic which is at work in the practice of philosophy'
(p. 86) (11) returns us once more to a formulation consonant
with action-research's dialectic of theory and practice,
since it is in both cases (as a dialectic) a formulation
concerned with the theorizing of <u>change</u>, whereas functionalism (without a notion of contradiction or of dialectic)
cannot articulate change except through 'deviance' (see
Talcott Parsons, 1951, p. 321) - ie. a failure of functionalism's own theoretical framework. Hence the paradox of a
Marxist functionalism, and hence the inevitability of
Althusser's recantation.

What remains after the recantation, is presented in the
work of Chantal Mouffe and Ernesto Laclau. Within a theory
of ideologizing 'the subject' they present a theory of
'articulations' (Laclau, 1979, p. 7 and Mouffe, 1981,
p. 174), which denies that the 'elements' of thought and
cultural practice serve specific class interests, even where
specific combinations of these elements do so. Thus
ideological systems may be 'disarticulated' into their
elements, so that these elements may then be re-grouped
('re-articulated') so as to transcend the class interests
served by the original combination. Instead of 'ideology'
as a unified structure imposed upon thought in general, we
have a level of 'ideological struggle' as a process of
<u>contested</u> dis-articulation / re-articulation, in which
social classes struggle for the appropriation of 'the
fundamental elements of a given society ... its "social
imagery"' (Mouffe, 1981, p. 175). In particular there is
a continuous contest between social classes for an
articulation of <u>its</u> class interests with the idea of 'The
People' in general (Laclau, 1979, p. 109). This emphasis
has points of contact with Foucault's suggestion (cited with
approval by Heinz Moser (Moser, 1978, p. 96) that although
'knowledge' and 'power' are intimately conjoined, this does
not imply a structure of centralized imposition, but rather
that power is a ubiquitous and immanent feature of the
social relationships within which knowledge is constituted
(Foucault, 1981, p. 91 and pp. 98-9).

How, then, might these various suggestions find a place within the previous arguments concerning the nature of the theoretic self and its theoretic resources?

The first step is to note the link between the ideological and the mythic. Paul Ricoeur (1981) seems to open up this possibility by his description of the features of ideology within a:

> 'fundamental thesis ... that ideology is an unsurpassable phenomenon of social existence insofar as social reality always has a symbolic constitution and incorporates an interpretation, in images and representations, of the social bond itself'. (p. 231)

According to Ricoeur, ideology presents 'the social bond itself' in terms of justifying and rationalizing the original basis (the 'founding act' - p. 225) of the particular social group; its tendencies are thus to simplify, to reduce to a taken-for-granted orthodoxy, to justify the authority which pervades and preserves the group, and to treat its own symbolic representation not as a representation but as reality itself (pp. 225-31). The crucial point for Ricoeur is that ideology does not 'thematize' (p. 227) what it represents. (ie. it does not treat what it represents as a <u>theme</u>, in need of analysis.)

But if ideology justifies without analysis the social bond which it takes for granted, why does ideology continue? Why cannot a taken-for-granted social bond simply <u>be</u> taken for granted? If ideology <u>justifies</u> authority, why is authority not simply <u>accepted</u>? Whence, in other words, the apparently auto-destructive quality of 'justification'? The point is, that a formulation of ideology needs to recognize ideology's own fragility as a justification, in order to explain ideology's necessity, as a widespread and endlessly repeated feature of the cultural process. This is perhaps the final irony for Althusser's functionalist theory: the notion of a <u>successful</u> imposition of an ideologized consciousness explains the reproduction of social relations but fails to address the reproduction of ideology itself. Conversely, only an ideological effort whose effectiveness was always in question would 'explain' (in functionalist terms) the necessity for a continuous ideological process, and it would also explain why social relations are not simply reproduced but (slowly) develop. Which is, after all, what Marxism would wish to argue.

Now, Ricoeur suggests that the converse of ideology is 'thematization' (see above) leading to his general proposal of 'science' as <u>critique</u> (p. 235), but a simple opposition of this type would lead to a confrontation which could be resolved only by a capitulation - and one typical outcome would then be a <u>prescriptive</u> 'critical science', which would 'defeat' ideology by revealing it as 'error'. But Ricoeur wishes, on the contrary, to establish 'an

72

intimately dialectical relation between science and
ideology' (p. 224), and for this (I would argue) it is
necessary to establish the possibilities for critique
within ideology, as an 'intimate' and inherent contradiction which would sustain Ricoeur's dialectic. And this
is where the notion of mythic thought, as founded in
contradiction, becomes crucial. Levi-Strauss argues:

>'For a myth to be engendered by thought and for
>it in turn to engender other myths, it is
>necessary and sufficient that an initial
>opposition should be injected into experience ...
>This inherent disparity of the world sets mythic
>thought in motion, but it does so because ... it
>conditions the existence of every object of
>thought'. (1981, pp. 603-4).

Elsewhere he says:

>'The purpose of myth is to provide a logical
>model capable of overcoming a contradiction ...
>it therefore grows spiral-wise until the
>intellectual impulse which produced it is
>exhausted' (1972, p. 229)

It is for this reason that Levi-Strauss's analyses of myth
work towards structures of 'binary opposites' (1981, pp. 559
692). Hence, for example, myth does not present a hero as
heroic except in a dynamic, dangerous, and problematic
relation with a force for villainy (a dragon or a
'traitor'). Myth is indeed the exciting story of their
struggle. Myth justifies the original social bond but
always at the 'political' cost, as it were, of 'thematizing'
it, ie. raising it to prominence as a theme by showing it
to be endangered.

My argument, then, is that ideology is not simply opposed
to thematization. Rather, there is an inevitable tension
within ideology, as part of ideology's process: any
elaborated justification implicitly 'thematizes' (makes
available for analysis) the questionability of the
justification, the possibility of alternatives (12). However,
it is not possible to 'thematize' everything at the same
time (Ricoeur, 1981, p. 227). In order to render X
problematic, Y must be taken for granted, and (perhaps) vice
versa. Hence, on the one hand science can never find a
position entirely 'apart', from which it can carry out a
'purely analytical' critique of ideology; and on the other
hand ideology always evokes the possibility of science at
the very moment that it denies science's accomplishment.
This is the dialectical relation desired by Ricoeur, a
relation founded ultimately on the reflexivity of consciousness and on the 'negativity' of language's relation to the
reality it speaks: to utter 'justification' is to recollect
the possibility of non-justification. Ideology and science
thus constitute a mythic pairing: hero and villain, locked

in a necessary, mutually constitutive, and unending combat,
rehearsing the possibility but also the fragility of self-
knowledge on the part of the social group, and, by the
dialectical progress of their struggle, transforming the
parameters of that self-knowledge.

Such a framework can accommodate the proposal, by Laclau
and Mouffe, of ideology as a _political_ struggle for a
particular articulation of social imagery, and also
Althusser's suggestion that the practice of philosophy is
'class struggle within theory'. Both proposals can be seen
as evoking the 'interests' of knowledge (cf. Habermas, 1972)
within a dialectical formulation both of political power and
of the understanding of that power, ie. a dialectics of
'interest' and a dialectics of knowledge.

In this way, the theory of myth-as-contradiction can help
to formulate dialectical and reflexive possibilities for
ideology. Can ideology perhaps help to reformulate myth?
Levi-Strauss's argument concerning myth is that an
'inherent disparity of the world (which) conditions the
existence of every object of thought ... sets mythic
thought in motion', and gives examples such as the
'disparity ... between the high and the low, the sky and
the earth, land and water, the near and the far, left and
right, male and female, etc.' (Levi-Strauss, 1981, (p. 603).
For Levi-Strauss the universalization of mythic themes was
an important project, but for the argument here the generality of his examples is something of a limitation, if myth
is to be considered as a resource for theorizing an
industrialized society. In other words, we need to consider
the concrete binary operations of the 'social imagery'.
(Mouffe, 1981, p. 175) with which the members of an
industrial society represent to themselves the 'social bond'
(Ricoeur 1981, p. 231) in which specifically they are
constituted.

Much of Durkheim's work argues precisely this point, that
in industrial society the articulation of the social bond
is analytically different in nature from that which
characterizes the type of 'primitive' society observed by
Levi-Strauss, and the same argument poses a problem
concerning the relevance of the Jungian 'archetypes', which
point always towards the archaic as the resource whereby
modern society might recover its 'mythopoeic imagination'.
Hence also the 'pastoral' theme which underlies Jung's view
of non-industrial cultures, so that he refers, for example,
to 'arab culture' as 'the paradise of childhood' (1967,
p. 272). In a sense Jung seems to view primitive man as the
unconscious for the European, but not to envisage the
possibility that the European could embody the unconscious
for a primitive civilisation, as in 'cargo cults'. For
Jung, the 'mythopoeic imagination' seems to be not so much
a formulation of the process whereby the members of a
modern society might recover an intelligible sense of self-
reflection (which is the problematic for this study) but a

74

nostalgic invocation of <u>direct</u> access to a consensual social
meaning, which (Durkheim would argue) the differentiating
structures of industrialization have for ever banished.

This, then, is what 'ideology' could contribute to myth-
ology: the social imagery of a society structured by
hierarchical difference and contested power relations,
including, therefore, the imagery of class, bureaucracy, and
the state. As a resource, therefore, ideology as it were
'updates' the vocabulary of myth. (See Barthes, 1976).
This 'updating' is, I would argue, a necessary process,
given the complex relationship in industrialized societies
between their past and their present, as mythic locations
for their ideals. While still haunted, as was the Greece of
Homer and Sophocles, by the imagery of past 'golden ages'
inhabited by gods and heroes, we <u>also</u> glamorize the
contemporary, as part of the myth / ideology of industrialization's progressive achievement: thus, alongside the
mythic images of Helen of Troy and Mary Queen-of-Scots, we
also install 'Princess Di' and, in capitalism's own
dynastic Olympus: Joan Collins.

In the institutional context of the educational action-
research worker, symbolic possibilities are also articulated
in terms of mythic figures both from the distant past
(Socrates: 'critical rationality', Archimedes: 'practical
innovation', Einstein: 'intellectual genius') and also more
recent examples (A.S. Neill: 'creative freedom', Paul
Freire: 'curriculum as cultural revolution', Piaget:
'stages of cognitive development', Arthur Jensen:
'inherited intelligence'). And, even without being person-
alized, the imagery of the institutional forces which make
up the educational context (government departments,
industrial training agencies, local educational authorities,
teacher unions, even 'the school') do not form a unified and
self-legitimating system of norms which determine our
comprehension of them, any more than, at the political level
itself, they form a stable, static, and integrated set of
practices. If, on the contrary, the institutional context
is seen as structured by political conflict (rather than as
a pacified 'system') then our thinking of that context can
also, without inconsistency, be characterized, not as a
determined reflection of that context, but as a dialectical
process, both within the oppositions of ideological imagery
<u>and</u> within the reflexive dialectic between ideology and
theoretic analysis.

To sum up, then: in this section I have argued that
action-research's ideal of critical reflection upon its
institutional context is not be be undermined by a theory of
ideology: on the contrary, theories which would assimilate
reflection to its context are themselves undermined by the
overwhelming irony created by their lack of reflexive
awareness. Rather, I would argue that a dialectical
formulation of institutional processes <u>and</u> of ideological
processes preserves the possibility of <u>critical</u> theorizing

and gives precision to its aspirations. At the same time,
the unending dialectic between ideology and theory is
another formulation of action-research's grounds for
proposing the specific intimacy of theory and practice, of
research and action. However, the characterization of
analysis as a dialectical process returns us to its basis
in the Self-Other relation and thus to the question of the
form of the social interaction within which theorizing may
be constituted.

The Social Relationships of Theoretic Reflection

Having established that theory is not necessarily encapsulated by a merely institutionalized authority (see previous
section), the question becomes: wherein lies the authority
for theorizing itself, or indeed: what is the relationship
between theory and authority in a relationship constituted
as a search for enlightenment? It has already been argued
that for action-research this question has a specific
urgency, since action-research wishes to refuse the theoretic authority of Nature, as uttered by a would-be oracular
positivism. In wishing to locate theory within the domain
of practitioners, to define research as action-research,
action-research must reject a simple polarized authority
relation between the theorist who knows and the actor who
is known. Otherwise, if it tries to theorize itself within
such a relationship - as, indeed (as we have seen) it often
does - action-research would be assimilated either to a
ramshackle format for applied social science or to the
apologetics for a sophisticated version of management
theory - as indeed (as we have seen) it often is. For this
reason this section will only be concerned with formulations
in which the authority of theory has already been rendered
problematic by the 'counter-authority' of the knowledge
available to the object of theory, the 'social actor'.
Only a genuinely 'balanced' opposition of this type (in
which indeed the problematic of action-research is
constituted) could originate a sustainable dialectic. This
necessary and poised ambiguity, which action-research
writers have presented, for example, through the notion of
the 'facilitation' (of actors by theorists) will be
approached by comparing it on the one hand with 'therapy'
(for actors by theorists) and on the other hand with
'emancipation' (of actors into theorists). It is for this
reason that I begin once more with Freud, and with
Habermas's criticism of Freud.

Although Freud apparently aspires to a determinism based
on causal origins which are positively known within the
structure of a general descriptive theory, these causes and
origins are necessarily manifested in ways which are
irremediably personal to the particular patient. It is for
this reason that the 'training' of an analyst must take the
form of the psycho-analysis of the would-be therapist (see
'The Question of Lay Analysis' Freud, 1962, p. 109). Hence
the ambiguity of the process of inquiry into those causes

and origins: inquiry cannot be 'a causal therapy in the
literal sense' - that a cause identified by the therapist
thereby becomes available to remedy by the therapist (Freud,
1952, p. 443). Rather, the therapy depends on the
contribution of the patient (the 'resistance', p. 445), and
indeed the process of inquiry becomes its own object (the
'transference' - pp. 449, 452); ie. inquiry is recognized
as inherently reflexive. Hence:

> 'The labour of overcoming resistance is the
> essential achievement of the analytic treatment:
> the patient has to accomplish it, and the
> physician makes it possible for him to do so by
> suggestions which are in the nature of an
> education ... Psycho-analytic treatment is a
> kind of re-education'. (p. 459, my emphases)

But in this passage we have a statement of the basic
ambiguity at the level which Freud did not address: the
accomplishment is the patient's, but the terms of that
accomplishment are 'suggested' by one in the role of
'physician'; the accomplishment is thus the acceptance of
a re-education, whose content is conceived by Freud in terms
of a biologically based causal theory.

It is precisely to this contradiction (between accomplishment and acceptance) that Habermas points, in a chapter
called 'The scientistic self-misunderstanding of meta-
psychology' (Habermas, 1978, p. 246 ff.). Habermas's basic
argument is that Freud confuses the different epistemological bases underlying respectively a natural, empirical
science (with its knowledge created by experimentation), and
a hermeneutic science 'embedded in the context of self-
reflection' (namely a dialogue 'involving both partners,
doctor and patient') (p. 252-3). Freud, says Habermas,
wishes to claim that his science is simultaneously both,
'because he considered the analytic situation of dialogue
quasi-experimental in character' (p. 253), while Habermas
emphasizes the incompatibility between 'the controlled
observation of predicted results' and 'the intersubjectivity
of mutual understanding' (p. 253). For Habermas, and for my
argument here, it is important to disentangle from Freud's
'scientistic' claim a formulation of analysis in which the
authority for 'enlightenment' arising 'intersubjectively' is
not obscured by the prescription of a supposedly prior
scientific expertise. This would of course entail
questioning the basis of a relationship based on the role of
'the physician', whose 'training', once it is 'completed'
allows him to 're-educate' others.

Jung's criticisms of Freud are helpful at this juncture.
Jung emphasizes that there is no set of 'rules for
interpretation' which a therapist can bring to particular
cases: he claims to abandon what he terms 'so-called
"methods"' and 'theoretical assumptions' (Jung, 1967,
p. 153) and instead locates the authority of the therapist

in a rigorously pursued self-understanding which (more unambiguously than for Freud) is not the acquiring of 'a set
of concepts' but learning 'to know (one's) own psyche and
to take it seriously' (p. 154). Further, this
'seriousness' is not the familiar 'scientific' seriousness
of 'systematic rigour': quite the contrary (see p. 153).
Rather, in more Heideggerian terms it is a willingness to
make a commitment to the situation. Therapists must bring
their whole personality 'into play' along with that of the
patient. They cannot 'cloak themselves in authority';
they are 'part of the drama' (p. 154). The seriousness of
the therapist is thus not a defence, but on the contrary a
specifically recollected vulnerability: the 'play' of the
drama is its unpredictability; uncloaked, the therapist is
at risk; he is, indeed 'effective only when he himself is
affected. "Only the wounded healer heals "'. (p. 155).
And - the final reflexive twist of the argument - 'the
healer heals himself' (p. 242). The condition of the
therapeutic relationship, then, ceases to be the resistance
of patients (Freud's version of reflexivity) but therapists'
lack of resistance to their own sense of need. Jung thus
introduces the notion of a 'counter-transference', whereby
not only the patient but the therapist also focusses
unconscious themes into the interaction (see Fordham, F,
1978, p. 80 ff.) (13)

Underlying this radical abandonment of a cognitive
authority are two important strands in Jung's thought. One
is his emphasis on the uniqueness of the individual:
'Interpretation ... requires a study of the whole symbol-
producing individual' (Jung, 1977, p. 250). Each case
requires 'a new language', the grasping of a separate
'personal myth' (Jung, 1967, pp. 153, 224). Secondly, the
sense of the unique individual is in turn grounded in what
might be termed a theological epistemology, in which a
radical protestantism - the direct access of the individual
psyche to the divine - is constituted in an equally radical
deism - the divine manifested in both nature and culture -
hence Jung's interest in both alchemy and archetypes, as
points of intersection between the apparent availability of
human symbolism and the numinous mystery of the grounds of
that symbolism. For Jung, therefore, there is a ready and
potent analogy between the therapist as a wounded healer
and Christ as 'the suffering servant of God' (Jung, 1967,
p. 243). But is it possible to interpret these ideas
within the analytical limits of social inquiry itself, to
'bracket out', as it were, the theological problematic in
which indeed inquiry might be seen in terms of 'the care of
souls' (p. 242) and to understand in analytical (rather
than ethical or spiritual) terms what Jung seems to present
as the necessary vulnerability of the would-be theorist?

In The Elementary Forms of the Religious Life Durkheim
says: 'The exceptional authority of ... Reason' is 'the
very authority of society ... transferring itself to a
certain manner of thought which is the indispensable

condition of all common action' (Durkheim 1915, p. 17).
And in 'The Determination of Moral Facts' (in Durkheim,
1974) he says that he is 'indifferent' as to whether the
basic formulation of 'collective being' is taken to be God
or Society, since he sees 'in the Divinity only society
transfigured and symbolically expressed'. (p. 52).
Durkheim's sociological 'indifference' in this respect
permits the following analogy: the prophet of the divine
'serves God' by recollecting the basis of the relationship
between the divine and the earthly; the prophet is
condemned to call for the sacrifice of earthly advantage,
as a manifestation of the seriousness of its grounds in the
divine. Such a sacrifice cannot merely be preached - it
must be exemplified: the prophet's destiny is martyrdom,
an earthly death signifying the life of the divine.
Similarly, the social theorist 'serves Society' by
recollecting the basis of the relationship between the
theoretic and the pragmatic; the theorist is condemned to
call for the sacrifice (the 'interruption') of the pragmatic
as a manifestation of the seriousness of its grounds in the
theoretic. Such a recollection of the theoretic grounds
for social action cannot merely be preached to others, but
must be exemplified: the theorist must suffer the
demonstration that his/her own social action (of providing
theoretic grounds for others) is grounded in the same
theoretic basis. The theorist's destiny is the unremitting
recollection of reflexivity, a pragmatic death, signifying
the life of theory.

There is however, a further important step to the analogy.
For the conventional religious 'believer' (such as Jung's
father, whose views he rejected - see Jung, 1967) the
martyrdom of the prophet is not so much a tragic irony as a
triumph. Similarly, conventional social science proclaims
theory as a triumph - not a wound but a weapon, not an
ironic awareness but a prescriptive interpretation. In
contrast, the analytical reflexivity of the theorist-as-
wounded-healer is not a theory-which-prescribes-for-action,
but a 'meta-theory' - a theory, that is, of the relationship between theory and action, of their mutual neediness
within a constitutive dialectic. The recollection of the
'life' of theory does not, then, signify the 'death' of
pragmatic action; rather, that both are moments in an
unending cycle, the cycle of theory and action to which
action-research aspires. The theoretic 'authority' of the
meta-theoretical analysis of reflexivity does not create a
relationship whereby the theorist-as-physician provides
diagnosis and prescription for the social practitioner:
rather, it is a continuously self-cancelling, self-
questioning authority which constitutes a mutual dependence
between practitioner and theorist, as a 'questioning
dialectic' (see previous chapter, final section).

A further way of grasping the mutuality of theory and
research, of theorist and practitioner, is in terms of
Kirkegaardian irony.

'Constantly engaged in leading the phenomenon
up to the Idea (the dialectical activity) the
individual is thrust back, or rather flees back
into actuality. But actuality itself has no
other validity than to be the constant occasion
for wanting to go beyond actuality - except that
this never occurs. Whereupon the individual
draws these exertions of subjectivity back into
himself, terminates them in himself in personal
satisfaction. Such is the standpoint of Irony'.
(Kirkegaard, 1966, The Concept of Irony, p. 183).

Irony itself therefore is the apparent triumph of
analytical reflexivity over action. But Kirkegaard later
continues:

'Only insofar as irony is mastered ... does
irony acquire its proper significance and true
validity' (p. 338).

'Irony as a mastered moment ... teaches us to
actualize actuality ... Actuality acquires
its validity ... as a history wherein consciousness
successively outlives itself ... actuality
acquires its validity through action' (pp. 340-1).

In other words, although irony 'establishes the disparity
between Idea and actuality ... and between possibility and
actuality' (p. 302), mastered irony does not allow this
disparity to be formulated merely as a negativity, which
illuminates the irremediable irony of action, from a
distance, but is itself in turn rendered helpless by the
equal irony of its own distance from action. Instead, the
mastery of the ironic moment formulates the disparity as a
constitutive relationship - between Idea and actuality,
between theory and practice. This relationship would always
subject action to the irony of theory, but would also
ceaselessly challenge theory to transcend its negativity, to
'outlive itself' by formulating its necessary relation to
action. Thus, through submission to irony, the irony of the
'healer' can itself (temporarily) be 'healed'.

These lines of argument enable us to make two vital points
concerning action-research. Firstly, that action-research's
desire to reject the prescriptive interpretative theory of
positivism makes a 'meta-theoretical' epistemological framework absolutely essential. Moser (1978, p. 140) dismisses
meta-theory, arguing that since discourse is a 'practice in
the life-world' ('Lebenspraxis') questions of validity can
be settled only within a given discourse and therefore not
'in general'. On the contrary, I have argued that unless
discourse is rigorously formulated in meta-theoretical terms,
ie. within an analytically reflexive dialectic between
action and theory, then action-research's epistemology will
be engulfed by positivism, and action-research's investigative relationships will be cast once more in the

authoritarian mould of the expert and the client, the physician and the patient.

Secondly, we can challenge action-researchers who suggest that they can act as 'catalytic agents' (Halsey, 1972, p. 198). The catalyst is a metaphor for an 'unchanged agent of change'. Hence both Halsey (p. 58) and Moser (1978, p. 169) anticipate a situation where action-research personnel transform social actors, by endowing them with previously absent qualities (theoretic autonomy), and then withdraw - themselves apparently untransformed. Similarly, Brown, et al. (1972) list the one-way traffic of facilitation between 'facilitator' and 'participants', but do not consider what might be facilitated in and for the facilitator. The facilitator is a teacher, but he / she is not taught. But, from Marx onwards, a question for all sociology of educational processes must be: how is the educator educated? ('Theses on Feuerbach', III - Marx, 1970) and it is this issue which has been reformulated in this section: the dialectic of analytical reflexivity challenges the theorist along with the practitioner, and denies the direct authority of one over the other by submitting both to the necessity of commitment and irony, and providing a set of metatheoretical auspices under which 'change agency' and 'facilitation' are mutually transform-ative processes for both theorist and practitioner. Hence: what remains unchanged by the process of inquiry is neither the theories nor the practices of either theorist or practitioner, but rather the auspices of irony, reflexivity and commitment, dialectical question and play, under which the interaction of the inquiry proceeds.

We have thus begun to reformulate the relation between authority and inquiry. It has been argued that inquiry's desire for critical enlightenment contests the authority given by institutional roles (and the previous section attempted to provide for the analytic possibility of this contestation). Also, inquiry (in the form required by action-research) denies the authority derived from specific corpuses of knowledge located externally to the situation under inquiry. The relationships of inquiry thus exclude 'scientists' and 'catalysts', and include only 'participants-at-risk'.

But authority is now embodied in the auspices whereby inquiry requires, precisely, risk. What form of authority could sustain these auspices?

Habermas presents an answer at the requisite level - that of a metatheory of valid discourse - and one that has appealed to action-research's aspiration to formulate the relationships of inquiry as a non-hierarchical 'collabor-ation'. In a paper first published in 1981 (14) I presented Habermas's argument as follows:

'In his paper 'Towards a Theory of Communicative

Competence' (1970), Habermas presents 'the dialogue constitutive universals ... of the ideal speech situation' as a symmetrical distribution of control by dialogue participants of the following dimensions of discourse:

1) The personal pronoun system;

2) The system of logical expressions of space, time, identity, and causality;

3) The system of speech acts concerning truth and value ie.

   (a) being and appearance (claims and disputes)

   (b) being and essence (revelations and concealments)

   (c) being and ought to be (prescriptions and refusals)

Habermas summarizes the significance of these as follows:

> 'Pure intersubjectivity is determined by a symmetrical relation between I and You (We and You), I and He (We and They). An unlimited interchangeability of dialogue roles demands that no side be privileged in the performance of these roles: pure intersubjectivity exists only when there is complete symmetry in the distribution of assertion and disputation, revelation and hiding, prescription and following among the partners of a communication'. (p.143)

Only under the conditions of such 'pure intersubjectivity' can there be a discourse about truth in which all can share who are affected, in which the absence of constraint allows only genuinely common interests to be agreed, in which there is no deception because each individual's interpretation is subjected to scrutiny, and in which no force except that of the better argument is used. (Habermas, 1976, pp. 108-110)'

The paper continues by arguing directly from this account of Habermas to the possibility of 'emancipatory' dialogue and collaboration as the essential format for inquiry.

Now, if the ideal of speech is taken to be the 'unlimited interchangeability of dialogue roles', then it is possible to say, as Habermas does: 'With the very first sentence the intention of a general and voluntary consensus is unmistakably enunciated' (Habermas, 1974, p. 17). Hence the ideal of 'dialogue' provides the authoritative auspices for the search for enlightenment, since it provides analytically for agreement that the outcome of dialogue is enlighten-ment, and it also provides auspices for the necessary relationships, ie. egalitarian mutuality. Hence Habermas's appeal for action-research writers. (See, for example, Carr and Kemmis, 1986, p. 158 and pp. 203-4).

But this argument moves through a series of abstractions which ignore their reflexive basis. To begin with, language is equated on the one hand with the form of utterances ('pronoun system') and on the other hand with its social function ('speech acts'), and this ignores the reflexive processes by which utterances and social interactions are mutually constitutive - the processes described, for example, by Lacan and Garfinkel. Then, having thus dismantled the complexity of symbolization into its notional 'components', Habermas then reassembles them into an 'intersubjectivity' whose 'purity' seems to represent the final cessation of dialectic, and is postulated precisely so that it will offer no resistance to 'consensus', as a static moment of changeless unity. Finally, the invocation of 'logic' in terms of Kantian universals is significant: an unproblematically valid 'logic' would indeed prescribe the 'better' argument and thereby endow it with 'force'. My argument against Habermas here parallels Heidegger's criticism of Kant's abstraction of the cognitive subject and of the a-temporal moment of 'intuition' from the dialectics of Being (Heidegger, 1962, pp. 366-8, p. 410 - see Chapter One, above). Habermas's argument is 'utopian': the auspices for theorizing which it proposes are illusory: it provides a theory of language's ideal which cannot enter into relationship with the practice of language, but remains as a disabling irony. Unlike Kirkegaardian irony, it does not limit itself with an ironic awareness of its own self-contradiction: for Kirkegaard, irony itself must, as it were, be seen ironically, and hence provide for the mastery of its own moment. The inert unity of Habermas's ideal of speech simply 'makes a mockery' of actual speech, just as the ideal of science, says Garfinkel, mocks the actual practices of comprehension.

And yet this discursive ideal rendered inert by the purity of its intersubjectivity and the finality of its consensus is far from what Habermas himself requires. On the contrary, he wishes to formulate a 'universal pragmatics of speech' as an ideal which can guide the adjudication of validity claims in practical life (Habermas, 1979, pp. 2-5). Elsewhere he states that he rejects 'pure theory' in order to urge that knowledge and interest are related in a 'dialectic' (1978, pp. 314-5) and that 'it is not unconstrained intersubjectivity itself that we call dialectic, but the history of its repression and reestablishment' (p. 59).

A metatheory of the auspices for a reflexive dialectics of inquiry, then, must provide for its own history, of which consensual intersubjectivity would be an evanescent and self-cancelling moment, rather than a teleology or a prescription. The relationships whereby these auspices might be maintained remain (so far) problematic: my argument against Habermas is that auspices for theorizing cannot in practice be equated with the notion of an egalitarian dialogue formulated as the 'interchangeability of roles'. As Habermas himself says, enlightenment could only be equated with agreement (among those whose roles have ceased to be differentiated) in a society which was 'already emancipated' (Habermas, 1978, p. 315), and where, in consequence, inquiry's own interest and necessity would seem to be in question.

But does not the requirement of a reflexive dialectic also imply a symmetrical distribution of initiative and responsibility in a sense which preserves implicitly at least something of Habermas's egalitarian ideal? Are not all at risk? Are not all to be transformed? Admittedly, analytical reflexivity is not a corpus of knowledge which one might authoritatively possess and transmit; rather it would be exemplified, and its exemplification would begin with a question addressed to its own possibility. But can anything be said concerning the distribution, symmetrical or otherwise, of the initiatives for such questioning among the participants of inquiry? Are we perhaps even talking of a theoretic practice which requires a specific prior 'education' and thus reconstitutes a hierarchical relation between 'theorists', for whom the reflexive dialectic is a familiar risk, and 'practitioners', to whom its challenges must be unfamiliar, and whose attempts at reflexive analysis will be, initially at least, 'unskilful'? Our question has thus become: what is the relationship between the mundane reflexivity of interaction and the analytic reflexivity of theory?

At this point we must consider more carefully the familiar dichotomy between hierarchy and equality. At the level of role relationships, hierarchy and equality are related in a dimension of power, and present their difference in the form of a question: what might be the legitimate grounds for a difference in power? In contrast, the difference between theory and action is not a question but a necessity: to abandon their difference is to annihilate both (see previous Chapter). However this difference does not constitute a power dimension (except within the positivist version of theory, which presumes to dictate its interpretations and explanations as the 'real meaning' of action). Instead, analytic reflexivity is related to mundane reflexivity as an irremediable difference, not within a power relation but as an analytic necessity. Indeed, the very problematic of this section - what is the appropriate social relation for an investigative enterprise? - must be queried, since it presupposes the possibility that a theoretic stance could be equated with a social relationship, which action-research writers have taken to be Habermas's suggestion, but which previous arguments enable us now to reject in principle. This in turn helps to justify action-research's claim that investigation can be an individual process of self-transcendence, that collaboration or facilitation are 'helpful', but not necessary. Within a Habermasian frame of reference this is hardly intelligible.

There are two main dimensions to the suggestion that there

is no power dimension constructed by the difference with which analytical reflexivity confronts the mundane reflexivity of action as the auspices of theoretic work. First, as we have noted previously in this section, it is a challenge to its own grounds as well as to the grounds of action. Secondly, this very difference is constructed within a particular intimacy between analytic and mundane reflexivity, as follows.

Analytical reflexivity always has as its occasion and potential starting point social members' implicit grasp (within a dialectic of consciousness and action) of the ambiguities and contradictions which characterize the symbolic processes of familiar cultural forms (see Chapter One). The most vivid examples of this are in the realm of the aesthetic: advertisements, rock videos, theatre, films, novels: all play with the crucial meanings which structure collective self-representation, and thereby constitute their massive appeal, as 'entertainment'. Often, their 'play' is explicitly quite 'risky': only 'in the end' do they turn aside from their subversive course and gloss their own challenges as within the realm of mundane order. Indeed, earlier in the discussion - of ideology as 'justification' - I hinted at the inherent link between play and risk at the level of language itself: to play with language is to risk the revelation of the inherent fragility of language's reflexive processes; and yet that experience of 'communication', in which we are so deeply dependent on language, is jocularly presented - through jokes, puns, quibbles, and crosswords - as but a question-able assumption. At one level, certainly, mundane reflexivity is, as Garfinkel says, 'uninteresting': what is, on the contrary, of absorbing interest (and thus 'entertaining'), is to play with the limits of mundane reflexivity - to move 'thrillingly' or 'comically' close to an analytic rupture. The difference of analytic reflexivity, however, is that its auspices are actually to make that rupture, to suffer the fall from the high wire, to plunge into symbolizations own reflexive abyss. But my argument here is that although only theorists 'do it', everyone could do it, because everyone can envisage it, and does so, all the time, for fun.

In other words, the resources for analytic reflexivity are provided for as possibilities in the richly ambiguous meaning structures of culture itself, ie. in their mythic, metaphorical, dialectical, and ideological features. As Blum and McHugh would say: everyone can be a theorist; any experience can be the occasion for theorizing (see McHugh et al., 1974, Introduction). It is this tension between the familiar and the different, between play as entertainment and play as critical analysis, that the auspices of analytical reflexivity can provide for a dialectic between theorist and practitioner which can realistically call upon the contribution of both - a dialectic which formulates an epistemological relationship quite precisely, but which has no necessary implications for the institutionalized interaction in which it might be embodied.

I conclude, then, that 'critical reflection' may be formulated as a possible stance: it may be established, as action-research requires, independently of specific role-relationships and independently of specific corpuses of academic knowledge; in other words, it establishes Subjectivity in a resource-ful, rather than a determined, relation to the symbolizing processes of both psyche and culture.

NOTES

(1) 'in konkreten gesellschaftlichen Situationen... welche Kluft zwischen Anspruch and Realität, zwischen formulierten demokratischen Prinzipen und faktischer Herrschaft im Spätkapitalismus uns besteht'. (All translations from Moser are by R. Winter)

(2) 'Das Sein und Schein, Wesen und Erscheinung, Sein und Sollen unterscheiden kann ... welche über die bloss vorgegebene Situation hinausgeht und den übergreifenden Zusammenhang, welcher diese Situation bestimmt, mit in die Diskussion nimmt'.

(3) 'Die Betroffenen selbst ihr Schiksal in die Hand nehmen'.

(4) From an analytical point of view, one would wish to see jokes as sudden reflexive twists, revealing both the limitations of their own conditions and the hitherto concealed possibilities which these conditions might otherwise facilitate or provoke.

(5) 'ma tendence théoriciste' (translations from Eléments d'Autocritique by R. Winter)

(6) 'théorie de la différence entre la science et l'idéologie en général'.

(7) 'le jeune chiot du structuralisme nous a filé entre les jambes'.

(8) 'le marxisme n'est pas un structuralisme, non pas parce qu'il affirme le primat du procès sur la structure, mais parce qu'il affirme le primat de la contradiction sur le procès'.

(9) 'La lutte des classes dans la théorie'.

(10) 'Le primat de la fonction pratique sur la fonction théorique dans la philosophie même'.

(11) 'La dialectique très particulière qui est à l'oeuvre dans la pratique de la philosophie'.

(12) This _ambiguity_ inherent in justification underlies Habermas's thesis of the current 'legitimation crisis' of the modern state. (Habermas, 1976, p. 71)

(13) For this last point I am indebted to my colleague Steve Decker.

(14) 'Social Research as Emancipatory Discourse', in P. Holly and D. Whitehead (eds): _Action-Research in Schools_, Cambridge Institute of Education, 1984; first published as _Occasional Paper No. 1_, Essex Institute of Higher Education, 1981.

4 Action - research and the improvement of professional practice

'IMPROVING PROFESSIONAL PRACTICE'

So far we have pursued action-research's assumptions and aspirations down two avenues: the intelligible unification of theory and practice (Chapter Two) and the theoretic competence, resources, and independence of the reflective individual (Chapter Three). This chapter is concerned with a further theme which is widely invoked as a basis for action-research investigation - both as a defining characteristic and even as an implicit criterion of adequacy - and which thus serves to provide a further elaboration of action-research's inherent problematic: action-research, it is almost universally claimed, is founded upon 'the improvement of professional practice'.

The initial problem is illustrated by the following statement by Brown, et al. (1982, p. 2):

'Action-research ... has as its central feature the use of changes in practice as a way of inducing improvement in the practice itself, the situation in which it occurs, the rationale for the work, and in the understanding of all these. Action-research uses strategic action as a probe for improvement and understanding. In fact the action-researcher selects a particular variation of practice with these two criteria uppermost'.

The argument of the passage enacts a crucial ambiguity: on
the one hand it seems as though 'changes' in practice might,
by 'probing' a situation, disclose hitherto concealed
possibilities, unpredicted outcomes, and thereby create
improved understanding; on the other hand such changes are
presented as 'strategic', ie. as planned with a clearly
envisaged end in view, so that improvement in both understanding and in practice will be induced, as though the
range of outcomes were predictable. Hence the direct
question becomes: will any changes in practice lead to an
improved understanding, or only a special type of change?
The answer suggested (only those changes which lead to an
'improvement' in practice) begs the question: how are
criteria for practice grounded, such that those leading to
'improvement' may be distinguished from those leading to
'deterioration'? Unless this question is addressed, the
recommendation that 'improved practice' can generate
'understanding' becomes merely another form of unexplicated
prescription: whereas positivist evaluation fails
(inevitably) to explicate its grounds for prescribing
methods for investigation (see Chapter Two), action-
research (in this formulation) threatens to allow the
methods and outcomes of investigation to remain open merely
at the cost of failing to give grounds for its prescription
of methods for professional practice. Thus the relationship between Brown et al.'s 'two criteria' ('improvement'
of practice and 'understanding' practice) becomes a central
issue, one which their juxtaposition above tacitly avoids.

The difficulty is not lack of elaboration of the relationship, as may be seen by a summary of the argument which the
writers present: practices, they argue, can only be
understood in conjunction with their rationale, and thus
they are open to critical self-reflection. This in turn
requires collaboration with other practitioners, who may
otherwise stand in a hierarchical relationship to each
other, and any such relationships must be 'suspended' so
that an 'unconstrained' critical self-reflection can take
place. Action-research is thus an expression of Habermas's
'emancipatory knowledge-constitutive interest ......
fundamentally concerned with democratic values as these are
expressed in the idea of a self-reflective community'
(Brown et al., 1982, p. 3). In this way the development of
understanding and the development of social practices are
encapsulated within a notion of 'emancipation'. (See, also,
Carr and Kemmis, 1986, p. 164, p. 185).

The limitations of this type of argument were presented
in general terms in the final section of the last chapter.
However, a more direct problem with the argument as
presented is its central lacuna: changes in practice are
envisaged in terms of teachers' professional work, but the
scenario of 'emancipation' concerns only the teachers'
freedom to reflect and to innovate; it is not seen as
constituting the nature of the work itself, namely the
practice of teaching. The question therefore becomes: on

what basis is such a boundary for the principle of
'emancipation' constructed? In other words, the problem
concerns the relationship between authority and
emancipation in the research activity and that same tension
in the professional practices which the research activity
claims to be able to use both as a topic and as a resource.
It is this relationship on which Brown et al. are silent.

Suppose, for example, that a group of teachers (including
a head of department and a scale 1 staff member) reflected
upon their 'habitual and traditional' practices, and
determined to liberate themselves from the 'constraints'
imposed upon their work by a taken-for-granted professional
ideology of active contributions to lessons by pupils, and
decided instead - mounting a thorough critique of
institutional policy - to translate an area of the
curriculum into predetermined behavioural objectives for
which massive and carefully planned practice would be given,
reinforced by a calculated system of rewards and punish-
ments, in order that the curriculum should be 'more
effectively learned'. Such an example would exploit the
lacuna in the argument, since the hypothetical case
describes the liberation from 'constraint' of a group of
teachers (as a Habermasian 'speech community') in order to
enable them to increase the constraints upon the learners
within their classrooms. Thus: the innovative discourse
would deconstruct the hierarchical relation between the
Head of Department and the Scale 1 teacher, freeing them to
interact on the basis only of 'the better argument' and of
their 'common interests' (Habermas, 1976, p. 108), but as a
result, the hierarchical relationship of the classroom
would be intensified by an increased didacticism: a more
prescriptive curriculum backed up by a more intensive
application of external sanctions would reduce the
opportunity for pupils to present 'arguments' concerning
the curriculum and would necessitate that pupils'
'interests' be defined by teachers (cf. Brown et al.'s
quotation from Habermas above). So the question is: upon
what grounds is staff discourse to be considered in
relation to the Habermasian ideal, but not classroom
discourse?

Certainly, this exclusion is not explicitly intended by
action-research writers. For example Holly (1984)
indicates the 'emancipatory' thrust of action-research by
means of the following diagram:

The Institution	Action-research
Hierarchical; vertical relationships	Horizontal relationships
Divided; compartmental- ized (subject based)	Unified; collaborative across subject boundaries
Bureaucratic; 'Top-down' management style	Democratic; 'Bottom-up' management style

The Institution	Action-research
Closed	Open
Formal (teacher-pupil relationships)	Informal

Holly's argument is that action-research generates relationships among staff which are incompatible with the requirements of the school as a societally determined institution.
His vocabulary suggests a clear debt to Bernstein
(Bernstein, 1971a, 1971b) and hence, indirectly, to
Durkheimian arguments concerning social order in general,
the wider implications of which will be explored in more
detail later (see the final section of this chapter). This
echo makes it clear that for Holly action-research will
challenge institutional structures inside the classroom as
well as outside, so that, for example, 'informal' teacher-
pupil relationships may be thought of as 'horizontal', and
as a 'democratic' style of classroom management.

But these are of course metaphors for a supposedly
dichotomous mutual exclusion, which itself evokes one of
the central difficulties of an 'emancipatory' problematic
for action-research: if the opposition between action-
research and its institutional setting is of the categorical
nature suggested by such pairings as vertical/horizontal,
open/closed etc., then it becomes difficult to see in what
sense Holly recommends 'caution' (Holly, 1984, p. 100): is
he suggesting that by means of 'caution' action-research
might conceivably succeed in 'overthrowing' institutions
into a diametrically opposite form? If so, how could this
be understood? In fact Holly's pairs of terms are
schematic, evoking rather than analyzing the contrasts they
present: 'open' and 'closed', for example, are a rather
crudely ideological formulation for the issue of
'democratic' relationships, and every student of 'organizational theory' knows that a 'formal' structure generates
an 'informal' structure as part of the inevitable texture
of institutional life (see Selznick, 1964).

Heinz Moser (1978) argues even more explicitly than Holly
for the intimate relation between the processes of
investigation and the aims and criteria for professional
practices, by making clear that for him the notion of a
critical social science of education must also in principle
inform pedagogical practices, ie. he explicitly does not
make the separation which is so problematic in the work of
Brown et al. Indeed, he says: '... Pedagogy, in the sense
of a critical theory of education, is taken to be a theory
of society'. (p. 12) (1) This 'critical theory of
education' is conceived as requiring the autonomy of youth
and as tending to render the educational relation itself
superfluous (p. 14), and Moser continues: 'A science of
education which is not devoted to the maintenance of the
status quo but which includes in its programme this process
of substantial liberation must therefore identify with the

emancipatory interest which characterizes science as the enablement of a liberating praxis'. (p. 13) (2) In other words, for Moser, a theory of educational research which liberates the teacher is inseparable from a theory of teaching which liberates the learner. Hence Moser contrasts education for the progressive liberation of youth _from_ education _into_ autonomy, with education as the instrumental practice of the educating Subject _upon_ the child Object (p. 14), and generalizes from this: 'Education therefore becomes the sine qua non of any (social) scientific programme, which must first of all 'create' self-reflective Subjects' (p. 19) (3)

However, this argument - although more sophisticated than Holly's diagram - by its abstract and programmatic form seems to neglect action-research's specific concern: the creation of a principled relation between theory and _practice_, between research and professional work within an institutional context.

In contrast, Elliott (1975) is much more specific about what he envisages as action-research's programme for improving professional practices. His Ford Teaching Project is an action-research investigation devoted to the implementation of 'Inquiry/Discovery Learning' in the classroom, ie. to a specific pedagogy which is explicitly described as the removal by teachers of the 'constraints' upon their teaching method fostered by their own institutionalized authority, such as their general tendencies to impose 'preconceived problems', to reformulate problems in their own words, (p. 7) to impose changes in the direction of discussion, to probe 'too deeply' into pupils' personal lives (p. 12), etc. In each case 'the principles of Inquiry / Discovery Learning' involve recommending to teachers 'constraint removing strategies' (p. 6). The generality of the principle of 'constraint removal' in the classroom is shown in another of Elliott's papers (Elliott, 1982a) where he suggests that Stenhouse's Humanities Curriculum Project, in which the teacher's role is reformulated as that of the 'neutral chairman', was an attempt to set up in the classroom a Habermasian 'ideal speech situation' (p. 22), and Elliott describes his own work as located within a similar problematic (p. 23).

For Elliott also, then, 'emancipation' provides a criterion which guides both the relationships of the action-research investigative process and the professional / client relationships of the 'practice' which forms both a topic and a resource for that process. What Elliott fails to consider, however, is the irony implicit in proposals to realize 'ideals' in practical situations. This is a version of Garfinkel's argument (see Chapter Two, final section): the presentation of practice in terms of a failure to realize ideals merely directs attention from the actual processes of that practice. Thus, given that teachers

cannot simply 'remove constraints' without abandoning
fundamental parameters of their institutionalized roles, we
are left wondering what sort of judgements action-researching teachers can actually make: which 'constraints' are
removeable, and which are not? action-research must
formulate (as the essence of its proposal to unify theory
and practice) what 'emancipation' could mean as a form of
feasible action within an institutional context.

Elliott structures his argument around two suggestive
pairs of terms: a contrast between Habermas's 'ideal
speech situation' and Bureaucracy' (Elliott, 1982a,
pp. 22-4), and between 'ethical' and 'technical' theories
of teaching (Elliott, 1982b, p. 20), where he argues that
criteria for the 'validity' of an educational process reside
in the values guiding the activity rather than in measurable
qualities of the outcome. But the work of this latter
project ('Teacher Pupil Interaction and the Quality of
Learning') makes clear the nature of the problem when
action-research attempts to enact its 'emancipatory'
aspiration. The first aim of the project is defined as:

> 'To help teachers monitor the extent to which
> the higher level understanding tasks they plan
> for pupils ... qualitatively differ from those
> which pupils actually come to work on in class-
> room settings' (Elliott, 1982b, p. 12)

Later Elliott writes:

> 'I would claim that the idea of 'teaching for
> understanding' is entailed by educational action-
> research. The latter has as its general focus
> educational action, but what makes action
> educational is not the production of extrinsic
> end states but the intrinsic qualities expressed
> in the manner of its performance ... The general
> idea of teaching for understanding simply
> specifies a quality of educational action, and as
> such guides, rather than directs, teacher
> deliberations about how to improve the educational
> quality of their teaching'. (p. 21)

Elliott's argument is that 'understanding' is entailed as a
pragmatic consequence of the educational enterprise; hence
to be engaged in educational action-research is ipse facto
to be engaged in teaching for understanding and thus in
'improving the quality' of educational practice. But this
is merely to take for granted the conventional normative
form of the term 'education', in the same way as 'the
philosophy of education' used to justify current practices
by unexplicated appeals to normative linguistic usage, a
form of philosophic practice whose theoretic weaknesses are
cogently analyzed by Ernest Gellner in Words and Things
(Gellner, 1968). Elliott wishes to attenuate the
prescriptiveness of his appeal to usage ('guides rather than

directs') in accordance with action-research's desire to preserve practitioners' autonomy, but the residual prescriptiveness remains unaddressed. 'Education' is taken as a <u>unitary</u> meaning which can be insisted upon, rather than as a moment in a dialectic, whose contradictions (say: authority versus autonomy) can be explored but not resolved: the educational practitioner as reflexive theorist would need to <u>pose</u> the nature of 'education' as a <u>question</u>, rather than utilize it as an authoritative usage.

The notion of 'levels of understanding' seems to be an even more concrete instance of taking for granted precisely what should be an issue (the questionable relationship between the rationalities of teachers' plans on the one hand and of pupils' 'work' on the other) in order to invoke a cognitive hierarchy quite at variance with action-research's proclaimed desire to ground criteria for action in an ideal of emancipation.

Elliott's paper is programmatic for the 'TIQL" (Teacher-Pupil Interaction and the Quality of Learning) project as a whole. When one turns to some of the reports produced by the teachers involved, one finds even clearer examples of the failure to address the grounds of the professional practices which have been 'researched' or the grounds of the research process itself. Thus Ingham (1984) reports:

> 'I very soon became aware through my observation
> that children often return to lower order concepts
> when acquiring those of a higher order, if they
> consider it relevant to the situation. I was
> able to show that if there is a deficiency in
> the lower order network, then it will be
> difficult for pupils to attain a higher level
> until this has been made good'. (pp. 5-6)

The claims to <u>observe</u> 'higher' and 'lower' orders of conceptualization represents an 'unreflexive' prescriptive-ness towards pupils' meanings which demonstrates quite dramatically the dangers of action-research's failure to articulate an alternative to positivism: Ingham's research stance is accomplished by <u>assuming</u> the 'instrumental' stance of 'the educating Subject upon the child Object', ie. by ignoring its necessarily reflexive basis. This, as Moser suggests (see above), is the antithesis of the desire on the part of action-research and of a critical social science to found their practices upon the constitutive possibility of 'self-reflective Subjects'.

Not surprizingly, Ingham does not point to the system of unexplicated norms in the following recommendations which she quotes from another professional practitioner / action-researcher in the project:

> 'The desire of children to re-negotiate and
> simplify tasks is widespread. Children will

frequently go against given instructions if
they can see a short-cut to the answer.
Work should be scrutinized when set to avoid
leaving these short-cuts open' (Ingham, p. 7).

Only by noting the reflexive processes underlying notions
of 'higher' and 'lower' levels of understanding would
Ingham have been able to examine what children as well as
teachers see as relevant and rational features of a
situation which children will inevitably be formulating for
themselves. Classroom practices are constituted in a mutual
difference between teacher and taught, which action-research
aspires to address as a problematic intersubjectivity
between 'reflective Subjects': if educational practice is
conceived as the setting of a task and as a requirement of
the answer, this difference will be glossed by an
authoritarian imposition, presented nevertheless as that
consensus which (as Elliott implies above) education's norm
of autonomous rationality always necessarily invokes. In
other words, criteria for the 'improvement' of practice
must be theorized independently of the institutional
authority by which practices are routinely evaluated (eg.
ideologies of higher and lower levels of understanding, or
of obedience to instructions which gloss their constitutive
contradictions). Otherwise action-research lapses into a
managerial rhetoric which takes for granted precisely the
judgements it should be questioning.

However, Ingham's paper, though significant, is
exceptional: on the whole action-research work has indeed
been concerned to formulate the improvement of practice by
questioning its prescriptive version. Thus, Michael
Armstrong says, at the beginning of the article which Nixon
uses to open his collection of action-research writing
(Nixon, 1981a):

'Part of the art of teaching consists ... in
asking children questions, discussing their ideas,
exchanging experiences with them ... There is a
self-consciousness implicit in this aspect of
a teacher's activity that makes those teachers who
manage it successfully - however fitful and
fragmentary their success - students of those
they teach as well as their teachers'.
(Armstrong M., 1981, p. 15).

Further examples are given in Carr and Kemmis, 1986,
pp. 167-174. Even more explicitly, Stephen Rowland says:

'It is only by committing ourselves to ... a
process of self-education that we can fully
appreciate the endeavours of the children we
teach as they strive to make sense of their world'
(Rowland S., 1983, Introduction)

This may be construed as a specific denial of the

authoritative <u>separation</u> of teacher and taught, of
professional and client: the educator's resource for a
reflexively conceived educational enterprise is not a
realization of his or her knowledge and of the children's
ignorance but rather of his or her own ignorance and of the
children's understanding. In general terms: a reflexive
analysis of professionalism would render problematic a
series of normative definitions and their attendant systems
of authoritative decision-making: a reflexive social-work
profession would problematize its basis for distinguishing
between and responding to 'deviant' and 'normal' ways of
life, a reflexive medical profession would question its
conceptions of health and treatment, and reflexive
journalism its conceptions of newsworthiness and reportage.

A concrete example of how an action-research project might
begin to work towards such an awareness of the problematic
nature of professional practice is given in John Crooke's
paper (Crookes J., 1983) in Stephen Rowland's collection.
Crookes tape-recorded a conversation during a science lesson
with two 15 year old pupils (Rob and Anthony) concerning why
crystals grow, and what relationship there might be between
the growth of crystals and the growth of human beings. He
observes:

> 'My early reactions on transcribing the tape
> were confused, as I had expected the conversation
> to turn largely on the differing mechanisms
> each boy employed to explain growth' (p. 9)

In fact the two boys kept 'digressing' onto the topic of
destiny and hence to their own identities and futures. He
analyzes his sense of confusion as follows:

> 'The importance of the learner's own knowledge
> in the growth of understanding ... can be viewed
> as largely one-way ... The teacher encourages
> the learner to tell of what he knows already
> (so that) the learner's own knowledge is a resource
> to be used by the teacher. (But) the learner's
> knowledge cannot be circumscribed in this fashion ...
> For as well as using his own knowledge to interpret
> and understand new events, the learner also uses
> these phenomena as vehicles for the interpretation
> and understanding of his own preoccupations and
> concerns ... (Hence) one of the reasons for
> my initial confusion was an inability to see
> Anthony's using the crystal as a starting point to
> re-explore an issue that continued to perplex him'
> (p. 10)

The first step in Crookes's analysis, then, is his
recognition that what an educational practice is <u>about</u> (ie.
'the curriculum') is constituted as problematic within that
practice: the teacher's definition of the nature of his
professional practice ('a lesson <u>about</u> crystals') is

challenged by pupils to be simultaneously intelligible as a discussion about their own destinies. The second step is to recognize that the problematic nature of this intersubjectivity, its 'digressiveness', is not an inadequate realization of a normative 'pure' intersubjectivity (as Habermas might argue) in which an 'improvement' might be to avoid such 'digressions', but on the contrary a condition of the creative process of understanding. To this end, Crookes cites the 'digressions' in the work of Kepler, with its 'analogies from every phase of life ... exhortations ... textual quibbles ... personal anecdotes ... delighted exclamations' (p. 10) and observes that Rob and Anthony 'stand in an analogous position to an early scientist' and that 'their interest and concerns spread more widely and deeply than the usual mundane events of the classroom'. (p. 11) In this way Crookes questions the authority of the teacher by providing as it were a counter-authority for Rob and Anthony to play an autonomous role in the constitution of their education: education itself becomes no longer a professional practice 'carried out' by teachers but the achievement (between teachers and pupils) of an imaginative intersubjectivity which enables the exploration of the metaphors ('growth' in this instance) whereby such intersubjectivity accomplishes its communicative process. (This argument is generally indebted of course to the work reported in M.F.D. Young - 1971)

However, a pointer to an interesting limitation in Crookes's paper is contained in his reference to Kepler as an 'early' scientist. Elsewhere he develops a contrasting account of the procedures of 'modern' science in highly normative terms. This suggests the difficulty of recognizing the reflexive basis of one's professional authority. Crookes seems to have succeeded in retreating from his conventional authority as a teacher by taking up a defensive position behind his authority as a scientist! Nevertheless Crookes's analysis of this 'science lesson' does suggest how a reflexively conceived professionalism might begin to point beyond what Crookes himself refers to as the 'mundane' realizations of its practices to its own inherent possibilities, without having recourse to a normative ideal for those practices which would render such possibilities 'only theoretical'.

What Crookes fails to do, however, is to consider how such insights could be related back to the institutionalized practice of education. In a sense he illustrates only the theoretical moment in the dialectic articulated at the end of Chapter Two. Thus, in a different way, like the other writers discussed so far, he does not address the issue of how the improvement of institutionalized professional practices could feasibly be action-research's aspiration. We have seen how this aspiration is generally enacted as the adoption of a consciously 'progressive' stance on such questions as ethical v. technical rationality, instrumentality v. the self-reflective Subject, and teachers' v.

pupils' versions of relevance. In other words we have seen
how action-research writers have tended to present these
various issues in terms of an overarching 'liberationist'
dichotomy: ideal speech v. bureaucracy, emancipation v.
constraint, democracy v. hierarchy. Such formulations evoke
rhetorically and metaphorically action-research's <u>challenge</u>
to its institutional context, the general dimension on
which professional improvement is sought, but it fails to
formulate action-research's possibility <u>except as</u> a
challenge, ie. as an 'idealistic' aspiration whose practic-
ability is always potentially undermined by the unaddressed
ironic relation between ideal and actuality, between the
individual and the institution. In order to do otherwise,
to formulate action-research's <u>constructive</u> relation
between theory and practice, the inert ironies of the
dichotomies presented so far must be reformulated in
dialectical terms, so as to provide analytically not only
for opposition but also for resolution, transformation, and
thus for change. It is to this task that the argument now
turns, by considering the nature of professional practices
and the sense in which they themselves offer opportunities
for the improvements which action-research seeks.

PROFESSIONALISM AND BUREAUCRACY: MYTHS OF NORMATIVE RATIONALITY

Professionalism is presented by Talcott Parsons as the
historically achieved resolution of the principles of
rationality and morality, the application of objective
<u>science</u> to everyday experience (Parsons, 1954). Hence the
institutional power of the professional over the client is
immediately legitimated by the form it takes, namely
expertise, ie. authority derived from scientific knowledge
and structured by Weberian notions of bureaucratic form:
functional specificity, systematic disinterest, and univers-
alistic rules. (4) The enormous <u>mythic</u> appeal of this
fusion of science and morality into an axiomatically
authoritative rationalism may be seen in the genre of
professional-as-hero (in radio and TV series, and in films,
novels, etc.) which endorses simultaneously the
righteousness and the expertise of such professions as the
doctor, the nurse, the vet., the pathologist, the solicitor,
the journalist, and (most of all) the policeman, and the
detective. Where there was error and hence injustice, there
shall be truth and justice.

But mythic structures are created by contradictions.
Levi-Strauss says (1981, p. 604):

> 'For a myth to be engendered by thought and
> for it in turn to engender other myths, it is
> necessary and sufficient that an initial
> opposition should be injected into experience'.

And (on p. 603):

'This inherent disparity of the world sets
mythic thought in motion, but it does so because
... it conditions the existence of every object
of thought'.

The 'initial oppositions' within professional work may be
thought of as those between individualized authority and
universalized truth, and between science and morality.
Both oppositions are mythically resolved in the figure of
the hero, who reveals the objective error of other
professionals, whose expertise is axiomatically on the side
of Good, and whose version of 'the case' is thus by
definition 'the Truth'. The Good of the hero is both
highly idiosyncratic (hence the emotionalism of Quincy, the
rudeness of Kojak, the vanity of Poirot, the artistic
introversion of Sherlock Holmes, etc.) and universal
(scientifically expert).

Perhaps it is an echo of the myth of the professional-as-
hero which enables Brown et al. to see the emancipation of
the professional from bureaucratic authority as a sufficient
formulation of 'improvement': the forces of error against
whom hero-professionals score their triumphs are very often
their own professional superiors. And in this element we
have, as it were, a mythic treatment of the contradictions
of a cultural form: the Weberian bureaucracy and the
Parsonian profession both express the progressive rationalization of institutionalized action; the rationalized
format for authority. Yet this authority is in contradiction with itself: bureaucracy creates a hierarchy of
jurisdictions in which practitioners at each level can
decide the means but not the ends of action; whereas (in
contrast) the status of 'professional' gives the practioner
precisely that principled autonomy which bureaucracy with-
holds, ie. the autonomy which comes from possessing a moral
as well as technical jurisdiction. Since professional
practitioners are also members of more of less bureaucratized institutions, the authority by which they practise
is enmeshed in ambiguity; and this ambiguity is mythically
opened out into a confrontation between apparently
dichotomous principles (autonomy / constraint, professional
/ bureaucrat, 'red-tape' / 'what justice demands') which is
worked out in the adventurous confrontations of the
professional-as-Rebel.

But a myth reveals its fragility at the same time as it
asserts its possibility - hence the need for continual
repetition, hence, indeed its 'appeal': the hero only just
triumphs, by means of the 'arduous journey' (Levi-Strauss,
1981, p. 65⁹) through the series of 'dangerous'
confrontations (on the street, in court, in the lab.) with
the forces of error or injustice by which professional work
is always threatened. That professional work will always
sense this threat is guaranteed by its origin in the
ambiguity, the instability, of professionalism's own
auspices: the rationality by which it claims authoritative

jurisdiction is the same authority by which, in the name of
bureaucracy, such jurisdiction is circumscribed. Hence the
powerful appeal of the figure of the action-researching
professional, who is continuously aware that his or her
authority possibly might not correspond with the practice
of justice and truth, while sensing a general requirement
that it should.

But although this version of professionalism shows the
inherent possibilities for action-research's 'heroic' calls
for 'improvement', there is a danger (clearly seen in many
of the examples considered so far in this chapter) that
action-research might merely subscribe to the myth which it
should be examining, namely the struggle for the
emancipation of the authority of the individual professional
against the constraints upon that authority provided by his
or her institutional context. We need therefore to look
more closely at the contradictions which constitute the
form of professional life, to establish an analytic rather
than a mythic formulation of 'improvement'. We may begin
by considering the crucial role of the notion of
'rationality' in Parsons's presentation of professionalism,
as the point at which the unproblematic authority of the
professional is established.

Weber's ideal types of 'Zweckrationalität' and
'Wertrationalität' were originally conceived - of course .-
as analytical devices, so that for Weber the formulation of
an instrumental rationality was not descriptive but was
rather constituted analytically in contrast to 'the great
bulk of everyday action' which (for Weber) is essentially
tradition-orientated, even (in other words) 'almost
automatic reaction to habitual stimuli', and thus 'lies
very close to the borderline of what can justifiably be
called meaningfully oriented action' (Weber M., 1971,
p. 139). However, it is this contrast between rationality
as an analytic norm and as an empirical norm which Parsons
often seems to lose: 'The starting point, both historical
and logical (my emphasis - RW) is the conception of the
intrinsic rationality of action ... The rationality of
action ... is measured by the conformity of choice of
means' (Parsons, 1968, p. 698-9). When the historical and
the logical are thus elided, we have a metaphysics of
instrumentality, in which action's rationality is
'intrinsic' and axiomatic because it has been merely
equated with the postulate of subjective purpose. Thus for
Parsons a 'system of action' is a 'set of variable
relationships 'between an organism' and its 'objects'
(Parsons et al., 1962, p. 6). But such a conception of the
subjective instrumental rationality of action makes it
difficult to conceive of everyday interaction except as
either authoritarian, in which I successfully manipulate
the Other (as an 'object'), or as irrational, in which the
Other (as a 'subject') obstinately frustrates the
possibility that my actions can attain predictability, and
this in turn leads to Weber's concession that the ideal of

instrumental rationality relegates everyday action to the
borderline of the meaningless. Hence the authoritarian
option, the subject/object model, reminiscent of Hegel's
primal Master / Slave relation, cannot (in the end) be
challenged by any thoroughly intersubjective articulation of
rational action.

At this point in the argument the metaphor of social
action as the selection of an appropriate instrument for a
subjective purpose joins the myth of the professional-as-
hero. Professional practices are conceived as fusing the
moral authority of Society with the technical authority of
Science: the professional as Subject thus possesses a
knowledge of the client, (as an Object of science), an
'expertise', to which the client's own life-world offers no
challenge, since it appears to have no theoretic resources,
being indeed merely an 'almost automatic reaction to
habitual stimuli'. Hence the cultural mandate for action-
research's unreflexive call for the improvement of
professional practice in terms of greater diagnostic or
therapeutic discretion for the professional over the client,
in terms of emancipation from bureaucratic constraint or
from the residues of 'unscientific' common-sense. The
authoritative stance of the professional towards the
client's life-world is thus closely linked to the social
scientist's deficit theory of the common-sense social actor.
But we have frequently noted Garfinkel's critique of this,
his counter-assertion of the rational properties of the
life-world, and the consequent need to theorize the nature
of science's difference, rather than (by positing only one
form of rationality - the instrumental) imposing science
upon the life-world as an unproblematic authority.

In other words, in 'professionalism', in 'bureaucracy'
and in 'instrumental rationality' we have normative
principles which gloss the reflexive processes for their
production as norms. And indeed, to explicate the requirements of practice in terms of normative ideals is to
present consensus as what can theoretically be envisaged
but never achieved at the level of practice: normative
usages (of 'education' or 'understanding', or 'bureaucracy'
or 'professional practice') attempt to prescribe for action
but cannot provide for the processes whereby their own
prescriptions could possibly be acted upon. More
specifically, to speak for a normative version of consensus
is immediately to enact its opposite: in any actual
situation such speaking makes a prescription which is
inevitably open to contestation on an unpredictable variety
of dimensions. What the action-research writers reviewed
in the early part of this chapter have done is to embrace
the norm of professionalism and to contest the norm of
bureaucracy without realizing the intimate relation between
the two, constituted by the normative version of rationality
which underlies both. The analysis so far shows how both
action-research's embrace and its contestation represent
mythic responses to a set of contradictions surrounding all

three concepts. The final argument in this chapter will be a consideration of how these contradictions may be addressed in terms which sidestep the invitation to mythic identification with a 'maverick' professional, since this threatens to lead action-research into an 'idealistic' confrontation with its institutional context, and this in turn undermines action-research's aspiration to be a form of investigation which can unite a theoretical stance with practitioner activity. Meanwhile it is important to look (at last) in detail at Habermas's theory of emancipatory discourse, which authorizes the self-mythologizing stance adopted by so many writers on educational action-research when they attempt to make a 'critical' move against their positivist inheritance (see Carr and Kemmis, 1986, for the most elaborated version).

HABERMAS AND THE THEORY OF EMANCIPATION

The appeal of Habermas's work for action-research in an educational context lies perhaps in that it addresses directly one of action-research's central concerns - the problematic relationship between emancipation and authority - while the proposed solution (in terms of an ideal fusion of Reason, Truth, and communicative participation) articulates one of the deepest ideals and hopes of the professional educator. A further 'attractive' feature of Habermas's ideal is that it appears to relate both to theory and to action; it combines a communicative possibility (rational discourse) and a political possibility (interaction freed from contingent power relations):

> 'Only in an emancipated society, whose members'
> autonomy and responsibility had been realized,
> would communication have developed into the
> non-authoritarian and universally practised
> dialogue from which both our model of recipro-
> cally constituted ego-identity and our idea of
> true consensus are always implicitly derived.
> To this extent the truth of statements is based
> on anticipating the realization of the good
> life'. (Habermas, 1978, p. 314).

Only in such an emancipated society would an 'ideal speech situation' allow 'an actually attained consensus the claim of a rational consensus' and constitute 'a critical standard against which every actually realized consensus can be called into question and tested' (Habermas, 1976, p. xviii). Thus, by means of the perfectly free and symmetrical procedures of Critical Reason, interaction could be both emancipated from any constraint other than its own constitutive features ('Reason'), and authoritative (grounded in consensus).

At one level this is a restatement of the liberal concept of the constitutive relationship between freedom, reason, and truth, which stems from Kant and J.S. Mill:

> 'Reason has no dictatorial authority; its
> verdict is always the agreement of free
> citizens'. (Kant: Critique of Pure Reason,
>   1933, p. 593).

and:

> 'Complete liberty of contradicting and disproving
> our opinion, is the very condition which justifies
> us in assuming its truth for purposes of action;
> and on no other terms can (we) have any rational
> assurance of being right'. (J.S. Mill, 'On Liberty',
>   1961, p. 271)

But Habermas's argument also derives a particular strength
from its specification at the level of language (Habermas,
1970, p. 141-3) and also from a commitment to an intersubjective conception of consciousness and of the
constitution of knowledge:

> 'The subject of the process of inquiry forms
> itself on the foundation of intersubjectivity ...
> Every dialogue develops on (the) basis ... of
> the reciprocal recognition of subjects ... (and
> thus) investigators are always already situated ...
> on the ground of intersubjectivity'. (Habermas
> 1978, pp. 137-9)

An ideal for inquiry is thus formulated as an ideal for
dialogue:

> 'Pure intersubjectivity is determined by a
> symmetrical relation between I and You (We and
> You), I and He (We and They). An unlimited
> interchangeability of dialogue roles demands
> that no side be privileged in the performance
> of these roles: pure intersubjectivity exists
> only when there is complete symmetry in the
> distribution of assertion and disputation,
> revelation and hiding, prescription and follow-
> ing among the partners of communication'.
> (Habermas, J. 1970, p. 143).

It is this ideal which action-research wishes to interpret
in directly practical terms as the formulation of a feasible
mode of interaction between investigator and investigated,
and between educator and educated.

Now, Habermas is indeed concerned with the practical: his
whole argument in Legitimation Crisis (Habermas, 1976) is
that the increasing dependence of social authority upon the
technical rationality of 'science', by removing the choice
of goals from the citizen, presents a political choice
between submitting to the imposition of values through
power relations and developing universal discursive forms

for testing the validity claims of moral norms (p. 105). The 'ideal speech situation' in other words is an ideal which can (and should) guide action. But it is precisely the relation between an 'ideal' and any practice which it might 'guide' which is so problematic. Weber's concept of the ideal is explicitly analytic: actual phenomena may be understood in terms of their variable distance from a 'logically deduced' ideal type of that phenomenon. But the possibility of such a deduction rests on a restricted, instrumental view of rationality in terms of which social phenomena may be conceived. Habermas's ideal, in contrast, is presented not only as analytical but as a development of a Kantian imperative: from the constituent conditions for the possibility of consciousness and inquiry arise the political ideals of pure intersubjectivity, emancipated speech, and hence the critical analysis of social norms. The political arises directly from the analytic: to question the Habermasian ideal is self-contradictory, since the question itself presupposes and expresses the necessity of the ideal whose necessity it purports to deny. Hence 'the transcendental character of ordinary language':

> 'In taking up a practical discourse, we un-
> avoidably suppose an ideal speech situation that
> on the strength of its formal properties,
> allows consensus only through generalizable
> interests. A linguistic ethics has no need
> of principles. It is based only on fundamental
> forms of rational speech that we must always
> presuppose if we discourse at all'. (Habermas,
> 1976, p. 110)

But does this normative ideal of emancipatory reason arise from engaging in the explicitly reflexive practices of theorizing or from the apparently 'unreflexive' communic-ative practices of the life-world? This is a crucial question for exponents of action-research, who make the latter interpretation and thus claim that Habermas's ideal, though unattainable, provides a criterion and a direct ambition for the improvement of mundane professional practices:

> 'In the real world, discourse is to some extent
> distorted or biassed by assymetrical power
> relations between participants. But one can
> make progress towards the ideal situation by
> identifying and coping with negative instances
> of distorted discourse'. (Elliott, 1982a, p. 19).

Is this the relation between ideal and actuality, between theory and practice? Are theoretical ideals to be posited as states of affairs which one can intelligibly but always unsuccessfully 'progress towards'? If so, then social action is forever condemned to a lamentable deficiency: theory will be conceived as normative, ideal types will be treated as moral aspirations (cf. Parsons on professional-ism) and ironies inherent in the inevitable difference between the theoretic and the actual will not be 'mastered' as analytic resources for grasping the contradictions of experience (see Chapter Three) but bemoaned as lapses of experience.

The intrinsic weaknesses of Habermas's argument have already been presented (see Chapter Three, final section) The point to be made here, rather, is that the widespread invocation of Habermas by action-research writers rests on a misunderstanding. Habermas does not derive his ideal from everyday communicative practices among practitioners: when he uses the term 'discourse', he specifies that he means the specific modes of talk in which the 'naive' assumptions of everyday speech are topics for critical analysis (Habermas, 1974, p. 18). Thus, Habermas is concerned to articulate emancipatory possibilities at the level of theory, which involves for example the recovery of unconscious determinants of (the) self-formative 'process' and the making explicit of general rule systems (Habermas, 1974, p. 22-3). Indeed he is explicitly dismissive of 'the fashionable demand for a type of action-research' (p. 11). In other words, Habermas, unlike Elliott - and unlike Carr and Kemmis (5) - does not forget that symmetrical discourse is an ideal - in a Weberian sense - and thus a theoretical principle rather than an intelligible practical goal.

It is because of this implication in Habermas's work that Heinz Moser, wishing to argue that action-research makes a necessary contribution to 'critical theory', is (apparently alone among writers on action-research) strongly critical of Habermas. For Moser, Habermas's notion of emancipated discourse rests on a rationalistic notion of consciousness (Moser, 1978, p. 99) and of history (p. 95) and on an over-optimistic view of the possibilities for unforced consensus and individual autonomy (p. 100). Moser urges, rather, that 'in discourse itself, power is still at work, compelling us without our noticing'. (p. 97) (6) Hence, the discursive recognition of the 'validity' of norms may either conceal 'overpowering and irrational motives' or simply calculative tactics (p. 99). Further:

> 'If one considers ... how humanity is actually
> enmeshed by the coercive relationships of
> society, and the individual devalued ... it
> seems that Habermasian discourse overestimates
> itself. It sees itself as a counter-force
> to the concrete power relations of late capitalist
> society, and thereby forgets that, by restricting
> itself to a mere willingness to cooperate, it
> yields up all possibility for building opposition ...
> For this reason, discourse itself needs criteria
> which might prevent those taking part in discourse
> from introducing the ideological arguments of
> false consciousness'. (p. 100) (7)

Moser would thus not be surprised to find Elliott unable to

put into practice the Habermasian ideal, and indeed he is critical of his own earlier attempts to list practical procedures for action-research (Moser, 1978, p. 131). However, there are powerful ambiguities in Moser's formulation, of which he hardly seems aware. His presentation of individuals as 'enmeshed' and 'coerced' by 'concrete power relations' makes it difficult to see how 'ideology' could be avoided merely by framing discourse criteria. And, conversely, if ideology and false consciousness are embodied merely in 'arguments', which might be recognized and excluded from discourse, then what possible meaning can be attached to 'coercion' and 'power'? It seems as if Moser's account rests upon precisely the purely rational notion of historical and psychic processes he criticises in Habermas. The explication of this ambivalence takes us back once more to the ever-present irony of determinist theories of the subjection of consciousness to its politico-cultural context: Moser, like so many other writers, wishes to present a strong version of the cultural determination of the mundane social actor and yet to exempt from this determination the social theorist (see the discussion of ideology in Chapter Three above).

The constructive relevance of Habermas's work for action-research is that it presents a metatheory of investigation. His arguments concerning language, intersubjectivity, rationality, and the unconscious present the theoretical possibility of the autonomous theorizing Subject, which (as was argued in Chapter Three) is indeed an analytical requirement for action-research. Unlike the argument of the present work, however, Habermas is neither concerned with nor sympathetic to action-research's project. When action-research writers attempt to treat Habermas's meta-theory as though it were (or could be) directly programmatic for action-research as a social practice, they are using Habermas's vocabulary of emancipation and dialogue as metaphors while claiming that such a vocabulary can, for action-research, be literal. Hence they fall into claims (for action-research's 'emancipatory' process, for example) which seem both idealistic (concerning the possibility of action-research's institutionalizability) and rationalistic (in relation to the complexity of the psyche - as discussed in Chapter Three). It is this misuse of Habermasian arguments concerning ideals of speech, role relationships, and rationality which frequently leads action-research to oversimplify all three - to treat speech as literally relatable to facts (rather than as essentially reflexive and metaphoric), to treat symmetrical role relationships as constitutive of the process of theorizing and to treat rationality as instrumental and prescriptive (rather than as dialectical and critical). In short, by taking Habermas's theoretic ideal as a practical goal, action-research creates a mythic scenario for emancipation rather than an analytic theory of investigation. Hence, 'the improvement of professional practice', as an essential dimension of action-research's format for investigation, is itself presented in mythic terms - as the 'removal of

constraints' imposed by bureaucraticized roles, for
instance - and thus it is to an analytical account of
professionalism and its relation to bureaucracy that the
argument now turns.

PROFESSIONAL AND BUREAUCRATIC PRACTICES: DIALECTICAL POSSIBILITIES

How can professionalism be understood as a potentially
self-transformative set of dialectically related contradictions, rather than as the inert and unitary ideal evoked
by Parsons? Following on from the series of contradictions
noted earlier in this chapter it is important to notice
that professionalism regularly invokes not one but at least
two 'opposites'. Firstly, professional work is not 'trade':
professionals are not supposed to be motivated by profit
(but by service); they may not advertise for customers nor
operate competitive pricing. Hence the professional's
proclaimed commitment to the good of the client: the
professional is the servant of the client's interests;
their interaction is confidential: the professional is
trusted to protect the client from investigation by police,
tax-collector, life-insurance company, or even (contro-
versially) by parent. Secondly - and in marked contrast -
the professionals are not 'amateurs'; they may accept and
will indeed require payment for making an appearance; they
have a skill and a living to make; they are committed, in
the sense of serious: they are not 'amateurish', and can
thus be relied upon to do an expert and effective job under
difficult conditions. Hence a professional relationship is
not concerned with persons but techniques: amateurs will
perform for (or give services to) friends and relations for
free: professionals will refuse to do so on principle:
their expertise is only available to anyone who will pay.

Thus, even without recourse to the Marxian critique of
professionalism as an ideological disguise for the
construction and exploitation of a cultural monopoly (see
Larson, 1977, pp. 220-244) we have two very different
versions of the professional authority (as an ethic or as
an expertise) and of the professional relationship (as a
commitment or as a technical service). The argument is not
that these contrasts could be or need to be denied (by the
heroic stances described earlier in this chapter); nor,
evidently, does it prevent the accomplishment of professional work with sufficient coherence for its mundane purposes.
The argument is rather that to note the contradictions
within the conventional auspices of a mundane practice
(given here as examples, with no pretension to exhaustive-
ness) is to note the opportunity for a questioning of the
grounds of practice, ie. for the instigation of the type of
questioning dialectic proposed at the end of Chapter Two as
a general format for action-research's process. Such a
process (as was made clear) will not confront professional
practices with their errors, nor will it prescribe an
improvement on the basis of either an ethic or a technical

authority: rather it will install <u>within</u> professional work
a moment which makes explicit the reflexivity by which
alone the complexities of professional judgements are
handled.

Focussing specifically on the <u>contradictions</u> within which
professional judgements are carried out makes it possible
to recognize that the normative forms in which judgements
are presented as mundane accomplishments cannot be taken as
literally descriptive of the practice of those judgements:
professional judgements such as pupils' 'higher' and
'lower' orders of conceptualization (noted in the first
section of this chapter) would be recast as problematic by
the elaboration of the contradictory versions of the
authority, and the relationships in which they are grounded.
Similarly, given the grounding of communicative competences
in the Self-Other dialectic (see Chapter One) the
elaboration of the reflexivity of professional judgements
would render problematic a series of normative definitions
and their attendant systems of authoritative decision-
making, since the client's rationality would be recognized
as a constitutive element in the formulation of adequate
practice. In this sense 'the improvement of practice'
would be bound up with an explicit grasp of the reflexive
grounds for practice. This would not be the - by now
familiar - proposal of a move from 'constraint' to
'emancipation' but rather the recollection that practices
are in principle grounded (as the condition of their
intelligibility) in the <u>intersubjective</u> dialectic between
self and other, between professional and client. This
recollection would be a moment in the dialectic between
theory and practice, action and research (see Chapter Two)
and equally a moment in the dialectic between ideology and
theory (see Chapter Three): in both cases the reflexivity
of each moment provides for a dialectical <u>self</u>-transcend-
ence, and thus prevents 'critique' becoming merely the
assertion of an ideal <u>against</u> practice.

Furthermore, we may recollect (from Chapter Two) that
practice itself is intrinsically guided by a complex set of
criteria for rationality and by a further complex set of
interpretive procedures for the enactment of those criteria.
If this is true analytically of action in general, then we
will expect that professional practice (as a set of actions
whose discursive elaboration is relatively accessible and
widespread among practitioners) will certainly have
available its own resources for 'improving upon' the
literal invocation of conventionalized rules concerning how
this or that situation 'ought to be dealt with': such
resources are mundanely presented by professionals as the
'discretionary' quality of their practice, whereby
professionalism denies that a normative rule can exhaust
the rational properties of professional work, but rather
welcomes the recognition of the complexities which are
glossed by such rules. More concretely, professionals deny
that a single prescriptive rule can exhaust the properties
of the individual case, which thus always remains in need

108

of specific diagnosis by the professional worker, within
the complexities of a) the dialectical contradictions
between different rules, and b) the reflexive and interpersonal process by which any rule or combination of rules
is applied. (At this point we may note the significance
for arguments about the improvability of practice of the
analyses in Chapter Three concerning the intersubjectivity
of the therapeutic relationship.)

However, in emphasizing at this point the discretionary
quality of professional work, as action's own auspices for
analysis, we are perhaps in danger once more of formulating
a 'herioc' opposition between the action-researching
professional and his or her 'bureaucratic' role definition.
It is thus important to emphasize now that a bureaucratic
role, like professional practice, may be formulated in
terms of a set of dialectical contradictions rather than as
a unitary ideal type.

Clearly for Weber, bureaucracy represents the historically
evolved institutional form for the ordering of social
decision-making according to the canons of reason, justice,
and authenticated knowledge. But Weber also presents
bureaucracy as the historical enforcement of centralized
control:

> 'The triumph of princely power and the
> expropriation of particular prerogatives (ie. of
> local feudal 'estates') has everywhere signified
> at least the possibility, and often the actual
> introduction, of a rational administration'.
> (Weber, 1964a, p. 133)

Hence Weber emphasizes 'a firmly ordered system of super-
and subordination in which there is a supervision of the
lower offices by the higher ones' (Weber, 1964b, p. 465),
and this is made possible because 'the management of the
office follows general rules, which are more or less stable,
more or less exhaustive' (Weber, 1964b, p. 467). This does
indeed emphasize the oppressive nature of institutional
order, and in the end Weber seems to forget his own
principle of the analytic status of ideal types, and finds
himself in 'despair' at the vision of combined 'timidity'
and 'mechanization' in social affairs (Weber, 1964c, p. 473)
which his own theory of bureaucracy conjures up, not merely
as a heuristic device but, apparently, as a description.

But Garfinkel would have comforted Weber by reminding him
that even if general rules are 'stable' in themselves, they
can never be 'exhaustive' of the cases to which they
purport to refer, and thus in principle bureaucrats cannot
be 'timid' because their work is not 'mechanized': rather,
they always require a specific confidence in their capacity
for improvising the application of rules to cases. It is
this sort of awareness which leads, for example, Selznick
to argue that 'Every organization creates an informal
structure' in which 'professed goals' are substantially

'modified' by the 'operational goals' of groups of workers within the organization (Selznick, 1964, pp. 477-9).

However, this line of argument only serves to <u>ameliorate</u> the sense of bureaucracy as 'constraint'. In order to find an argument which establishes a clear contrast of principle, so that we may formulate bureaucracy itself in strictly dialectical terms, we can turn to Durkheim. Durkheim interprets the same historical processes of rationalization and industrialization which for Weber are the origin of 'bureaucracy', as leading to the division of labour and thus to the development of 'organic' social solidarity. For Durkheim this is the opposite of a historical move towards the subjugation of the individual to a centralized rule system: on the contrary, it represents the relative <u>decline</u> of the <u>collective</u> consciousness which a centralized rule system implies: under organic solidarity:

> 'It is necessary ... that the "conscience collective" leaves open a part of the individual consciousness in order that special functions may be established there, <u>functions which it cannot regulate</u>'. (Durkheim, 1972, p. 140 - my emphasis).

Hence:

> 'The "conscience collective" ... comes to consist of very general and indeterminate ways of thought and sentiment, which leaves room open for a growing variety of individual differences'. (p. 145)

In a sense Durkheim's theory of organic solidarity itself presents a dialectic between individualization and social coordination, in which interaction becomes necessarily more intense as its basis becomes more problematic. This in turn provides an interpretation of bureaucratic organiz-ations as institutions where opportunities for discretionary judgement are increased by the specialization of functions, and thus where the integration of such functions becomes necessarily more and more a focus of concern as it becomes more questionable. Hence, bureaucracy's principle of hierarchical jurisdictions is in a dialectical contra-diction with its other principle of expertly qualified officials, especially if expertise (as 'knowledge') is no longer taken to be a law-like corpus of warranted propositions but rather as a capacity for and experience of essentially reflexive interpretation. If rationality is, as Garfinkel argues, an inherently pluralistic set of possible interpretations, then the very notion of 'legal-rational' authority immediately expounds a contradiction, since social rationality denies the possibility of general laws and thereby renders authority subject to a continuous process of individual interpretation.

In conclusion then, as with professionalism, bureaucracy

is not a monolithic format for authority-as-oppression, with which action-research's project of transformational development must needs do battle, but rather a context with its own developmental dialectic, which thus offers to action-research its own inherent opportunity for the devolution of decision-making.

Now, all this is not new: Bernstein's well-known work on education is explicitly presented as an interpretation of largely bureaucratized institutions according to Durkheim's problematic of organic solidarity; and Bernstein ends the first of his papers on this theme by emphasizing that he is not contrasting 'order' with 'flux' nor lamenting 'the weakening of authority' but rather exploring 'changes in the forms of social integration' (Bernstein, 1971a, p. 169). It is in this spirit that Bernstein presents a change in the institutional order of the school from 'closed' to 'open' (Bernstein, 1971a, p. 169), from subject-based to across-subject teaching roles (p. 167), from vertical to horizontal relationships between teachers (Bernstein, 1971b, p. 62) and towards 'increased discretion of the pupils' (p. 60).

For Bernstein, following Durkheim, institutional order itself has become a problematic pattern of interaction, not a hierarchy of prescriptions. How ironic, then, that Peter Holly, in his diagrammatic representation quoted in the first section of this chapter, uses Bernstein's vocabulary to articulate not a Durkheimian but a crudely Weberian model of institutional life, as a hierarchy of prescriptions, which action-research must 'painfully' and 'cautiously' oppose. The particular irony is that Holly's vocabulary for the principles of action-research reproduces Bernstein's vocabulary for the basis of the institutional order, thereby undermining the very distinction which Holly wishes to put forward and thus implicitly and accidentally putting forward the counter-suggestion which is the theme of this section: that the institutional order is in itself available to action-research's project.

To avail itself of this opportunity, what action-research needs is not the oppositional 'caution' recommended by Holly, but a grasp of the complex but ultimately enabling relationship between (on the one hand) the potentially reflexive interactive processes of institutional life and professional practice, and (on the other hand) the reflexive processes of action-research's own dialectic between theory and practice. In this way action-research 'improves' institutionalized practices by exploring to their uttermost limits the discretionary possibilities within which they are (institutionally as well as epistemologically) constituted.

In this way, also, action-researchers may differentiate between those dimensions of their professional and institutional lives which are amenable to concrete projects for 'improvement', and others which - determined by

political and economic forces beyond any influence from
within their immediate institutional setting - must indeed
be treated as 'constraints' and thus as beyond the scope of
the particular project. This argument is in its own way
'cautiously' balanced between an emphasis on possibilities
and an equal emphasis on limits: it would be beyond the
scope of this work to attempt to estimate the likelihood
of a world in which professional practitioners in all
institutions were simultaneously pressing to their limits
the possibilities inherent in their roles! However, it may
be that through envisaging such a state of affairs, and by
examining the conditions of its feasibility, that one might
begin to reformulate the relationship between the
epistemological radicalism which action-research requires
and the political radicalism which it wishes to claim.

NOTES

(1)   'Pädagogik wird ... im Sinne einer kritischen
      Erziehungswissenschaft als Gesellschaftwissenschaft
      verstanden'. (Translations from Moser by R. Winter).

(2)   'Erziehungswissenschaft, die sich nicht dem
      bestehenden status quo verpflichtet, sondern jenem
      Prozess substantieller Befreiung in ihr Programm
      aufnimmt, hat sich deshalb jenes emanzipatorische
      Interesse zu eigen zu machen, dass Wissenschaft als
      Ermöglichung befreiender Praxis charakterisiert'.

(3)   'Erziehung wird damit sine qua non für eine
      Wissenschaftsprogrammatik, welche die sie (sic.
      'sich'? - RW) anerkennenden Subjekte erst "schaffen"
      muss'.

(4)   What Parson's presentation fails to address, of course,
      is the gap between action and explanation, between
      description and rationalization, between actuality and
      ideal type.

(5)   Carr and Kemmis are particularly ambiguous in their
      treatment of Habermas. On the one hand they note
      Habermas's 'failure to offer a detailed clarification
      of the epistemological basis of critical social
      science' (Carr and Kemmis, 1986, p. 139) and hence
      'the frustration (of) those who look in vain to
      Habermas's work for the praxis of critical theory: its
      use in real social action' (p. 151). Yet on the other
      hand they go on to assert: 'Action-research can pre-
      figure an ideal situation in which community self-
      interests coincide with the emancipatory interest in
      freeing all people from ideological constraints.'
      (p. 197)

(6)   'Im Diskurs (ist) selbst noch Gewalt am Werk, die uns
      aufzwingt, ohne dass wir es bemerken'.

(7)   'Bedenkt man ... die reale Verstrickung des Menschen
      in die gesellschaftlichen Zwangszusammenhänge und die
      Entwertung des Individuums ... so scheint sich der
      Habermassche (sic) Diskurs selbst zu überschätzen.   Er
      betrachtet sich als Gegenmacht gegen die faktischen
      Herrschaftsverhältnisse in der spätkapitalistischen
      Gesellschaft und übersieht dabei, dass er selbst durch
      sein Beharren auf blosser Kooperationsbereitschaft,
      alle Möglichkeiten zum Aufbau eines Widerparts aus der
      Hand gibt ... Aus diesem Grunde braucht der Diskurs
      selbst Kriterien, welche verhindern, dass die
      Diskursteilnehmer ideologische Argumente des falschen
      Bewusstseins in den Diskurs aufnehmen'.

5 Action - research and the problem of validity

The previous chapter began to engage with an issue that
must be analytically necessary for any project of
formulating a mode of investigation, namely its criteria
for validity. So far the argument has centred on only one
of action-research's criteria - its aspiration to 'improve'
practice. In this chapter the argument will be broadened:
it will consider how action-research might conceptualize
'validity' in accordance with its own inherent problematic,
i.e. independently of such echoes of positivism as:
accounts which purport to correspond 'accurately' to an
external object world, and interpretations which aspire to
be 'generalizable' propositions.

   Generalizability is of course the direct claim with which
positivism challenges its rivals: its hypotheses are
derived from 'laws'; its experimental method produces
statements of 'significance' concerning 'representative'
populations, so that in turn its results can be claimed as
potentially 'law-like' or, at least, essentially
'replicable'. Action-research, by appearing to eschew such
claims, opens itself to the charge that its validity is
limited to the concrete instances in which it is constituted. This is another way of accusing action-research of
failing to be more than a mundane action strategy, rather
than an alternative, non-positivist research strategy.

   It is for this reason, perhaps, in order to authorize its
validity claims, that action-research has claimed to draw

upon 'established' methodological traditions such as symbolic interactionism (see Elliott, 1982b, p. 31). Hence also the importance of the notion of 'case study' as a format for action-research inquiry (Elliott, 1978b, p. 356), which also enables action-research to claim kinship with institutionalized social science, eg. 'anthropology' (see Walker, 1980, p. 33). The purpose of this chapter is, then, to analyze the forms of general validity which may be claimed (or which action-research has claimed) for inter-pretations of the specific action contexts with which action-research is concerned.

Elliott's article in the Journal of Curriculum Studies (Elliott, 1978b) presents action-research's claim in a passage which raises many of the central questions, and it will thus serve as a starting point for the analysis of (in turn) 'naturalistic theory', 'concrete description', and 'narrative form', as versions of 'validity' for action-research accounts:

> 'In explaining "what is going on", action-research tells a "story" about the event by relating it to a context of mutually interdependent contingencies, ie. events which "hang together" because they depend on each other for their occurrence. This "story" is sometimes called a case study. The mode of explanation in case study is naturalistic rather than formalistic. Relationships are "illuminated" by concrete description rather than by formal statements of causal laws and statistical correlations. Case study provides a theory of the situation but it is a naturalistic theory embodied in narrative form, rather than a formal theory stated in propositional form'
> (p. 356)

'Naturalistic Theory'

The phrase itself embodies a grand epistemological irony, which appears to propose the annihilation of a central philosophical issue: how could theory be natural? how could nature be theoretical? how could either claim be grounded? We have here, then, not a routine category nor a methodological device, but rather a contention and a dilemma. Nevertheless, the writers in the symbolic interactionist tradition which Elliott seems here to be invoking also treat the elision as achievable. For example Schatzman and Strauss, in Field Research: strategies for a natural sociology (1973) - often used as a methodological text by action-research practitioners - claim that it is a basic property of 'the human scene' that social action is always an outcome of actors' theories or 'perspectives' (p. 5) and that the researcher is a naturalist' by direct analogy with the researcher in 'zoology, archeology, and geology' (p. 14) in that he works by observing 'the natural properties of his field' (p. vii), namely actors' perspectives. This seems at first to be the fairly simple point that it is the task of

the researcher to discover actor's rationalities, so that
it is those actors in their 'natural' world who are the
arbiters of what is to count as an adequate understanding.
This would be a straightforward relativism argument, and it
would coincide with Elliott's suggestion, at another point
in the article quoted above, that action-research
'interprets "what is going on" from the point of view of
those acting in the problem situation' and indeed 'in the
same language as they used' (Elliott, 1978b, p. 356).

However, the apparently non-ironic invocation of zoo-
logical parallels accomplished by the category 'naturalistic theory' is indicative of a larger and even more
problematic claim. In their account of 'naturalistic'
inquiry Schatzman and Strauss admit that researchers will
begin their work with concepts ('classes') presumed in
advance on the basis of an academic discipline, but that
the process of 'observation' will make available the
'classes' used by the members of the situation under
observation. These two sets of 'classes' will be synthesized in the course of 'the experience of observation'
(Schatzman and Strauss, 1973, p. 112) and it is specifically this synthesized set of categories which is termed
'theoretical'. They conclude: 'thus we can anticipate the
researcher will continue shifting his grounds as he creates
or changes his classes, until all his presumed classes are
displaced by those based upon observation' (p. 113). To
suggest, in this way, that concepts can be derivable from
observation is to present a metaphysics of naturalism, in
which theory is encapsulated by nature. The rhetoric of
the naturalist is used to suggest the possibility of an
account which has 'nature's' authority, thereby implying
metaphorically what they analytically deny: that the human
world is a world of objects available to inspection. The
symbolic interactionist argument (to which Schatzman and
Strauss ostensibly subscribe) is, on the contrary, that the
world of social actors is a world of subjects and their
interacting 'perspectives': the further interaction
between actors' perspectives and researchers' perspectives
can thus in no way be reduced to 'the observation of
nature', but is rather a central analytical problem in
formulating the category of 'theory' itself, and (as Becker
himself says, in 'Whose Side Are We On'? - Becker, 1971) a
dilemma in the social relations of validity claims.

That symbolic interactionism and action-research should
thus use the positivist metaphor of nature's passive open-
ness to observation, when both wish also to emphasize the
independent interpretive competence of the social actor, is
highly suggestive. It relates to a failure to articulate
fully the relationship between science and common-sense and,
in particular, a failure to come to terms with positivism's
powerful challenge in this respect, which is of crucial
significance for the issue of generalizable validity.

Zetterburg's argument (Zetterburg, 1962) concerning the
relationship between social theory and social actors'

relevancies offers an instructive contrast. For Zetterburg
social theory is a set of general laws, eg. 'A person tends
to modify his communications ... so that they approximate
those found among his associates' (Zetterburg, 1962, p. 81),
and specific action contexts can be understood at the level
of theory by being classified under a 'systematic'
combination of these laws (p. 132). 'Commonsense' on the
other hand is 'unable to make the right combination of
ideas' (p. 132). Thus for Zetterburg, 'case study' is
merely 'descriptive' and 'intuitive': it lacks 'analysis
of the principles at work' (pp. 27-8). Zetterburg's
analytical problem is that he treats the relationship
between law and instance as deductive - the practitioner
can deduce an understanding of the specific from the lesson
of the law (see Zetterburg, 1962, p. 166 ff.: 'The
Calculation of Solutions' - a most suggestive heading!)
But this is to ignore the process of inductive generalization by which the laws were originally formulated. This
process is acutely complex even for natural science: for
social science it is the problematic for the whole enterprise, since it raises the central theoretical and methodical issue of the relationship between observers' categories
and those of the social actors being observed. In thus
treating 'induction' as an available procedure, whose
resources can be glossed as established, Zetterburg ignores
more or less every sense of social science's specific
challenge, and in particular - of course -the issue of its
inevitable reflexivity.

   In formulating 'grounded theory' or 'naturalistic inquiry'
(Denzin, 1978, p. 6) symbolic interactionism has tried to
remedy Zetterburg's 'problem', but has failed to do so
because it has retained a positivist notion of theory
construction as organized according to a classificatory
logic. We have already seen that for Schatzman and Strauss
'analysis' is a process of 'class-ification' of instances
under concepts, as though 'analysis' could be a process of
reducing language's metaphoricity to literalness. But such
literalness could only be a prescription or a pragmatic
interpretation (see Garfinkel, 1967, p. 192), and thus not
an achievement of analysis, but itself the occasion for the
analysis of that reductive process. Denzin makes the issue
even clearer. He is 'committed ... to theory that is
grounded in the behaviours, languages, definitions,
attitudes, and feelings of those studied' (Denzin, 1978,
p. 6) and yet also to 'processes of sampling, generalization,
(p. 19) and measurement' (p. 24), and to providing 'causal
explanations (p. 16) which are 'repeatable and reliable'
(p. 22). But if 'languages, definitions, attitudes, and
feelings' could be sampled and measured, they would have to
be formulated as observable behaviours, and this would
dramatize Denzin's lack of a reflexive awareness; for we
would then need analytic grounds for the crucial differentiation between those 'languages and definitions' which are
to be measured and the 'languages and definitions' by means
of which the measurement would be accomplished. Otherwise
theory and the object of theory ('commonsense', say) would

117

remain undifferentiated. Zetterburg himself notes that
each of the 'theoretical' generalities he adduces is itself
'well known to common sense' (Zetterburg, 1962, p. 132).
Thus the notions of 'system' and 'law', in terms of which he
presents the analytic difference at issue, are essentially
unaddressed metaphors for theory's <u>claim</u> to authority. As
metaphors they evoke theory's difference as a set of
interesting problems, e.g. the relation between 'law' as a
social prescription and 'law' as a general truth. As
metaphors, 'law' and 'system' evoke social science's
<u>aspiration</u>, its sense of its own difference (from common-
sense) as its ideal of 'validity'; however, as Zetterburg
presents them, they are proposed as rules-of-thumb, which
could operate the difference to which they refer as though
it were a mere methodological device.

For symbolic interactionism and action-research to
address the irony inherent in 'naturalistic theory', the
question of general validity would have to be approached in
terms quite other than as a process of classification by
progressive abstraction. Such a process denies in principle
the need to address the grounds for its own selectivity,
since it presents itself as having the warrant of an
algorithm, and ignores the creative doubtfulness of the web
of metaphors which alone make classification possible.

Illumination by Concrete Description

Ironically, the notion of explanation as 'illumination'
echoes a paper (Parlett and Hamilton, 1977) in which
'evaluation as illumination' is presented as diametrically
opposed to what those writers call 'the agricultural-
botanical paradigm'. It is thus an explicit rejection of
the analogy between the human and the biological sciences
which informs the 'naturalism' of Schatzman and Strauss.
The basis of the distinction for Parlett and Hamilton is
that, whereas innovatory programmes in agriculture can
utilize an 'experimental testing' format for evaluation,
educational programmes cannot do so (see Chapter Two above).
Instead: 'the task is to provide a comprehensive understanding of the complex reality (or realities) surrounding
the programme, in short to 'illuminate'' (Parlett and
Hamilton, 1977, p. 21). Illumination thus involves an
account of the 'milieu' (p. 11) surrounding the specific
programme, and how therefore the latter is affected by 'a
network or nexus of cultural, social, institutional and
psychological variables' (p. 11). Hence Elliott's emphasis .
(see the introductory quotation, above) on relating 'the
event' to 'its context', and on the description of these
'relationships'. Thus, whereas the focus of the experimental method upon single variables leaves the event
'obscure' (to follow up the metaphor), <u>light</u> is shed by
tracing the 'complexity' of which it is a part (Parlett and
Hamilton, 1977, p. 11). Such complexity cannot be tested
or measured directly so 'the primary concern (of
illuminative evaluation) is with description and interpretation' (p. 10). The question then becomes: how can

'description and interpretation' be methods for the
creation of valid accounts of this complexity? This is a
crucial theme for writers on action-research in general and
writers on case study in particular.

For Midwinter 'interpretative description' is 'the
attempted medium for relating the results of the (action-
research) project' (Midwinter, 1972, p. 52), as a way of
meeting the need to balance action and research' (p. 54).
In other words, the justification for 'interpretative
description' is that it is compatible with the rapidly
changing, flexible and interactive procedures of action-
research (Midwinter, op cit, p. 53): he admits that this
'is not often academic method research' (sic) (p. 52) but
his whole argument for action-research is that inquiry is
too <u>urgent</u> to be left to the slow pace of 'theory-based'
research (p. 51). He goes on to quote E.H. Carr on 'the
continuous process of interaction and the unending dialogue
between facts and their interpreters' (p. 53). In other
words, 'interpretation' can be 'valid' precisely <u>because</u> it
allows the structure of experience to proceed uninterrupted.
But this would return us to our original problem: What
forms of reflection does action-research <u>add</u> to the
pragmatic reflection which is the basis of mundane action?
This is particularly important for Midwinter, since his
projects and the case studies which report them are all
predicated upon a specific 'theoretical' ideal of 'community
education', and thus require a principled basis for
evaluative judgement if they are to constitute a form of
inquiry at all, rather than a managerial process of
'implementation'.

Midwinter's 'anti-academic' emphasis is at variance with
Parlett and Hamilton, for whom the method of 'description
and interpretation' placed educational evaluation
'unambiguously within the ... anthropological paradigm'
(p. 10) which also includes 'participant observation
research in sociology' (p. 7). Now these traditions of
inquiry <u>do</u> have a basis for claims to general validity, and
this basis is (again in contrast to Midwinter's emphasis on
speed and non-intrusiveness) the comprehensive, lengthy
and painstaking <u>variety</u> of the investigative process. Thus
Denzin emphasizes 'triangulation of methods' (Denzin, 1978,
p. 21), Glazer and Strauss (1967) emphasize the need for a
continuously 'comparative' analysis and Becker stresses the
importance of checking interpretations against possible
negative instances (Becker, 1971, pp. 31-2). It is this
emphasis which is found in the work of Rob Walker, who is
concerned in general to relate the case study tradition in
social science to educational research with a direct commitment to change professional practice. For example, he says
that anthropology succeeds in preserving complexity of
meaning through a research process which is highly time
consuming (Walker, 1977, p. 18), and, in another paper:
'Long term study is justified in terms of the need to
determine areas of significance and to check the relia-
bility and consistency of data' (Walker, 1980, p. 30).

At this point we can see, however, that the notion of validity being presented here presupposes a correspond-ential conception of knowledge. If 'validity' resides in recognizing the 'complexity' of the factors influencing a situation, ie. if the aim or inquiry is to 'describe' this complexity, then the longer the time spent in doing so, and the more varied the sources of information, the greater the chance that the resulting 'interpretation' will correspond to the complexity it describes. But this returns the problem of adequate understanding to the infinite number of variables, which Parlett and Hamilton recognized as under-mining the feasibility of the positivist paradigm they rejected, but which also undermines their own project of 'description'. Similarly, Elliott (see the introductory quotation) refers to 'a context ... of events which "hang together" because they depend on each other for their occurrence'; but how would such dependence be knowable except by invoking those same 'causal laws' which he rejects? Illumination by concrete ... description' evokes the ancient metaphor of knowledge as light, but to propose that by means of 'description' the object of knowledge is 'illuminated' does not formulate the process of knowledge; rather, it presupposes its accomplishment: to call the process 'illumination' presupposes that what is being shed is, indeed, light.

It is particularly important that action-research should be able to dissociate itself from a positivist notion of correspondential description, since as Walker himself goes on to argue (following Midwinter at this point), the time constraints of an inquiry which is intended to be of direct value to practitioners mean that a description which is adequate in positivist terms can never be achieved before the situation itself changes (Walker, 1980, pp. 31-2). Underlying Walker's argument is the general principle of dialectical understanding (see chapter one) which would make any project for the exhaustive description of phenomena self-contradictory: its implicit ambition of achieving finality is incompatible with the temporal, developmental quality of its object. Further: a recog-nition of the reflexivity of language means that description cannot, in principle, merely 'correspond' with the phenomenon described.

How, then, have exponents of educational action-research and educational case-study attempted to formulate 'description' in terms other than this implicitly positivist version? Robert Stake presents 'description' as a necessarily intersubjective process, with its own inherent principle of generalizability: 'Our methods of studying human affairs need to capitalize upon the natural powers of people to experience and to understand' (Stake, 1980, p. 66). Understanding and experience involve 'naturalistic generalization', which is a process whereby 'intuitive expectations based on 'tacit knowledge' lead to 'a full and thorough knowledge of the particular, recognizing it in new and foreign contexts' (p. 69). Hence, if 'the target

case is properly described ... readers recognize essential
similarities to cases of interest to them, (and thus) they
establish the basis for naturalistic generalization'
(pp. 70-1). 'Nature' here is no longer the nature which
the 'naturalist' observes, but in which he participates, as
a member of a shared, culturally and linguistically
constituted reality. In this sense Stake's argument has
links with Hegel's analysis of the generalizing property of
language (quoted in chapter one). However, whereas this
intersubjective and generalizing property of the symbol is
for Stake a methodical resource, for Hegel it presents an
irreducibly problematic quality: concrete objects cannot
be referred to except through the universalism of language;
the ontology of the concrete is thus a 'whirling circle',
and 'it just is not possible for us ever to ... express in
words a sensuous being that we MEAN' (Hegel, 1977, p. 79,
p. 60). Indeed, if the issue of generalization were as
straightforward as Stake suggests, then his argument would
apply to any descriptive communication, and we would still
lack grounds for inquiry's claim to be other than mundane
interaction. For Stake, the complexity of the symbol is
the basis for an affirmative answer to the question: can
concrete meanings be generalizable? For Hegel, in contrast,
this complexity poses the question: how can generalization
be related to the concrete?

Addressing this issue, Eisner presents the notion of
'thick description', which 'aims at describing the meaning
or significance of behaviour as it occurs in a cultural
network saturated with meaning', and which 'also aims at
using language in a way so vivid that it enables the reader
to participate vicariously in the quality of life that
characterizes the events being described. It is in this
sense that educational criticism is an art form' (Eisner,
1977, p. 97). A similar argument (linking description with
aesthetic form and with an effect of 'vicarious' experience)
is made by Whitehead and Foster (1984, p. 44). The various
ways in which aesthetic qualities have been invoked as part
of a declaration against positivism will be the topic of
the next section; meanwhile it is notable that for Eisner,
as for Stake, 'description' is not the transmission of
exhaustive information, but involves the dialectical
participation of writer and reader in a shared symbolic
culture, and is thus constituted in the transcendental
properties of language. However, it is clear that these
properties are much too superficially presented by Eisner
as 'vividness', and that 'vicariousness' (as a claim for
the effect of such vividness) is either exaggerated or
merely cryptic. Both 'vividness' and 'vicariousness' are
glosses for the intersubjective dialectics of language's
effectiveness: how such effectiveness may be either sought
or invoked as a criterion for validity remains to be
analyzed.

Theory Embodied as Narrative

In the passage originally quoted above, Elliott suggests

that it is by constructing a 'story' that the case studies
of action research programmes find coherence, that
contingencies 'hang together' and 'events' are related to
their 'context'. In this way 'theory is embodied in
narrative form'. Similarly Kemmis suggests 'case studies
work by example rather than by abstract argument ... just
as Tolstoy's theory of history is embedded in the story of
War and Peace'.(Kemmis S., 1980, pp. 136-7). But we need
to ask: how might a theory be 'embedded' in a story?
McDonald and Walker declare: 'Case study is the way of the
artist, who achieves greatness when, through the portrayal
of a single instance locked in time and circumstance, he
communicates enduring truths about the human condition.
For both scientist and artist, content and intent emerge in
form'. (McDonald and Walker, 1975, p. 3). The notion of
an enduring truth within the specific instance is focussed
in the idea of the 'typical', and they cite Zola, the
'naturalist', who achieved 'scientific generalization' by
'carefully researching the factual settings ...(and)
creating characters to represent the social type' (p. 3).
This would make of Zola a 'documentary' novelist, and
McDonald and Walker do indeed also cite the 'documentary'
as a possible format for the presentation of case studies
(p. 9). But both the documentary and the 'naturalistic'
novel raise the question: how are certain events and
characters deemed to be 'typical'? And this question is
crucial if we wish to consider how Zola's 'factual'
research created social types rather than merely concrete
reportage, and, in general, by what process either fiction
or documentary can structure particular experiences into
forms which might aspire to a validity beyond those
particulars.

Lukacs begins to answer this question through a distinction between 'Naturalism' (as 'mere' reportage) and
'Realism', as the selection of detail through criteria of
significance relating to an overall perspective (Lukacs,
1964, p. 51, p. 56). This 'perspective' is embodied in a
'typology' of significant, typical actors ie. 'characters',
who thus act out the meaning of the narrative as the 'plot'
of their interaction. In other words: 'Characters are not
in a novel; they constitute it, just as a typology - a
range of hypothetical possibilities - constitutes a form of
sociological theory. In both cases we are presented with a
series of hypotheses set up in order to investigate the
nature of the world' (Winter R., 1975, p. 34). For this
argument the theoretical problem then becomes the origin
and the grounds for the 'perspective' which operates as the
criterion of relevance for setting up the 'typology'. Lukacs
relates it to a positively known 'history', and he is in
general opposed to the reflexive turn of 'modernist'
fiction which addresses the grounds of the writer's
perspective as a central issue. On the other hand McDonald
and Walker point to the issue without engaging it:
'Clearly, representativeness is an important consideration
... instance and abstraction go hand in hand in an
iterative process of cumulative growth' (McDonald and

Walker, 1975, p. 4). 'Hand in hand', 'accumulation', and
'growth' are metaphors for the desirability of a theoretical relationship between instance and abstraction but do
not specify what this relationship might be.

The argument so far has presented a parallelism between
positivist social science and realist fiction, a parallel
which enables Becker to propose the valuable contribution
of 'Life Histories' to the 'mosaic' of available 'data'
(Becker, 1971, pp. 70, 72) and to suggest that the sociologist's hypotheses can be inspired by reading novels as
well as by reading sociological theory (pp. 21-3). But
this parallel, although it rescues description from mere
data collection, simply interposes a third term, 'typology'
or 'perspective', to bridge the gap between 'narrative' and
'theory': the theoretic processes which might be involved
remain unaddressed. In particular, it does not address the
grounds of the analytical work carried out by the producer
of a documentary in selecting interviewees, settings, and
background 'information', nor that of the fiction writer in
devising a set of characters and their interaction in a
narrative. Rather the notion of 'typicality' is used as an
unexplicated resource for generalization, a resource which
can be treated as available for two reasons: i) by
reliance upon what Stake calls 'naturalistic generalization',
which the symbolic process itself seems to facilitate as
soon as the symbol is treated as non-problematic, divorced
from the reflexive issue of its invocation; ii) by
reliance on the rationalist model of action invoked by both
Weber and Schutz to create 'ideal types' for actors'
perspectives. In other words, the documentary and realist
fiction are examples of how generalization from the
concrete can be treated as achievable through cultural
convention - the 'vivid example, the 'typical' illustration.
It is precisely the grounds for these conventions - the
grounds for the possibility of generalization - which are
not addressed.

It is an indication of the significance of these issues
for action-research that Walker has attempted to elaborate
a methodological link between fiction and research, in an
article called 'On the Uses of Fiction in Educational
Research', (Walker, 1981). Walker suggests, following
Terry Denny ('Story Telling as a First Step in Educational
Research'), that the format of a story can 'communicate the
general spirit of things' which is true to what people
'mean' rather than what they merely (according to a tape-
recorder) 'say' (Walker, 1981, p. 155). But how is this
achieved? Walker suggests: 'A story sets limits, it
controls what the writer lets the reader see. In this
sense a story is analogous to a theory' (p. 157). But this
is, of course, to use a prescriptive version of theory,
which is alien to action-research and to 'grounded theory'-
both of which desire to generate theory from participants'
own interpretations. Walker's implicitly positivist theory
of knowledge and his exclusive focus on realist forms of
fiction finally lead him to say: 'The attraction of

fictional forms ... is that they offer a license to go
beyond what, as an evaluator / researcher, you can be
fairly sure of knowing' (p. 163), and to propose that
fictional forms can be 'adopted' by a case study researcher
as 'a means of disguise' (p. 159), so that he can report
his data-gathering while preserving its confidentiality.
In this way, presenting no principled basis for addressing
the theoretic quality of fiction, fiction's particular form
of truth, Walker does not follow up his earlier statement
that 'a story is analogous to a theory' except in the
superficial sense that a theory, like a story, is an
observer's point of view. Hence fiction is finally aligned
in opposition to 'real' knowledge, as a form of 'licensed'
subjectivity: fiction is not itself a knowledge-constitutive form; hence it can be 'used' strategically in
relation to knowledge, which is constituted as 'objective',
presumably, on other grounds. What is thus in urgent need
of consideration is the sense in which fiction constitutes
knowledge through its own forms, ie. fiction as a
structuring of reality, fiction as a reflexive structuring
of the relation between subject, object, and symbol. This
involves questioning precisely the conventions concerning
art, science, reality, and knowledge, on which scientific
positivism and aesthetic realism both rely.

ACTION-RESEARCH AND THE VALIDITY OF THE CONCRETE

So far I have considered three aspects of action-research's
quest for a principle of 'validity' which might guide its
accounts of social situations. The argument has been, that
the notion of 'naturalistic' theory needs to be recast in
terms of the reflexivity of theory and the metaphoricity of
language, that the notion of 'concrete description' raises
the issue of the relation between the general and the
specific in terms which necessitate a dialectical theory of
intersubjectivity, culture, and symbolization, and that the
notion of 'narrative-as-theory' cannot simply utilize the
assumptions of realism, but requires also an awareness of
the reflexivity of aesthetic structuring. In the final
section of this chapter these arguments will be developed
in a more positive and detailed form. But in order to
prepare for that argument the next two sections will
consider in general terms the relation between action-
research's requirement of non-positivist formulations of
validity and the principles of 1) reflexivity and 2)
dialectics.

Action-Research, Validity, Reflexivity

In Chapter One the reflexive quality of symbolization was
emphasized, and it was argued that it is by addressing
(rather than glossing) this feature that acts of communication (ranging from the spoken comment and the anecdote to
the novel and the social research project) can attain a
form of 'completeness' and thus of 'adequacy'. (1)
Reflexivity was taken to be the underlying structure of the

relation between consciousness and its objects (including of course, and in particular, 'other' consciousnesses). Reflexivity (it was argued) is conventionally glossed, leaving communication open to the cultural contingencies of 'bias', ie. the political and psychological pressures which socially distribute the plausibility and authority of interpretations. Such pressures cannot be abolished, although it is precisely the claim of positivism to do so by means of methodology, and thereby to transform interpretation into scientific knowledge. Rather it is by <u>analyzing</u> the irreducibly reflexive dimension of communicative acts (including such analyses themselves) that their grounds are revealed. 'Validity' is thereby approached by taking as a topic the form and nature of communication itself, ie. the 'conditions of its possibility', (see Chapter One). 'Bias' is thus neither glossed nor abolished but rather confronted, through an analytically 'complete' examination of the theoretical basis of the communicative act in the general (reflexive) structure of the relation between subject, symbol, and object. Validity, in other words, becomes a quality of the interpretive <u>process</u> whose grounds are adequately theorized, rather than a quality of a particular interpretation which itself can claim to be everyone's interpretation.

How does this relate to action-research? Action-research certainly recognizes the importance of its own process. Does that mean that it envisages the need for reflexive awareness?

Lippett says: 'Probably the best resource every group has for studying the problems and techniques of human relations is the life of the group itself' (Lippett, 1984, p. 110). However, this seems merely to point to the group as a conveniently available 'example': the 'life' of the group is said to exemplify the problems of human relations: a reflexive analysis would note rather that in attempting to address 'the problems of human relations' those same problems would manifest themselves, so that the <u>theoretical</u> 'life' of the group would exemplify 'the problems of attempting to address the problems of human relations'.

Elliott, in the paper quoted at the beginning of this chapter, refers to criteria guiding the <u>process</u> of action-research by saying: 'Action-research ... can only be validated in unconstrained dialogue' (Elliott, 1978b, p. 356). He goes on to specify:

> 'The participants must have free access to the
> researcher's data, interpretations, accounts,
> etc. and 'the researcher' must have free access
> to 'what is going on' ... Action-research
> cannot be undertaken properly in the absence
> of trust established by fidelity to a mutually
> agreed ethical framework governing the collection,
> use and release of data'. (pp. 356-7)

For McDonald and Walker (1975) the process is one of
negotiation: the case-study worker does not produce one
summative interpretation but rather engages in a negotiating
process: 'the evaluator acts as broker in exchanges of
information between differing groups' (p. 7). For Elliott
the 'process' is constituted in an 'ethical framework',
whereas for McDonald and Walker there is also a related
political dimension: the 'process' they outline is termed
'democratic' evaluation, which they say is predicated on
the notions of 'confidentiality','negotiation', 'access-
ibility', and 'the right to know' (p. 7). In both cases
the process of investigation is indeed the topic of
grounding principles, in which the epistemological adequacy
of an account is described in terms of the interpersonal
conditions of its possible production. However, both
Elliott and McDonald and Walker formulate the investigative
process at the level of practical prescriptions, which fail
to consider the further reflexive processes by which such
mundane rules would have to be interpreted. How would an
adequate degree of 'faithfulness to an ethical framework'
be decided? How accessible is 'accessible'? What are the
structures and (inevitable) limits of 'a right to know'?
In remaining at this level, these writers rely for their
intelligibility upon the glossing procedures which a
reflexive analysis would take as its topic.

Another writer, Kemmis, invokes the principle of reflexivity quite explicitly: 'The insights reached through case
study are impermanent ... (they) must therefore be treated
historically. Any useful social science is reflexive, and
must be treated as such' (Kemmis, 1980, p. 133). But
'history' itself needs to be formulated reflexively, rather
than being treated (as it often is within such arguments)
as a taken-for-granted origin, relating insights to their
contextual causes, and thereby conjuring forth all the
problems of 'ideology', discussed at length in chapter
three. However, Kemmis is more precise. He says:

> 'In reporting the study, the case study worker
> demonstrates how, in his own case as a cognitive
> subject, the imagination of the case and the
> invention of the study have exerted controlling
> influences on one another' (p. 126).

Kemmis calls this a 'dialectical process' involving the
subject, the object (ie. 'the case'), and the method (ie.
'the study') (p. 124). This, he says, is 'a new
perspective' which preserves 'the interdeterminacy of
knowledge' as a constructive alternative to the untenable
claims of positivism (p. 117-9).

Although the general theme of Kemmis's argument is
compatible with the discussion presented here, his
formulation displays, nevertheless, an interesting
ambiguity. On the one hand he proposes a cognitive subject
who 'imagines' and 'invents', and yet (strangely) the
activity of exerting the power of imagination and invention

is presented in terms of 'control' and 'influence', rather than in terms of a reflexive theory of symbolization in general and of language in particular. Instead of this, Kemmis oscillates between formulating a controlling subject who uses language ('In all knowing, the knower ... brings to bear his language and perceptual habits' - p. 108) and references to Wittgenstein where language seems to be an independent structure which controls the subject, by means of 'conventions' and 'games' (p. 135). By thus reducing the complex reflexivity of language to an unaddressed dichotomy, Kemmis can only imply the parameters of the reflexive awareness which must underlie a non-positivist process of inquiry, ie. imagination and symbolic resource, indeterminacy and validity, contingency and necessity. He leaves us with the problem of how such a reflexive awareness could be formulated: analytically, in order to conceive of that form of validity which is compatible with the indeterminacy of knowledge; and yet concretely, as a form of theorizing to which an action-research study could aspire.

In previous Chapters I have made two suggestions concerning a possible reflexive dimension to action-research - both embodying the form of the question - the mutual questioning of action and theory (Chapter Two) and the mutual questioning of professional and client (Chapter Four). In examining the nature of the 'validity' with which reflexivity might be concerned, it is once more the possibilities of the questioning mode of thought I wish to explore. Heidegger says that to understand 'a thinker' is 'to take up his quest and pursue it to the core of his thought's problematic'. In this way, he continues, 'we are taking a way of questioning (Heidegger's emphasis) on which the problematic alone is accepted as the unique habitat and locus of thinking' (Heidegger, 1968, p. 185). Now, whereas questioning is taken to be the quintessence of 'thinking', Heidegger's whole effort in the second half of What is Called Thinking is an elaborate dismantling of the syn-tactical structure of the assertion, in order to reveal the thinking which asserting conceals and, layer upon layer, glosses. In this he seems to be engaging directly with Hegel's problem (already cited): 'It is not possible for us ever to say, or express in words, a sensuous being that we MEAN'. In this respect both writers seem to suggest an argument that the 'performative' functions of language's indicative, non-questioning mode (noted by Austin: How to Do Things With Words, 1962) constitute the problematic nature of language as an analytical means. To assert a meaning is to take part in the mundane world of unexplicated actions (listed by Austin as: giving verdicts, exercising power, making commitments, and, in general, adopting roles). Extending this argument, then, one might suggest that it is the question which can interrupt this mundane interchange by addressing the grounds of its intelligibility: since assertions can never give their own grounds, they can always only address one problematic by creating another; hence questioning alone is the 'habitat' where the problematic in general may be addressed.

How, then, could 'questioning' establish such a habitat within action-research? Action-research studies have frequently been described as 'dialogue' between participants and as 'brokerage' between the multiple viewpoints of those involved (eg. Elliott, 1978b, p. 356; McDonald and Walker, 1975, p. 7). The image of a 'broker' neatly evokes, in a context of commercial trafficking, the ambition of a format acceptable to all 'parties'. But what would be its theoretic equivalent? And in what sense might it address reflexivity?

Any set of viewpoints within a mundane situation will manifest a range of tensions or even incompatibilities. Merely to 'exchange' the viewpoints among the parties, as McDonald and Walker suggest (p. 7) is not necessarily more likely to generate a single mutually acceptable interpretation than to reinforce existing oppositions. And for the researcher to adopt a viewpoint on the basis of an elaborately justified adjudication between members' interpretations would still be to operate within that set of oppositions. To this extent, any justification of a particular preferred viewpoint will be 'polemical' and thus, according to Heidegger, unlikely to constitute nor to develop 'clarification'. As Heidegger says, 'Any kind of polemic fails from the outset to assume the attitude of thinking. The opponent's role is not the thinking role. Thinking is only thinking when it pursues whatever speaks for a subject'. Heidegger, 1968, p. 13). 'Polemic' is the language of assertion, the language of what one might term 'oppositional interpretation': it asserts the adequacy of this interpretation and the inadequacy of others. When this process is extrapolated one can see that the justification of asserted interpretation will merely serve to maintain the pressure of the mundane power struggle, within which any claims to validity will immediately be contested. The oppositional stance justifies one interpretation by attempting to annihilate the intelligibility of what it rejects; this is the rhetorical mode of the law-courts, of parliament, of competitions for power, of wars, rows, and divorces.

In contrast, reflexive interpretation is the language of questions: it questions my own interpretation along with others; its extrapolation poses as problematic the origin, the coherence, the grounds, of all perspectives; it is a form of questioning which attempts to speak for not against its interlocutor (a formulation conventionally espoused within 'counselling' for example). It creates a theoretic space by means of a general withdrawal from interpretation to problematic. This is a space therefore within which discourse can proceed under the auspices of theoretic grounds, which may be shared, and which thus may come to be agreed as valid theoretic grounds for the whole set of interpretations at issue. Further, and of crucial importance for action-research's commitment to 'change' and 'improvement', the withdrawal from interpretation to problematic may create not only a theoretic space but also as it were a potentially political space, allowing for at least the possibility of a redefinition of the interpretations themselves, and hence, in turn, of new possibilities for action.

In this way, Heidegger's notion of 'thinking' as reflexive questioning can suggest a possible analytical form for action-research's metaphors of 'negotiation' and 'brokerage': it shifts the criterion of validity from the level of a consensus concerning interpretation to consensus concerning theoretic grounds for a plurality of interpretations. But then a further question arises: if reflexive questioning can constitute a theoretical space which allows the possibility of change, what form might this change take, such that change itself might be formulated analytically, rather than as mere contingency? It is in this context that I wish to examine the significance of the <u>dialectic</u> as a basis for critique and thus for transformation. Can the dialectic be formulated reflexively and thus constitute for action-research a further dimension for the process of theorizing?

Action-Research, Validity, Dialectics

Action-research has frequently invoked the rhetoric of dialectics as a way of presenting its commitment to action and to change, and some of these presentations were considered in Chapter Two in order to explore the possible form, within action-research, for a dialectic between action and theory: in this section I wish to examine how far the form of the dialectic might allow the writing of the action-research study report itself to approach its inherent problem: how can the study of a single concrete situation claim a validity beyond that of a possible interpretation of a mundane actor's perspective?

In one simple sense, 'dialectic' can enable us to address once again the problem of 'grounded theory', which (as I have argued earlier) is also action-research's problem. Theorists of grounded theory suggest that validity can be sought through 'triangulation' of methods and viewpoints (Denzin, 1978, p. 21; Becker, 1971, p. 58; Elliott, 1981, p. 19); but when they do so, what are the grounds for the difference which produces the triangulation AS a triangulation, and thus creates the force of a metaphor for validity derived from trignometry? Problems in navigation can be solved by invoking Euclid's theories of the forms of triangles, but what are the equivalent theories and forms which problems in social science might require? A straight line identifies an infinite number of points: only the difference created by a triangular form enables the One point to be identified. Similarly, the listing of a multiplicity of interpretations does not generate a basis for choice between them (nor for the construction from them of a further transcendental interpretation) until they are structured in terms of a principled conception of Difference.

129

In the previous section this principled Difference separated reflexive from assertive analysis; in this section Difference is examined in terms of Contradiction, as a principle which leads us to 'dialectic' as a process of theorizing.

Underlying the image of triangulation is the desire to create validity through the structure of inquiry, rather than by the multiplication of the objects of inquiry: for positivist social science, validity can be located in the replication of similarity (generalization of the object-as-a-unity); for action-research and case study, the object itself is non-replicable - only by comprehending the structure of the object as the set of differences which constitute it, can validity be claimed in terms of a generalizable structure. However, grounded theorists and action-researchers are concerned that this structure should be grounded in the object of the inquiry, rather than in an independent system of categories brought to the inquiry. Hence the relevance at this point of one of the major questions concerning the dialectic: where are contradictions located?

Debates within Marxist theory have attempted at times to provide clear-cut answers to this. For example, Colletti (1975) wishes to make a clear distinction between conflicting forces in nature and logical incompatibilities in thought, but finally recognizes that such a dichotomy, resting as it does on a further dichotomy between 'science' and 'philosophy' merely leaves the social sciences 'without a true foundation of their own', awaiting a 'reconciliation' (p. 29). In reply, Edgley (1977) proposes such a reconciliation by suggesting that social reality, being a symbolic constellation, is therefore both 'thought' and 'nature', and hence in itself quite intelligibly constituted in contradictions both of meaning and of political forces, which it is the task of analysis to expose and thus help to overcome. Yet, as McCarney says, 'the realization of (Edgley's) science would be a society without contradiction. It is far from clear that such a state of affairs could be coherently described in any detail' (McCarney, 1979, p. 29).

Yet each of these proposals seems to be an attempt to resolve an issue which seems in principle to be not susceptible of resolution, namely the problem of the irremediable tension between theory's desire for clarity of exposition, and the complexity of - on the one hand - its object (the contradictions of social reality) and - on the other hand - its relation with that object (theory's essential reflexivity). Formulations of the role of 'contradictions' in social analysis must - I would argue - embrace this complexity - a complexity which involves the symbol and the object, thought and reality, and indeed renders problematic those very categories. Hegel, for example, as we have seen, described 'The Thing' as 'a manifold' of contradictions: the One essence and the Many qualities, the universal and the concrete, the self-defined and the defined-in relation-to-other (Hegel, 1977, pp. 67-71). Further: the consciousness which perceives the Thing cannot simply distinguish the Thing, Consciousness, and the act of perceiving: instead the act of perceiving becomes 'a complex assumption of responsibility' (p. 74) whereby the constitution of the Thing in consciousness becomes an act of self-definition, and thus the complexity of the Thing becomes reflected back as a structuring of consciousness itself (pp. 73-5). The ontology of the Thing is thus a 'whirling circle' (p. 79) from which commonsense tries to escape by means of such simple dichotomies as single/plural, essence/qualities, concrete/universal, or - one might add - the contradictory/the logical.

In this respect, as noted in Chapter One, Lenin follows Hegel:

'Dialectics is general as a method since, as
Hegel noted, every proposition itself contains
the contradiction of the relation between universal
and individual' (Lenin, 1972, p. 361)

Thus, 'The universal exists only in the individual and through the individual' and conversely 'Every individual is connected by thousands of transitions with other kinds of individuals (things, phenomena, processes, etc.)' (p. 361) which seems to evoke not only a connected world of 'nature' but also, potentially at least, that metaphorical aspect of thought which gives the development of knowledge always the property of a dialectic (p. 362) - a 'spiral', so that for Lenin 'rectilinearity' of thought is equivalent to 'obscurantism' (p. 363). This emphasis is followed by Adorno for whom contradiction is that principle of ontology 'which indicates the untruth of identity, the fact that the concept does not exhaust the thing conceived' (Adorno, 1973, p. 5). What must be avoided therefore is the apparent self-sufficiency of the concept (p. 12) and the implicit claim to unity of 'systems' (p. 20). Instead, 'philosophy' must 'adhere as closely as possible to the heterogeneous' (p. 13). For these writers, then, dialectics proposes a way of encompassing the complexity of social experience, and the complexity of attempts to understand social experience, within a general structural principle, while allowing for the essential heterogeneity of the concrete. In other words, dialectics offers the possibility of grounding validity in experience, by formulating a principle for the structure of inquiry which is at the same time a principle for the structure of experience itself.

Such seemed to be the value of dialectics for action-research, and, as such, inspired my article 'Dilemma Analysis - A Contribution to Methodology for Action-Research', (Winter R., 1982) as an attempt to apply dialect-ical principles to action-research. (2) The following passage embodies the main line of the argument concerning validity and dialectics in an action-research context (in this example, a study of students on 'teaching practice'):

> 'A teaching practice, in common with many social
> situations, involves interaction between different
> parties who, as a consequence of their different
> roles in the situation have different aims,
> priorities, and definitions of reality. Also,
> the situation creates a hierarchy of power and
> status between these roles. Hence, <u>some</u> of the
> problems typically encountered will rest on a
> failure by one party to appreciate the point of
> view of the other parties involved. The task I
> formulated for myself, as a teaching practice
> supervisor/researcher, was to attempt to transcend
> my view as a supervisor in order to create an

1) account of the T.P. situation which would be
> faithful to the views of students, classroom
> teachers, and pupils, as well as those of
> fellow supervisors. This account had to gain
> the assent of all parties so that it could be
> used to illuminate for each party the point of
> view of the others, as a practical contribution
> to preparation for T.P. The different views
> therefore had to be presented plausibly as
> parallel rationalities, without the hierarchical
> valuation which conventionally discriminates

2) between them. In other words, the analysis had
> to gain acceptance as 'objective', evoking the
> main areas of tension in the situation without
> generating immediate controversy by seeming
> partisan, which would of course lead to its
> being rejected in such terms as: 'It's your
> point of view as a supervisor' or alternatively:
> 'You've gone over to the other side'. The
> action-research task then, in this case, and not
> (I think) untypically, was precisely that of

2) creating an account of a situation which would be
> seen <u>by a variety of others</u> as convincing, ie.
> as 'valid'.

The theoretical basis of the method

> ... The formal theory which guides the method
> of Dilemma Analysis is what could loosely be
> called the sociological conception of 'contra-
> diction', which is used here in the form of a
> series of general, indeed all-embracing postulates:
> that social organizations at all levels (from
> the classroom to the State) are constellations
> of (actual or potential) conflicts of interest;
> that personality structures are split and

3) convoluted; that the individual's conceptualization
> is sytematically ambivalent or dislocated;
> that motives are mixed, purposes are contradictory,
> and relationships are ambiguous; and that the
> formulation of practical action is unendingly
> beset by <u>dilemmas</u>. Hence a statement of an opinion in

an interview is taken to be a marginal option
which conceals a larger awareness of the potential
appeal and validity of different and even opposed
points of view. (This is an elaboration of
Winter, 1980b, p. 68). On this basis, then, it
became intelligible to analyze the interview
transcripts not in terms of particular opinions,
but in terms of the issues about which various
opinions were held. The method is called
'Dilemma Analysis' precisely to emphasize the
systematic complexity of the situations within
which those concerned have to adopt (provisionally
at least) a strategy. Beneath the analysis lie
the conceptual underpinnings of Marxian and
Freudian theory: at the literal surface of the
analysis is the relatively non-controversial
notion of the paradoxical nature of social
existence.' (Winter R, 1982, pp. 167-8)

A 'procedural sequence' is then given - followed by
examples - as to how this 'dialectical' theory could be
embodied as a practical method:

'The techniques .... involved (a) formulating the
dilemmas at roughly the same level of abstraction
at which they were originally presented in the
interview scripts, (b) choosing as a starting point
the most elaborated formulation of any given dilemma
from among the various statements in the scripts,
(c) formulating each dilemma so that it balanced
non-controversially between the potentially opposed
points of view ......'etc.

The strength of 'Dilemma Analysis' is that it attempts to
install dialectics as a methodological process. In this it
is more rigorous and self-consistent than the work of Carr
and Kemmis (1986), who, although they invoke a 'dialectical
view of rationality' (p. 184), do not carry forward their
original theory of 'contradiction' (pp. 33-4) into their
accounts of the action-research process: instead they
accept Lewin's 'spiral' of planning and observation as what
they mean by 'dialectical' method (an argument which was
considered and refuted in chapter two, above), and present
their series of concrete examples merely as illustrations
of Lewin's approach (pp. 168-74).

However, the 'Dilemma Analysis' article was written in
1980, before the present study was undertaken, and the
quoted extract clearly reveals a number of weaknesses, some
of which I have already criticized in other action-research
work. Hence, concerning the marginal numbers:
1) Its own practice is presented as the articulation of
viewpoints, a form of 'brokerage', which does not make
explicit the theoretical grounds of its process.
2) Its version of validity is seen as a consensus, without
any reference to a process by which such a consensus might
be created, except through the presumption of spontaneous

133

empathy (cf. Eisner's invocation of 'vicariousness', see above).
3) Although there is a reference to the 'ambivalence' of conceptualization, there is no specific reference to the reflexive problematics of language itself, and thus there is no awareness that the action-research worker is himself beset by the problematics he describes.

The last point gives rise to a crucial weakness of the article: it attempts to provide a quasi-mechanical 'methodology' based on precisely the literal specification of simple alternatives which Adorno dubs 'bureaucratic thinking' (Adorno, 1973, p. 31). (See the 'Teachers' Perspective Document' later in the article, which presents the various issues in terms of a repeated sequence of oppositions: 'On the one hand ... BUT on the other hand' - pp. 271-3). Thus 'Dilemma Analysis' attempts to be literal, where it should recognize the inevitability of metaphor; it attempts to be exhaustive, where it should recognize that it must remain 'inconclusive' (Adorno, 1973, p. 33); and it locates contradiction in an external world of actors' perspectives, where it should recognize that its own processes of cognition and expression are constituted in those same contradictions. Hence it attempts to prescribe a description by utilizing 'contradiction' as a resource which could provide a method, where it should attempt to transcend description by reflexive analysis of the problematics of that resource (in relation to its own process).

Finally, and most disabling of all, it denies the temporal dimension required by its own theory. Contradictions are constituted as such in terms in a dialectical _process_ of transformation. As Lenin (3) says: 'The condition for the knowledge of all processes of the world, in their '_self-movement_', in their spontaneous _development_, in their real life, is the knowledge of them as a unity of opposites' (Lenin, 1972, p. 360). In thus presenting contradictions as a series of static, if complex 'perspectives', Dilemma Analysis fails to provide for its own process of inquiry which constitutes them, a further failure of reflexive awareness, and, more curiously, a failure of the basic spirit of action-research, whose ambition is essentially to constitute its theorizing within the developing action of its own process. (4)

In principle, however, as the above critique implies, the dialectic _could_ provide a powerful theoretic basis for the conduct of action-research. It raises the possibility of an analytical basis for presenting the structure of concrete situations and thus for grounding the investigation of such situations in a general and coherent principle, namely an inherent epistemology which locates theorizing in relation to its own cognitive and interactive processes, as well as to its apparent object.

In this way, one might begin to formulate a constitutive relationship between the two principles of reflexivity and

dialectics, in terms of which I have tried to present
'validity' in this chapter. One might suggest that there is
an analogy between the questions which reflexivity poses to
interpretive assertion - questions of grounds and
possibility - and the dialectical logic which, as Adorno
says is 'one of disintegration ... of the prepared and
objectified form of the concepts which the cognitive subject
faces' (Adorno, 1973, p. 145). 'Dialectics is ... the
resistance which otherness offers to identity' (p. 161).
The important point is that investigators are themselves
'cognitive subjects', and their own interpretations take on
a quality of 'identity' as soon as they are expressed, so
that their own work must accept inevitable 'disintegration';
it must itself face the resistance of 'otherness', and thus
in the end 'enact its inconclusiveness' (p. 32). It is such
an emphasis that action-research requires, since action-
research by its very nature is constituted in a dialectic
between action and theory, and thus does not wish its
inquiry to provide a conclusive prescription for action, but
rather to allow action to open out developmentally on the
basis of such provisional enlightenment as has been achieved
by its inquiry, and on the basis of that achievement always
to invite and require further phases of action-research
itself.

It is on such a basis, I would argue, that action-research
could begin to formulate the 'validity' of its processes,
and it is thus within this formulation that we must now seek
a sense of 'validity' for action-research's descriptive
accounts of the situations which are its topic and its
occasion.

Dialectics and Reflexivity, Narrative and Description

It was noted at the very beginning of this chapter that
action-research has often attempted to authorize its
validity claims in terms of 'anthropological' case-study
methods, and it is with an anthropological approach to the
issue that this section commences, namely an analysis of
'thick description', so unsatisfactorily glossed by Eisner
(see above). The term originates with Gilbert Ryle, but its
relevance for the present argument is elaborated by Clifford
Geertz.

Positivism, he argues, seeks 'valid' description by
reducing phenomena to the 'thin-ness' of 'operational', ie.
behavioural, terms (Geertz, 1973, p. 5), so that a social
action such as 'winking' becomes 'rapidly contracting (the)
right eyelids' (p. 7). Validity here is: what-could-not-
possibly-be-contested-by-anyone. But this would be an
entirely unhelpful formulation of validity in social inquiry,
since it evades social inquiry's central task: to understand the significance of the action in question. (What-
could-not-possibly-be-contested-by-anyone risks being so
banal that it is not of the slightest interest or significance to anyone: hence the vacuousness of so many social
science 'research findings'.) Now, indeed, the rapid

eyelid contractor may have an involuntary muscular twitch
(and behaviourists could indeed collect such instances) but
he or she may be 'winking', in which case the significant
question is, whether the action is an enticement or a
conspiracy, or even 'practising a burlesque of a friend
faking a wink to deceive an innocent into thinking a
conspiracy is in motion' (Geertz, 1973, p. 7). In other
words, the description of social actions must be at least as
'thick' (ie. as complex, as multi-layered) as the meaning of
the actions described. Now, it is clear from Geertz's
example of how 'meaning' is structured into layers of
mutually imputed interpretation, that one such layer must be
the interpretation imputed by the describer. This in turn
implies that accounts of social meanings can never have the
finality of a behavioural definition: 'ethnographic
assertion is ... essentially contestable' (Geertz, 1973,
p. 29). But this does not mean that interpretation is
therefore merely a matter of private opinion or whim, which
is so often the despairing response to a recognition of the
impossibility of realizing positivism's ideal. On the
contrary, meaning (says Geertz) is inherently 'public'
(p. 12), ie. it is constituted essentially in the dialectical intersubjectivity and interplay of cultural symbols
(eg. 'winks', 'conspiracies', 'fakes'). Thus, although
interpretations can never be finally 'verified', they can
always be 'appraised' (p. 16), and this appraisal itself,
being a further interpretation, is available for further
appraisal, in the endless dialectic of inquiry.

In other words, description may be considered as a
hermeneutic experience and accomplishment: 'The structure
of the hermeneutical experience is ... the dialectic of
question and answer' (Gadamer, 1975, p. 340). In more
detail:

> 'The reconstruction of the question to which
> the text (5) is presumed to be the answer takes
> place itself within a process of questioning
> through which we seek the answer to the question
> that the text (5) asks us' (p. 337)

This dialectic interweaves with another, and one which is
particularly relevant to action-research:

> 'Understanding (is) an event, and the task of
> hermeneutics ... consists in asking what kind of
> understanding, what kind of science it is, that
> is itself changed by historical change'. (p. 276)

In a sense Gadamer begins to answer his own question when he
goes on to describe a third dialectical strand in his
presentation of the process of interpretative description,
'the great dialectical puzzle of the one and the many, which
fascinated Plato' (p. 415), and which in Hegel's version has
been cited frequently in this work. Gadamer presents it as
follows:

'The hermeneutical rule (is) that we must
understand the whole in terms of the detail
and the detail in terms of the whole' (p. 258)

a rule which would need some reformulation in the context
of social inquiry, of course, since social situations do not
have the finite boundaries of a 'whole' text. In fact,
Geertz's analysis of ethnographic meaning construction
(outlined above) could serve as such a formulation of
'hermeneutics' as applied to social actions, and in
particular to the process of action-research: meaning is a
relation between social actions and their cultural matrix;
interpretations of this relation and appraisal of those
interpretations must endlessly succeed one another, since
interpreters are situated within the same process of
historical change as the social actions they describe.

At this stage in the argument we have moved once more to
the central role of reflexivity. How can we approach
description in reflexive terms? We can begin to pursue this
question by considering Levi-Strauss's essay 'The Science of
the Concrete' (in Levi-Strauss, 1966). Levi-Strauss
approaches the issue of the relation between concrete
experience and validity of meaning by distinguishing between
'two strategic levels at which nature is accessible to
scientific inquiry: one roughly adapted to that of
perception and the imagination; the other at a remove from
it' (p. 15). These two strategies are labelled (with
specific reference to man's interaction with the world of
inanimate objects) 'engineering' and 'bricolage' (literally:
fixing things up by imaginative improvisation with resources
that lie ready to hand) (p. 17). The engineer operates with
'concepts' whereas the bricoleur uses 'signs', the
distinction being that, 'although either may be substituted
for something else, concepts have an unlimited capacity in
this respect, while signs have not' (p. 18). The bricoleur
therefore

'interrogates ... an already existent set made up of
tools and materials, to consider or reconsider what
it contains, and finally and above all to engage in
a sort of dialogue with it ... to widen the possible
answers ... to discover what each of them could
'signify' and so contribute to the definition of a
set which has yet to materialize but which will
ultimately differ from the instrumental set only in
the disposition of its parts'. (p. 28)

In other words, the bricoleur (as an improvising DIY
enthusiast) carries out an essentially reflexive review of
biographically situated resources and their possibilities.
Engineers, armed with the unlimited referential scope of
'concepts' can interrogate 'the universe': they can aim to
transcend the current resources of their culture, while
bricoleurs knows that those resources are their limits
(p. 29). In this way, Levi-Strauss's account of the

concrete science of the bricoleur evokes a way of formulating the possible achievement and the necessary limitation of the social scientist's descriptive case-study. He
allows us to reformulate 'concrete description' in terms of
the possibility of an analytical and reflexive strategy
based on the multiple meanings of the culturally defined
sign, leaving the larger claims of the logically constructed
concept to those who wish to define their social science in
positivist terms. (cf. Popper, whose apparent modesty in
restricting his claims to 'social engineering' is thus
revealed as mock modesty indeed!)

Now, the notion of 'concrete description' as carried out
by 'observers' (who could possibly - if they wished - choose
to do 'abstract' description instead) raises the familiar
and unanswerable question of how such observers could select
their concrete details from the infinite range available,
and thus of how any such selection could be either
replicable or representative. In contrast, Levi-Strauss's
notion of 'bricolage' as a science OF the concrete avoids
the epistemological trap of the residually positivist
formulation, by treating 'the concrete' as the inevitable
habitat of social inquiry, a habitat which delimits
cognitive resources as culturally constructed and contingently available, and constitutes 'validity' as a provisional, essentially temporary achievement. As 'bricoleurs',
in other words, interpreters of the social world know the
limitations of their resources and their achievements, as
constituted by their situational availability: only self-
styled 'engineers' could consider themselves able to ignore
the reflexivity of their work and thus to claim 'universal'
validity.

Levi-Strauss goes on to make the reflexive dimension of
his work quite explicit (6) and in doing so addresses the
other important theme raised by the action-research writing
reviewed at the beginning of this chapter, namely the
relationship between descriptive structuring and aesthetic
form. He suggests that any symbolic process (science, myth,
myth-ology, ritual, or art) can be considered as constituted
in a relationship between 'structure' and 'event', between
the contingent and the necessary (Levi-Strauss, 1966, p. 21
ff). In general this formulation seems to beg the question
of its original distinction: what event could be so simple
that it was not also a structure, and what structure could
be either so eternal or so instantaneous that it did not
also constitute a complex event? However, the value of
Levi-Strauss's argument is that he provides a level of
analysis which can encompass the aesthetic as a mode of
comprehension and expression in juxtaposition to other forms
of symbolization, and that it allows a consideration of the
nature of the aesthetic to be formulated, which is precisely
what the writers previously discussed have merely glossed as
an available convention. Levi-Strauss's proposal is that
the expression itself is the 'structure', and that this
structure must be considered in relation to its three

constitutive contingencies: the occasion of the work, the
execution of the work, and the purpose of the work: 'The
process of artistic creation therefore consists in trying
to communicate (within the immutable framework of a mutual
confrontation of structure and accident) either with the
model (ie. the reality-to-be-represented - RW) or with the
material or with the future use'. (Levi-Strauss, 1966,
p. 27). (These are not of course mutually exclusive
alternatives.)

The importance of this argument for action-research is two
fold. Firstly it enables us to envisage a 'reflexive
description' as one which makes explicit the relation
between, on the one hand, its own structure and, on the
other hand, its symbolic resources, its audience, and the
events which are its topic. Secondly, it makes possible an
analogy between social research and a formulation of art
which is not merely concerned with a model (which realism
and positivism might claim or admit), but also with both
the 'material' and the audience for the symbolic process,
ie. a reflexive formulation of the aesthetic. This in turn
would parallel action-research's own ambition to transcend
positivism by addressing the principled relation between
action and theory (the 'materials' of its research process)
and between research and its audience, namely its attempts
to formulate such possibilities as i) the action-researching
professional as one who is simultaneously artist and
audience, or ii) the case study researcher whose work is a
continuous negotiation with the practitioners whom he serves
and in whose concerns he wishes to 'ground' his theory. In
each case there is a constitutive relation between
expressive process, audience, and theoretic resource.

A reflexive formulation of the aesthetic would find
support in, for example, Kenneth Burke's contention that
(literary) 'form would be the psychology of the audience ...
the creation ... and the adequate satisfying ... of an
appetite in the mind of the auditor' (Burke, 1968, p. 31),
an emphasis which for Barthes leads to 'the realization of
the relation of writer, reader, and observer (critic)'
(Barthes, 1977, p. 156). The 'realization' is, that readers
and critics are collaborators in the construction of
meaning: author-itative meaning is no longer 'what (we
think) the author meant'; instead, the closure of the
author's descriptive work is transformed into the open-ness
of readers' (critics') interpretive interaction with a text
(Barthes, 1977, pp. 155-6). Hence, whereas literature
previously claimed to employ a transparent language for the
description of 'Nature', 'Literature is (now) openly
reduced to the problematics of language' (Barthes, 1967,
p. 8), (although this 'reduction' is better described -
without nostalgia - as a principled recognition). The
general thesis that the essence of a modernist aesthetic is
its reflexivity is the theme of Gabriel Josipovici: The
World and the Book: 'The modern writer ... makes his art
out of the exploration of the relation between his unique

life and the body of literature, his book and the world'.
(Josipovici, 1971, p. 291). This argument applies not only
to such explicit and well-known exponents of 'modernism' as
James Joyce, T.S. Eliot, and Samuel Beckett, but (as has
been previously argued) to aesthetic form in general, in its
widespread cultural manifestations.

The relevance of this for social science is taken up by
Michael Clarke, who contrasts literature's tradition of
reflexive self-questioning with science's strategy of
insulating the person of the scientist from his data by
means of his 'methodology' (Clarke M., 1975, p. 99). In
other words, whereas 'artists' have accepted (and indeed,
latterly, embraced) a role which casts them simultaneously
as hero and as victim, 'scientists' persist in attempting to
evade any destiny whatever, by seeking a role of principled
invisibility through an ideology of technicism (cf. the
analysis of Jung's notion of the 'wounded healer' in Chapter
Three, above).

The way in which action-research can learn from literature
is not, then, to borrow its 'realist' claims (of 'validity'
through 'typicality') as an alternative approach to the
generalizing format of scientific positivism. Rather, by
analogy with a 'modernist' aesthetic, its claims to a
theoretic status can be made through an explicit recognition
of the reflexive form of its own process.

The above argument constitutes the process and the effect
of art (and, by implication, of inquiry) as essentially
reflexive in terms of its confrontation with its contingent
conditions ('material', audience, and 'model'). What about
the aesthetic structure itself, which so far has only been
referred to (within a realist problematic) through the
positivist metaphor of a 'typology' expressing a
'perspective'? At this point it is once more helpful to
invoke the principle of dialectics as the inherent structure
of social phenomena. Here again, a lead is given by action-
research writers themselves, namely McDonald and Walker.
Having said, 'the kind of case-studies which we believe
education needs have characteristics which call for a fusion
of the style of the artist and the scientist', they go on
immediately to quote Freud: 'the case histories I write ...
read like short stories' (McDonald and Walker, 1975, p. 3).
Now a Freudian case history is a narrative rather like a
'whodunnit': the questionable meaning of a dream sequence,
for example, is progressively 'solved' into a structure of
'rationality'. Since dreams are themselves narratives, this
resolution is itself a narrative of a narrative. Freud's
theory of the representative strategies of the dream thus
becomes a possible entry to the question: how can narrative
'embody 'truth''? His argument concerns the two basic
dimensions of symbolization, synchronicity and diachron-
icity. The chronology of the narrative transforms causal
relations into an ironic sequence (Freud, 1976a, p. 427),
and logical relations into ironic contiguity (p. 424). The
metaphoricity of the narrative unifies opposites (p. 429)

and fragments similarities into contrasts (p. 431). In
general, dreams constitute a systematic distortion of an
original reality, often to the point of 'reversal' (p. 441).
To understand the dream, by means of the case history, is to
clarify the distortion, to reverse (as it were) the
reversal.

As with much of Freud's work, an ingenious insight into
symbolic processes is limited by an ambition towards a
mechanical methodology (leading, in the present argument, to
the apparent implication that 'rationality' may be 'decoded'
unproblematically out of 'distortion'), but what Freud does
seem to provide here is the notion of narrative <u>structure</u>
constituted in the <u>dialectical</u> contradictions both of
action and of meaning, such that one might tentatively
suggest that to understand the 'truth' of narrative is to
grasp its structure as the dialectic of its constitutive
contradictions.

It is of course dialectical structure which underlies
Levi-Strauss's analysis of the meaning of mythic narrative
(see Chapter Three). For example:

'For a myth to be engendered by thought and for
it in turn to engender other myths, it is necessary
and sufficient that an initial opposition should
be injected into experience, and as a consequence,
other oppositions will spring into being'.
(Levi-Strauss, 1981, p. 604).

In an analysis of mythic structures which has clear
parallels with Freud's previously cited account of the dream
process, Levi-Strauss suggests (1979, pp. 224-9) that
opposites may be resolved into an intermediate term,
producing a 'triad', that characters' contradictory
qualities involve them in relations which gradually mediate
an original opposition, and that the events of the myth may
'transpose' its original semantic terms. Levi-Strauss sums
up: 'The purpose of myth is to provide a logical model
capable of overcoming a contradiction' (p. 229). And we
may follow Northrop Frye in taking myth to be an underlying
pattern for aesthetic form in general (Frye, 1957, pp. 163-
225).

The 'logic' of mythic or aesthetic form creates a set of
possibilities made available by the ambiguities, metaphors,
contradictions, reversals, etc. embodied in the narrative
itself. This 'logic' is embodied in the narrative in the
sense that its constituent units are 'bundles of relations'
which are sufficiently large as to function both
synchronically and diachronically (Levi-Strauss, 1972,
221-2). Thus, meaning is constituted in the narrative at
the level of metaphorical structures (protagonists and
settings) and at the level of dialectical structures
(actions and transformations), or rather: at the level
where metaphor and dialectic are <u>mutually</u> constitutive,
namely, as Derrida notes, the level of symbolization's

intrinsic properties of 'Difference' and 'Deferral'.

In this way we can perhaps make sense of Elliott's original suggestion that action-research can seek, as part of a non-positivist approach to inquiry, to embody 'truth' in narrative. Narrative recognizes, in Levi-Strauss's original terms, the analytic confrontation between the necessary and the contingent, structure and event, general and particular. This confrontation is expressed in narrative's underlying pattern of metaphor and dialectic, ie. its pattern of transformation both at the level of meaning and of action, which parallels action-research's own ultimate ambition to transform meaning by means of action. Positivist description seeks to dichotomize the necessary and the contingent in terms of method and data: it seeks to isolate data so that they have no inherent structural or temporal properties, and so are purely available to be gathered (by means of 'method') into a literal and ahistorical 'truth'. In contrast, the form of representation accomplished by narrative allows truth to be dialectical: the narrative of action can show action's own semantic transformations. Furthermore, 'narrative' is not merely a single sequence of events, but a complex pattern of allusions, showing the interweaving of many destinities: the dialectics of 'narrative' tends towards the ironic collage of anecdotes indicated in the Brechtian aesthetic (See Brecht, 1974, p. 279).

Action-Research and the Descriptive Text (7)

How could these various considerations be related to a possible set of principles for action-research's descriptive accounts? Three of the central ideas seem to be related in the following way:

a) A reflexive description can only seek validity through a structure which embodies a principled recognition of the problematics of its own possibility (see references to Barthes, above).
b) The scope of this problematic, as applied to social inquiry, is given (following Levi-Strauss's formulation) by the relationship between the descriptive account and 1) its symbolic resources, 2) its audience, and 3) its 'model' - ie. the experience(s) 'described'.
c) The structure of each of the problematic relationships noted in (b), is dialectical as follows:

1) Symbolic resources for a descriptive account are, for example: reports of actors' perspectives, institutional documents, interpretive theories, and narrative structures which embody mythic/ideological patterns as the constitutive 'characters' and 'plots' of the 'anecdotal' events recorded by the researcher. There will be a dialectical relationship (ie. a combination of intimacy AND incongruity, similarity AND difference) between the various elements, eg. between ideals and experiences, between claims and actions, between long-term and short-term rationalities, and between the

ideals, ideologies, reported experiences, and rationalized interpretations of different social actors. (This is an extension of the principle behind 'Dilemma Analysis - see above).

The relationship between the description and such resources will be dialectical, ie. its coherence will take the form of making explicit the dialectical play between elements, in a structure whose unity is that of irony rather than of resolution and negotiated consensus. In this it may resemble the documentary or the news report, which presents 'different sides' in a studied stance of abstention from authorial imposition' (cf. Barthes on the 'death of the author' in the reflexively conceived text - (Barthes, 1977, p. 142). (8) In this respect, it may resemble a story (with a complex plot and characters and with one or several protagonists but - following the principle of ironic play - without a hero, taking 'hero' here as typically embodying a mythologized elaboration of an authorial perspective.) But more precisely, description - in this reflexive form - will embody the dialectical structure of an ironic collage, which juxtaposes a variety of elements. (See Brown R, - 1977, chapter 5 - for an elaboration of sociological accounts as structures of irony).

There is another sense in which description will have a dialectical relation with its resources: it will recognize the historically situated quality of its collection, and will explicitly present its collection as contingent and provisional, rather than as exhaustive or final. It will thus be structured by its principled and necessary anticipation of a continuation (ie. amendment and critique) by its readers, since description will have a dialectical relation with its audience.

2) The audience for descriptive accounts will have both necessary and contingent features (see the presentation of Levi-Strauss's argument in the previous section). At one level the rhetorical processes of writing are structured by the requirements of an analytically presupposed intelligibility to a readership. This is the dialectical structure of intersubjectivity necessarily required by acts of communication (see Chapter One). 'Validity', then, would be the achievement of persuasiveness. But audiences are also historically contingent. A description may anticipate a highly specific audience (one which shares a particular standpoint or set of relevancies) and may achieve a persuasive validity for that limited audience; while other audiences (with whom the description in question does not anticipate a dialectically constitutive relationship) would characterize such a description as, say 'tendentious', and would note 'inadequacies' in a variety of dimensions. 'Objectivity', within this argument, can then be seen as the quality of a description which anticipates a constitutive dialectic with a highly varied audience, ie. a description which structures a dialectical relation between a wide variety of its own heterogeneous elements, and thereby

achieves persuasiveness for audiences which begin their
reading of the description from a position of provisional
identification with only a limited range of those elements.
Hence the persuasive task of description can be seen as
establishing, through its own processes, that the heterogeneity of phenomena does indeed represent a dialectical
(ie. a mutually transformative) relation, rather than that
simple antagonism between 'similar' and 'different' in which
they are constituted by the pragmatic requirements of daily
life.

3) The 'model' for description is a set of experiences,
whereas description itself is, of course, constituted
symbolically, and - in particular, linguistically. (9) It
has already been argued at a number of points that
linguistic representations cannot be seen simply as 'labels'.
Rather their reference to experience must be seen as
metaphorical, and thus as always located within the
dialectic between reference and difference noted by Hegel.
Richard Brown makes this point explicitly and at length:
'A theory must be metaphorical: if it were literally
identical with what it theorizes about, it would not, could
not tell us anything new'. (Brown R., 1977, p. 101). This
would also hold true for description, as a communication
between One who-has-had-an-experience and Others, who have
not had that identical experience but who could be brought
to understand that experience in the light of different but
potentially similar experiences which they have had. Hence
the central function of metaphor's dialectic between
similarity and difference. (Description is not engaged in
between people who are both present at an event. Rather,
one says to the other for example: 'Just look - isn't that
a terrible/marvellous ... (painting, maths lesson, forehand
smash, etc) ...?' One might indeed say, 'It reminds me of
...' but that, precisely, would return us to the principle
of metaphoricity). 'Metaphor', then, is itself a metaphor
for the problematics of communicative description and
interpretation, the problem of the general and the
particular, of description's always ambiguous ambition to be
description (rather than - say - a random association or an
eccentric vision). Thus 'validity' for description must
ultimately reside in its recognition of the very ambiguity
of its own aspiration; it must explicitly recognize that
its metaphorical structure, no matter how densely and subtly
woven, can never claim a literal or final correspondence
with its object. For positivist description this would be a
matter for despair (as though 'validity' were to be given up
as impossible); for a reflexive and dialectally
structured description it marks a rigorous requirement for
critical awareness, and thus a dimension of validity itself.

The Analytical Text as Description and Commentary

Finally, what form might be taken by description's
'recognition' of its dialectical ambiguities and limits? In
general terms we may remember once more Gadamer's axiom that
'the structure of the hermeneutical experience ... is the

dialectic of question and answer' (Gadamer, 1975, p. 340).
But it is more helpful at this stage in the argument to
'reverse' - or rather to extend - Gadamer's statement and to
consider a dialectic of answer and question, in which
description's answers to its presupposed questions are
presented in conjunction with the questions it in turn
raises. This would then enable us to formulate 'description' as embodying a similar 'questioning dialectic' to that
relating action and theory, presented at the end of Chapter
Two). And the format that this might take in the context of
a descriptive account is in fact suggested by a comment of
Lawrence Stenhouse, the doyen of writers on educational
action-research - a comment which in fact makes curiously
little sense in its original context (a proposal for
Popperian 'scientific method') but which seems to have a
very precise relevance for the present argument.

Stenhouse says that, 'The dialectic between proposition
and critique ... is personified in the relationship between
artist and critique'. (Stenhouse, 1975, p. 124). Now although
much 'art criticism' displays a numbing combination of
blandly unreflexive evaluation and crude technicism, there
is a certain ideal for critical writing on works of art
which could indeed be taken as a formulation of the moment
of analytical recognition in the complex dialectic of
description. In this sense, the 'critic' (at best) writes a
commentary which accompanies the structure of a work in
order to make explicit the implicit pattern of the work's
complex internal relationships; in order to do so, it will
reveal ironies, point to dialectical relations between
elements, show ramifications, analyze the detail in terms of
the whole, and insist upon the irreducible complexity of the
whole as (at least) the sum of all its details -
hermeneutics, after all, originated as a method for textual
criticism. In this way, if 'description' is to be, as has
been argued, a dialectical structure of irony and metaphor
(rather than - positivistically - a unified structure of
consensus and literal reference), then perhaps the
descriptive text can be differentiated from, say, the novel
or the documentary (as an analytical from a rhetorical text)
by the inclusion within the text itself of a 'critical'
commentary in the sense outlined here, one which addresses
directly the text's own problematic and how its processes
address that problematic. (10)

Here, then, is a final dimension for the 'validity' of
descriptions, namely the adequacy of its own explicit
recognition of its reflexive and dialectical structure.
There is a link between this suggestion and the comments of
Peter McHugh et al. on the collaborative process of their
own text, in which 'response papers seek to enter into
relationship with the original by transforming its present
but unexplicated features' (McHugh et al., 1974, p. 5). The
point is, that texts are open, 'plural' structures,
(Barthes, 1977, p. 159) intelligible only in the light of
the reflexivity of language and the constitutive dialectic
between writer and reader. Textual openness and plurality

have been fully explored as principles for the understanding of literature (see for example Belsey, 1980), and this may explain the affinity for aesthetic forms expressed by a number of action-research writers, who thus perhaps sense the general argument of this chapter: that such openness is a necessary requirement for action-research, since action-research is predicated upon the assumption that a descriptive account will not be a final product by an observer, but a moment in a continuing process among writers and readers who are also practitioners.

The 'validity' of description, in this context, then, is not a matter of being 'correct', but of adequately representing 'the conditions for its possibility' (see Chapter One). In other words, following Levi-Strauss's argument (see previous section, above) 'validity' concerns the necessary rather than the contingent features of description, ie. the explicit recognition of its reflexively constituted ironies. Admittedly, the contingencies of 'correctness' will not be entirely unintelligible when the dialectic of action-research moves to the moment of action, when - as was argued at the end of Chapter Two - the question becomes: which of the possibilities made explicit through the open text of 'description' would be a feasible practical strategy now? Nevertheless, in general, the notion of 'validity', as applied to the complex process of action-research, is not to be sought in terms of a 'correspondence' between two simple entities - 'account' and 'reality' - but rather in the principles of reflexivity and dialectics, which (it has been argued in this chapter) can guide the internal, textual structuring of action-research's accounts, as well as - at the same time and without incoherence - the other moments of action-research's process.

NOTES

(1) I am indebted to Paul Filmer for this point.

(2) See also Whitehead and Foster (1984) p. 43.

(3) 'Lenin ... the master action-research officer of all time' (!) (Midwinter, 1972, p. 57)

(4) In this respect, the emphasis in Carr and Kemmis's work is well directed, towards dialectics as a relationship between theory and practice (Carr and Kemmis, 1986, p. 184) in spite of the weakness of their reliance on Lewin's wholly untheorized version of this relationship.

(5) For 'text' read 'social action' in the context of the present argument. The possibility of this equivalence is asserted by Ricoeur, in 'The Model of the text - meaningful action considered as a text', in the same volume as Ricoeur (1981).

(6) There is, however, a tension in Levi-Strauss's work between passages where he clearly describes his own

myth-ology as bricolage ('a precarious assemblage of odds and ends' - 1981, p. 562) and other passages where he seems to anticipate a <u>future</u> state of affairs when the human sciences will indeed transcend bricolage through an 'absolute' methodology (p. 686).

(7) One aspect of the argument in this section is presented more directly in R. Winter (1986): 'Fictional-critical writing: an approach to case study research by practitioners', in <u>Cambridge Journal of Education</u>, vol. 16 no. 3.

(8) In mundane examples of such reportage, this 'abstaining' stance is, of course, merely a carefully presented illusion: it is the <u>textual structure</u> which is being considered at this point in my argument.

(9) In principle, much of the argument of this section could be applied to descriptions embodied as painting, film, ballet, music, marble, or papier-mâché, and indeed as combinations of these! But to do so would further complicate an already complex set of ideas, and the verbal sign plays a central and - arguably - indispensable role.

(10) I am indebted for this argument to my colleague David Ball and to members of the Essex Institute M Ed course in Educational Research.

6 Conclusion

My aim in this study has been to reconstruct the intelligibility of action-research by disentangling the virtues of its inherent possibilities from the problems of its heterogeneous claims. Some of these claims are simply borrowed from positivist social science - claims to possess an authoritative methodology for the production of accurate descriptions or of 'grounded theory', for example - and others seem to be defensive counter-claims, made against positivism's rejection of action-research's adequacy - claims to flexibility, creative idiosyncracy, immediate practical relevance, democratic process, and aesthetic form, for example. The contradiction between these two sets of claims can be traced to the contradictions in the relationship between orthodox social science and the social world which is its topic and its resource. The virtue of action-research is that it glimpses the need to reformulate this relationship; the defect of action-research is its failure to carry through the reformulation. At various points in this study - especially in the final section of each chapter - aspects of this reformulation have been presented. In this concluding chapter I wish only to draw together an overall statement concerning the potential contribution of action-research (in the reflexive and dialectical formulation I have put forward) to social inquiry as a general project. As a 'conclusion' it is temporary and provisional: it draws together a phase of study into a moment of reflection which anticipates, now, explorative and variously transformative practical continuations, in particular action contexts. 'Conclusion', otherwise, would threaten to overwhelm one of the central

themes of the study with the irony of an implied finality,
and hence of an implied claim that 'theory' (such as this
study) might - after all - make prescriptions for practice.
It is to the danger of that irony that the following section
is addressed, as a summary statement of a non-prescriptive
relationship between theory and practice.

ACTION-RESEARCH, THEORY, FACTUALITY, PRESCRIPTION

At the centre of action-research stands its hyphen,
indicating an axiomatic and inescapable relation between
action (which must treat knowledge as adequate) and research
(which must treat knowledge as problematic). Yet the
clumsiness of the phrase 'action-research', as a mere juxtaposition - with or without a hyphen - expresses the irremed-
able problem of the relationship. Unlike other expressions
(such as 'applied science' or 'theoretical practice') which
have their syntactical point of rest in one term or other,
'action-research' merely vibrates with its own irony, its
unresolved difference, and hence its interminable question:
the dialectic of action-research-action-research-action ...
can begin anywhere, and once begun, it cannot end, since it
is without prescription, and thus without a principle for
completion.

It is through this unending quality of its dialectic that
action-research provides for the irremediably problematic
combination of irony and responsibility which characterizes
theorists' relation to their social context, a relation
which - in contrast - orthodox social science would wish to
formulate either as non-ironic (leaving the social scientist
as an employee of one sub-section or other of an institutional order which provides both topics and purposes) or as
non-responsible (leaving social scientists proclaiming both
their free-floating abstraction from all social interests
and their potential availability to any such interest.)

Now, action-research's principled commitment to both irony
and responsibility enables it to grasp the problematic
status of 'theory' in relation to the 'action' which
constitutes theory's social world. In a crucial sense,
there is no action which is not informed by theory, and this
applies in a broadly similar fashion to the following
series: a racist street brawl, police arrests of some but
not all protagonists, a government inquiry into urban law
and order, and a survey of attitudes carried out by the
Commission for Racial Equality. In each case 'theory' takes
the form of factual knowledge generalized into justificatory
principles for a range of envisaged action. In this way,
knowledge is continuously being socially constructed within
the technical / moral debates (concerning capitalism,
racism, social order, urbanization, etc., etc.) which
constitute everyday culture as a pattern of discursive
agendas. These agendas only exist because their relevance
is relatively urgent, and thus the theory with which they
are informed tends to be presented in a maximally persuasive

- indeed in a would-be prescriptive - form, namely as 'facts'. However, the irony of factuality is that, as a practical rhetorical format, it is utilized by all competing interest groups, with the result that, although claims to factuality are made in the name of an objective correctness which aims to silence opposition, such claims are immediately contested as 'biassed' selections. Hence the typical scenario in which a 'highly-significant-statistical-finding' is presented in a prestigious social science journal with all the mythic trappings of mathematical absolutism, only to be dismissed in the next issue as a random illusion created by some-one's crass technical blunder.

Of course, the sequence of cognitive claim and challenge within these technical / moral debates constitutes one of the basic processes of politics, culture, and the daily life of institutions and professions; but this is to character-ize such debates as, precisely, topics of the deepest sociological interest, whose theoretical grounds it must be sociology's task to address. And here the merit of a reflexive action-research begins to emerge. For it is clear that the political clash of rival factualities and their attendant prescriptive generalizations will not be addressed (but will, rather, be taken as given, sustained, and prolonged) by a social science which invokes a methodolog-ical warrant for its own factualities, its own theories-as-prescriptive-generalizations.

Instead, therefore, what a reflexive action-research would offer to its action context is not 'theory' in this sense at all. (See references to 'metatheory', à propos of Habermas and Moser in Chapter Three). It would propose, rather, to subject the theories (the factualities and organizing conceptions) of common-sense and of professional expertise to a critical analysis of their located-ness within the practices whose intelligibility they serve. Action-research thus proposes a move 'beyond' theories (whether mundane or academic) which prescribe and justify an interpretive basis for action towards a reflexive awareness of the dialectic between such theory and action, a dialectic which (as has been argued throughout this study) can sustain their mutuality while transforming both. It is in this way that a reflexive action-research can be essentially and inevitably committed both to the critique of action's interpretive rationalities and yet also to the continued possibilities of action in its mundane context.

In the following section this fundamental contention is illustrated by a summary of the general principles by which action-research's epistemology may be coherently embodied in its processes. Nevertheless, it follows from the previous argument that these principles cannot prescribe specific procedures for every action-research project, nor even for any project in particular. Rather, they indicate a series of parameters which mark out the limits of a reflexive, dialectical relationship between theory and practice in the context of social inquiry. The theoretical moment of this (unending) dialectic does not provide prescriptions for valid interpretation or for adequate practice. Rather, it provides complex questions and formulated contradictions, which require of any given practice that it should recollect and draw upon all its own particular interpretive resources, that it should live <u>with</u> those questions and live <u>out</u> those contradictions, in order to live <u>up to</u> its own fullest awareness of its own concrete possibilities. It is in this sense that the following statements are offered as 'principles'.

PRINCIPLES FOR A REFLEXIVE ACTION-RESEARCH

A (Critique)

Action-research is grounded in the topics of professional expertise, but also has grounds for transforming them. (Action-research will not simply organize and report members' topics and categories; neither will it encapsulate them as merely illustrative of prior theoretical systems). Action-research will begin by recording the cognitive resources which underpin the invocation of professional expertise in the specific context - its particular range of plausibly warranted 'factual' bases, and its particular set of concepts which provide for the intelligibility of those 'facts' in relation to the requirements of action in that context, ie. concrete versions of normality, predictability, event, motive, chance, relevance, etc. Action-research will then make explicit the essentially reflexive basis of this expertise, its grounds in contextually specific judgements, rather than in general laws. By drawing attention to the process and structure of these judgements, action-research transforms the assumed resources of expertise into topics, and transforms received topics into questions. By drawing attention to the contextual basis for claims to generality, expertise's 'necessity' is transformed into contingency, and 'irrelevancies' are transformed into thinkable possibilities.

B (Dialectic)

Action-research is grounded in the phenomena of practical experience, but also has grounds for transforming them. (Action-research will not simply treat members' meanings as criteria for its own adequacy; neither will it treat members' meanings as merely epiphenomena produced by supposedly objective societal processes). Action-research will begin by recording members' experiential accounts of the context - as sets of relatively unified phenomena organized into relatively fixed relations of similarity and difference. Action-research will then explore the dialectical basis of these phenomena, exploring the <u>differences</u> which have been collected as 'similar', the <u>similarities</u> which have been set apart as 'different', and the historical dimensions within which current categories of similarity and

difference may be seen as both contingent and transient. By
drawing attention to the developing contradictions within
the categories of experience, implicit necessities (as
labels of the present) will be transformed into explicit
possibilities (as metaphors for thinkable futures).

C (Collaborative Resource)

Action-research's resources are personal, but its transformative outcomes have valid grounds. (Action-research will
not simply claim to discover objective empirical generalizations: neither will its outcomes merely be expressions
of personal opinion). Action-researchers are constitutive
elements of their contexts-in-question: when they begin to
subject contexts to a principled reflexive and dialectical
critique (see A and B above), they are required by
those same principles to initiate and/or accept a reflexive
and dialectical critique of their own resources which have
provided for the original critique. Action-research must
accept and require the recognition of this risk as the
ontological and epistemological structure of its (reflexive
and dialectical) intersubjectivity, and this has two
important consequences. Firstly, by means of the interpersonal process of action-research, subjective commitments
to interpretation ('points-of-view') will be deconstructed
by a review of possible resources for such commitments, ie.
the pragmatic and rhetorical unity of subjectivity will be
required to recollect its fundamental potential for disunity, and hence its resources for alternative commitments.
Secondly, and consequently, subsequent commitments to
interpretation (re-made in the light of such recollections)
will recognize the limits of their specific personal and
contextual resources as part of a provisional, reviewable,
interpersonal, and contextual strategy. Reflexive action-
research does not seek to replace personal resources with
'im-personal' techniques or 'universal' theories, but rather
to push to their here-and-now limits the inherent resources
of interpersonal contextualized understanding.

D (Risk)

Action-researchers recognize they they will suffer the
transformations of the processes they initiate. (Action-
researchers' interactions with members will not simply
provide prescriptions for action; neither will they merely
result in interpretive insights which members can take or
leave). Action-researchers will require from themselves, as
well as from others, a recognition of the reflexive and
contextual limits of their interpretive judgements, and the
dialectical contradictions of their activities as action-
researchers (see C above). Only insofar as they enact their
requirements upon their own activities will they be able to
persuade practitioners that these requirements are indeed
requirements for all, including practitioners, rather than
special requirements typically inflicted upon others by,
say, 'theorists', and thus carrying no persuasive import
(but only a rejectable instruction) for those who are

'practitioners-but-NOT-theorists'. Hence, whatever understandings action-researchers bring to a context (in terms of
methods, interpretive theories, and anticipations of the
processes of action-research itself) will - they know - be
transformed by their enactment first in this and then in
that context. In this way, reflexive action-research will
not be a version of 'applied science' (as though procedures
for social inquiry had been created 'somewhere else', as
through action 'here', could simply learn from science) but
a formulation of social inquiry's own capacity to develop
('everywhere') as a dimension of social inquiry's
constitutive relation with its social world.

E (Plural Structure)

Action-research transforms the relationship between the
disparate elements in an action context, but it does not
attempt to construct them into a unity. (Action-research
will not simply attempt to negotiate a consensus in order to
supercede contradictions; neither will it merely record
contradictions as they present themselves). Given that
action-research's frames of reference will be challenged by
its own process, and are thus part of an unending development (see D above), the format for reporting action-
research's outcomes will not be an integrated descriptive
account, presenting a reader with a specific state-of-
affairs, but, rather, for example, a sort of 'collage-text'
which artfully sets in play a dialectical (and hence always
potentially ironic) pattern of relationships between
alternating elements, authored by various members of the
action context, including explicitly reflexive accounts (see
A above), dialectical analyses (see B above), reviews of
possibilities and of grounds for commitments (see C above),
and diaries of action. A key element in this 'plural text'
will be a series of contributions which attempt to make
explicit the structure of the relationships enacted in the
sequence as a whole. Such an 'open' text will express both
the contradictions of its origin and its non-prescriptive
availability to its varied audience for their varied and
unpredictable purposes and responses (including responsive
action). Action-research will thus be able to turn to its
own advantage the inescapable and fundamental tensions in
which it is constituted (between theory and action, between
the valid and the concrete) by learning from and drawing
upon the traditions of ironic and reflexive symbolization
(narrative, drama, rhetoric, counterpoint, and
hermeneutics) rather than merely the procedures for
enumeration and classification familiar to 'science'.

F (Theory, Practice, Transformation)

Action-research has grounds for the critique of action, but
these grounds require also action-research's commitment to
the (transformative) continuation of action. (Action-
researchers will not simply be observers, who can arrive
with a repertoire of skills, re-describe the action scene,
and depart unscathed and unimplicated; neither will they

simply be participants, who learn by taking part in the implementation of developmental programmes.) Action-research's moment of critique (see A and B above) assembles and expands a range of previously 'repressed' possibilities (see C above). But these possibilities are derived from action's own cognitive resources and will not be left merely as possibilities 'in theory' (as realizable in, say, an ideal world but <u>not</u> here-and-now) since action-research's dialectic requires that the possibilities created by critique be confronted by the requirements of action, always given that action's limits will have been transformed by the exploration of its possibilities. It is this double confrontation (the question posed to practice by theory, and the question posed to theory by practice) which ensures that no-one will escape the transformations of the action-research process (see D above), a process whose dialectic disqualifies claims either to be an observer who can leave to others any responsibility for the continuation of action, or to be a practitioner who can leave to others any responsibility for originating the transformation of action. Action-research formulates action as always potentially responsible to the grounds for its transformability by theorizing, and formulates theory as grounded in its responsibility towards action's transformed necessity. 'Action-research' thus expresses a double responsibility as well as a double irony.

The previous principles (A - E) formulate the nature of action-research's inherent resources and processes; this final principle refers most directly to action-research's fundamental capacity for structuring (however delicately, ironically, provisionally, and non-prescriptively) that crucial interplay between theory and practice, critique and responsibility, ideal and actual, Reason and politics, which constitutes the central problematic of social inquiry.

Appendix: 'Interpretive procedures'

For the convenience of readers who may not be familiar with the notion of 'interpretive procedures', I include the following brief summary, which is based on ideas in the passage referred to - ie. Cicourel, 1973, pp. 51-6.

<u>General</u>

Underlying the ability to use the 'surface rules' of a language (eg. this is 'a dog' but that is 'a cat') and of cultural norms for behaviour (eg. this is 'polite', but that is 'rude') there must be a set of competences involving a grasp of 'procedures' whereby experience can be 'interpreted'. This entails the ability to see particulars as 'examples' of categories, to select a particular rule as 'relevant', and hence, in general, to 'assign meaning' to phenomena. None of this is possible <u>simply</u> by 'following' a rule: rules only guide behaviour in conjunction with a whole range of '<u>ad hoc</u> considerations' (see Garfinkel, 1967, pp. 21-2) which must be invoked in order that a rule may be, on each occasion, 'interpreted'. These 'interpretive procedures' are therefore '<u>invariant</u> properties of everyday practical reasoning' (p. 52, my emphasis) in the sense that they are <u>presupposed</u> by any act of communication or of seeking 'accounts (of experience - RW) that can be viewed and accepted as recognizable and intelligible displays of social reality' (p. 51). Being 'invariant', they therefore underlie the activities of 'social science' as well as those of mundane social action. 'Interpretive procedures' are procedures for 'making sense'.

'A Few Properties' (p. 52) of Interpretive Procedures

1) 'The Reciprocity of Perspectives' is assumed. In order to make sense of what B says, A assumes that B means what A would mean if their roles were reversed. Hence, 'until further notice (the emergence of counter-evidence) the speaker and hearer (the writer and reader - RW) both assume that each can disregard, for the purpose at hand, any differences originating in their personal ways of assigning meaning....' (p. 53). Thus, each assumes the intelligibility of their utterances for the other.

2) The 'Et Cetera' assumption is filled in. The communication of meanings is not achieved through an explicitly established consensus; rather, utterances which are experienced as 'vague' or 'ambiguous' are tolerated, allowed to 'pass' as intelligible, by 'filling in' for oneself, from one's own resources, whatever seems necessary in order to create an acceptable degree of intelligibility in the particular context. (Occasionally this procedure is explicitly invoked, when one uses 'et cetera' as part of an utterance, indicating, 'Please fill in any further specification of detail you may need in order to render what I am saying sufficiently intelligible for your purposes'. But, implicitly, every communication relies on this process: every utterance carries with it a tacit 'et cetera' tag, asserting or pleading, 'You know the sort of thing I mean'.

3) 'Normal Forms' are assumed and recognized. The meaning of all experiences and utterances is structured around an assumption that all phenomena have a 'normal form', and consequently that "all communication is embedded within a body of common knowledge or 'what everyone knows'". (p. 54). In this way, even 'new' experiences are assimilated by being recognized (without consternation or bewilderment) as 'normal' forms of novelty, deviance, or incongruity. The assumption, recognition, and employment of 'normal forms' are procedures whereby experiences are rendered 'typical' of general categories, so that the potential uniqueness of each moment of experience (which would otherwise be massively confusing) can be satisfactorily managed.

4) 'Retrospective-Prospective Sense' is recognized and anticipated. The process of understanding a conversation, a lecture, or a piece of writing depends on speakers and hearers, writers and readers 'waiting for later utterances to decide what was intended before'. (p. 54). Speakers and hearers (writers and readers) both assume that what is said or written 'has, or will have at some subsequent moment, the effect of clarifying a presently ambiguous account .....
Waiting for later utterances.....to clarify present descriptive accounts, or 'discovering' that earlier remarks or incidents now clarify a present utterance, provide continuity to everyday communication.' (p. 54). More

precisely: without the 'retrospective-prospective'
procedure for making sense, communication of any sort would
be impossible, because it would <u>lack</u> continuity, and without
coherence in <u>time</u> there can be no intelligibility.

Bibliography

Adorno, T., (1973), Negative Dialectics, Routledge, London
Althusser, L., (1971), Lenin and Philosophy, New Left Books,
   London.
Althusser, L., (1974), Eléments d'Autocritique, Hachette,
   Paris.
Althusser, L., (1977), For Marx, New Left Books, London.
Armstrong, M., (1981), 'The case of Louise and the painting
   of landscape', in Nixon J. (ed.): A Teachers Guide to
   Action Research, Grant McIntyre, London.
Austin, J., (1962), How to Do Things With Words, University
   Press, Oxford.
Barthes, R., (1967), Writing Degree Zero, Jonathan Çape,
   London.
Barthes, R., (1976), Mythologies, Paladin, St. Albans.
Barthes, R., (1977), Image, Music Text, Fontana, Glasgow.
Becker, H., (1971), Sociological Work, Allen Lane, London.
Belsey, C., (1980), Critical Practice, Methuen, London.
Berne, E., (1967), Games People Play, Penguin, Harmondsworth
Bernstein, B., (1971a), 'Open schools, open society', in
   Cosin B. et al. (eds.): School and Society, Routledge,
   London.
Bernstein, B., (1971b), 'On the classification and framing
   of educational knowledge', in Young M.F.D. (ed.):
   Knowledge and Control, Collier Macmillan, London.
Blum, A., (1971), 'Theorizing', in Douglas J. (ed.):
   Understanding Everyday Life, Routledge, London.
Blum, A., (1974), Theorizing, Heinemann, London.
Brecht, B., (1974), Brecht on Theatre, (2nd Edition),
   Methuen, London.

158

Brown, L. et al., (1982), 'Action research - notes on the National Seminar', In Elliott, J. and Whitehead, D. (eds.): Action-Research for Professional Development and the Improvement of Schooling, Institute of Education, Cambridge.

Brown, R., (1977), A Poetic for Sociology, University Press, Cambridge.

Burke, K., (1968), Counter-statement, University of California Press, Berkeley and Los Angeles.

Carr, W. and Kemmis S., (1986), Becoming Critical, Falmer Press, Lewes.

Cicourel, A., (1964), Method and Measurement in Sociology, The Free Press, New York.

Cicourel, A., (1973), 'The Acquisition of social structure', in Cognitive Sociology, Penguin, Harmondsworth.

Clarke, A., (1976), Experimenting with Organizational Life - The Action-Research Approach, Plenum Press, London.

Clarke, M., (1975), 'Survival in the field', in Theory and Society, Vol. 2, No. 1.

Colletti, L., (1975), 'Marxism and the dialectic,' in New Left Review, No. 93.

Collier, J., (1945) 'The US Indian Administration as a Laboratory of ethnic relations', in Social Research, Vol. 12.

Cory, S., (1953), Action-Research to Improve School Practice, Teachers College Press, New York.

Crookes, J., (1983), 'Diversions, digressions, and destiny', in Rowland, S: Teachers Studying Children's Thinking, No. 2, Leicestershire Education Department.

Denny, T., (1978), 'In Defense of Story Telling as a first step in educational research', College of Education, University of Illinois - Urbana,(Mimeo).

Denzin, N., (1978), Introduction to Denzin, N. (ed.): Sociological Methods - A Sourcebook, McGraw Hill, New York.

Derrida, J., (1976), Of Grammatology, Johns Hopkins University Press, Baltimore.

Derrida, J., (1978), Writing and Difference, Routledge, London.

Durkheim, E., (1915), The Elementary Forms of the Religious Life, Unwin, London.

Durkheim, E., (1972), Selected Writings, (edited by A. Giddens), University Press, Cambridge.

Durkheim E., (1974), Sociology and Philisophy, The Free Press, New York.

Edgley, R., (1977), 'Dialectics - the contradictions of Colletti', in Critique, No. 7.

Eisner, E., (1977), 'Thick description', in Hamilton, D. et al. (eds.): Beyond the Numbers Game, Macmillan, London.

Elliott, J., (1975), 'Implementing the principles of Inquiry/Discovery Teaching - some hypotheses', Unit 3 of the Ford Teaching Project, Centre for Applied Research in Education, University of East Anglia, Norwich.

Elliott, J., (1978a), 'Action-research in schools - some guidelines', (Mimeo) Institute of Education, Cambridge.

Elliott, J., (1978b), 'What is action-research in schools?' in Journal of Curriculum Studies, Vol. 10, No. 4.

Elliott, J., (1981), 'Action-research - a framework for self-evaluation in schools', Working Paper No. 1 of Schools Council Programme Teacher-Pupil Interaction and the Quality of Learning, Schools Council, London.

Elliott, J., (1982a), 'Legitimation crisis and the growth of educational action-research', (Mimeo) Institute of Education, Cambridge.

Elliott, J., (1982b), Working Paper No. 12, Schools Council Programme:Teacher-Pupil Interaction and the Quality of Learning, Institute of Education, Cambridge.

Fay, B., (1975), Social Theory and Political Practice, Unwin, London.

Filmer, P., (1976), 'Garfinkel's gloss', in Writing Sociology, No. 1, Goldsmiths' College, London.

Fordham, F., (1978), Jungian Psychology, John Wiley, Bath.

Foster, M., (1971), 'An introduction to the theory and practice of action-research in work organizations', (Mimeo) Tavistock Institute of Human Relations, London.

Foucault, M., (1977), 'The political function of the intellectual', in Radical Philosophy, No. 17.

Foucault, M., (1981), The History of Sexuality, Penguin, Harmondsworth.

Freud, S., (1952), A General Introduction to Psycho-analysis, Washington Square Press, New York.

Freud, S., (1961), Beyond the Pleasure Principle, Hogarth Press, London.

Freud, S., (1962), 'The question of lay analysis', in Two Short Accounts of Psycho-analysis, Penguin, Harmondsworth.

Freud, S., (1976a), The Interpretation of Dreams, Penguin, Harmondsworth.

Freud, S., (1976b), Jokes and their Relation to the Unconscious, Penguin, Harmondsworth.

Frye, N., (1957), The Anatomy of Criticism, University Press, Princeton.

Gadamer, H.G., (1975), Truth and Method, Sheed and Ward, London.

Garfinkel, H., (1967), Studies in Ethnomethodology, Prentice Hall, Englewood Cliffs.

Geertz, C., (1973), 'Thick description - toward an interpretive theory of culture', in The Interpretation of Cultures, Basic Books, New York.

Gellner, E., (1968), Words and Things, Penguin, Harmondsworth.

Glazer, B. and Strauss A., (1967), The Discovery of Grounded Theory, Weidenfeld and Nicholson, London.

Habermas, J., (1970), 'Towards a theory of communicative competence', in Dreitzel, H.P. (ed.): Recent Sociology, No. 2, Macmillan, New York.

Habermas, J., (1971), Toward a Rational Society, Heinemann, London.

Habermas, J., (1974a), 'Rationalism divided in two', in Giddens, A.,(ed.): Positivism and Sociology, Heinemann, London.

Habermas, J., (1974b), Theory and Practice, Heinemmann, London.

Habermas, J., (1976), Legitimation Crisis, Heinemann, London.

Habermas, J., (1978), Knowledge and Human Interests (2nd edition), Heinemann, London.

Habermas, J., (1979), Communication and the Evolution of Society, Heinemann, London.

Halsey, A., (1972), Educational Priority. Vol. 1, HMSO, London.

Harris, T., (1973), I'm OK, You're OK, Pan Books, London.

Hegel, G., (1977), Phenomenology of Spirit, University Press, Oxford.

Heidegger, M., (1962), Being and Time, Blackwell, Oxford.

Heidegger, M., (1968), What is Called Thinking?, Harper and Row, New York.

Heidegger, M., (1971), Poetry, Language, Thought, Harper and Row, New York.

Holly, P., (1984), 'Action-research - a cautionary note', in Holly, P. and Whitehead, D. (eds.): Action-Research in Schools; Getting it into Perspective, Institute of Education, Cambridge.

Horney, K., (1962), Self Analysis, Routledge, London.

Husserl, E., (1965), Phenomenology and the Crisis of Philosophy, Harper and Row, New York.

Ingham, C., (1984), 'The role of teacher language, pupil language, and the relationship between the two in concept development and understanding', in Holly, P. and Whitehead, D. (eds.): Action-Research in Schools; Getting It into Perspective, Institute of Education, Cambridge.

Iser, W., (1978), The Act of Reading, Routledge, London.

Jenks, C., (1982), Introduction to Jenks, C. (ed.): The Sociology of Childhood, Batsford, London.

Josipovici, G., (1971), The World and the Book, Macmillan, London.

Jung, C., (1967), Memories, Dreams, Reflections, Collins/ Fontana, Glasgow.

Jung, C., (1977), Collected Works, Vol. 18, Routledge, London.

Kant, I., (1933), Critique of Pure Reason, Macmillan, London.

Kemmis, S., (1980), 'The imagination of the case and the invention of the study', in Simons, H. (ed.): Towards a Science of the Singular, University of East Anglia, Norwich.

Kirkegaard, S., (1966), The Concept of Irony, Collins, London.

Koestler, A., (1969), The Act of Creation, Hutchinson, London.

Krech, D. and Crutchfield, R., (1948), Theory and Problems of Social Psychology, McGraw Hill, New York.

Lacan, J., (1977), Ecrits, Tavistock, London.

Laclau, E., (1979), Politics and Ideology in Marxist Theory, Verso, London.

Larson, M., (1977), The Rise of Professionalism, University of California Press, Berkeley.

Lees, R., (1975), 'The action-research relationship', in Lees, R. and Smith, G. (eds): Action-Research in Community Development, Routledge, London.

Lenin, V., (1972), Collected Works, Vol. 38, Lawrence and Wishart, London.

Lewin, K., (1946), 'Action research and minority problems', in Journal of Social Issues, Vol. 2.

Lewin, K. and Grabbe P., (1945), 'Conduct, knowledge, and acceptance of new values', in Journal of Social Issues, Vol. 1.

Lévi-Strauss, C., (1966), The Savage Mind, Weidenfeld and and Nicholson, London.

Lévi-Strauss, C., (1972), Structural Anthropology, Penguin, Harmondsworth.

Lévi-Strauss, C, (1981), The Naked Man, Jonathan Cape, London.

Lippett, R., (1948), Training in Community Relations, Harper, New York.

Lukács, G., (1964), Realism in Our Time, Harper and Row, New York.

Marx, K. (1970), 'Theses on Feuerbach', in Marx, K. and Engels, F: The German Ideology, Lawrence and Wishart, London.

McCarney, J., (1979), 'The trouble with contradictions', in Radical Philosophy No. 23.

McDonald, B. and Walker, R., (1975), 'Case study and the social philosophy of educational research', in Cambridge Journal of Education, Vol. 5, No. 1.

McHugh, P. et al., (1974), On the Beginning of Social Inquiry, Routledge, London.

Midwinter, E., (1972), Priority Education, Penguin, Harmondsworth.

Mill, J.S., (1961), 'On Liberty', in Essential Works of John Stuart Mill, Bantam Books, New York.

Moser, H., (1978), Aktionsforschung als Kritische Theorie der Sozialwissenschaften, ('Action-research as a critical theory of the social sciences'), (2nd edition) Kosel-Verlag, Munich.

Mouffe, C., (1981), 'Hegemony and the integral state in Gramsci', in G. Bridges and R. Brunt (eds.): Silver Linings, Lawrence and Wishart, London.

Musgrave, A. and Lakatos, I., (eds.), (1970), Criticism and Growth of Knowledge, University Press, Cambridge.

Nixon, J., (1981a), Introduction to Nixon, J. (ed.): A Teachers Guide to Action-Research, Grant, London.

Nixon, J., (1981b), 'Towards a supportive framework for teachers in research', in Curriculum, Vol. 2, No. 1.

O'Neill, J., (1972), Sociology as a Skin Trade, Heinemann, London.

Parlett, M. and Hamilton, D., (1977), 'Evaluation as illumination', in Hamilton, D. et al. (eds.) Beyond the Numbers Game, Macmillan, London.

Parsons, T., (1951), The Social System, Routledge, London.

Parsons, T., (1954), 'The professions and social structure', in Essays in Social Structure, Collier-Macmillan, New York.

Parsons, T., (1968), The Structure of Social Action, The Free Press, New York.

Parsons, T., et al., (1962), Towards a General Theory of Action, Harper and Row, New York.

Phillipson, M.,(1975), 'Stratifying speech', in Sandywell, B. et al.: Problems of Reflexivity and Dialectics in Sociological Inquiry, Routledge, London.

Phillipson, M., (1981), 'Sociological practice and language', in Abrams, P. et al. (eds.): Practice and Progress - British Sociology 1950-80, Unwin, London.

Piaget, J., (1977), The Essential Piaget, Routledge, London.

Popper, K., (1963), Conjectures and Refutations, Routledge, London.

Ricoeur, P., (1981), 'Science and ideology', in Hermeneutics and the Social Sciences, University Press, Cambridge.

Rogers, C., (1983), Freedom to Learn for the 1980's, Bell and Howell, Columbus.

Rowland, S., (1983), Teachers Studying Children's Thinking, No. 2, Education Department, Leicestershire.

Sanford, N., (1976), 'Whatever happened to action-research?', in Clarke, A.: Experimenting with Organizational life - the Action-Research Approach, Plenum, London.

Sartre, J.P., (1969), Being and Nothingness, Methuen, London.

Saussure, F. de., (1974), Course in General Linguistics, Fontana, Glasgow.

Schatzman, L. and Strauss, A., (1973), Field Research - Strategies for a Natural Sociology, Prentice Hall, Englewood Cliffs.

Selznick, P., (1964), 'An approach to a theory of bureaucracy', in Coser, L. and Rosenberg, B. (eds.): Sociological Theory - a Book of Readings, (2nd edition) Collier-Macmillan, New York.

Silverman, D. and Torode, B., (1980)., The Material Word, Routledge, London.

Smith, G., (1975), 'Action-research: experimental social administration?', in Lees, R. and Smith, G. (eds.) Action-Research in Community Development, Heinemann, London.

Stake, R., (1980), 'The Case study in social inquiry', in Simons, H. (ed.): Towards a Science of the Singular, University of East Anglia, Norwich.

Stenhouse, L., (1975), An Introduction to Curriculum Research and Development, Heinemann, London.

Walker, R., (1977), 'Descriptive methodologies and utilitarian objectives: is a happy marriage possible?', in Norris,- N. (ed.): Theory in Practice, Centre for Applied Research in Education, University of East Anglia, Norwich.

Walker, R., (1980), 'The conduct of educational case studies - ethics, theory, and procedures', in Dockrell, W. and Hamilton, D. (eds.): Rethinking Educational Research, Hodder and Stoughton, Sevenoaks.

Walker, R., (1981), 'On the use of fiction in educational research', in Smetherham, D. (ed.): Practising Evaluation, Nafferton, Driffield.

Weber, M., (1964a), 'Types of authority', in Coser, L. and Rosenberg, B. (eds.): Sociological Theory - a Book of Readings (2nd edition), Collier-Macmillan, New York.

Weber, M., (1964b), 'Characteristics of bureaucracy', in Coser, L. and Rosenberg, B. (eds.): op. cit.

Weber, M., (1964c), 'Some consequences of bureaucratization', in Coser, L. and Rosenberg, B. (eds.): op. cit.

Weber, M., (1971), 'The definition of sociology, social action and social relationship', in Thompson, K. and Tunstall, J. (eds.): Sociological Perspectives, Penguin, Harmondsworth.

Whitehead, J. and Foster, D., (1984), 'Action-research and professional educational development', in Holly, P. and Whitehead D. (eds.): Action-Research in Schools - Getting It into Perspective, Institute of Education, Cambridge.

Wilkins, L., (1967), Social Policy, Action, and Research, Tavistock, London.

Winter, R., (1975), 'Literature and sociological theory', in Cambridge Journal of Education, Vol. 5, No. 1.

Winter, R., (1980a), 'Institutional research and institutional relationships - the methodological problem', in J. Elliott and D. Whitehead (eds.): The Theory and Practice of Educational Action-Research, Institute of Education, Cambridge.

Winter, R., (1980b), 'An attempt at self-evaluation research in a Faculty of Education'. Journal of Curriculum Studies, Vol. 12, No. 3.

Winter, R., (1980c), Perspective Documents on Teaching Practice, Educational Research Unit, Essex Institute of Education, Brentwood.

Winter, R., (1981) 'Social research as emancipatory discourse - the significance of the work of Jürgen Habermas', Occasional Paper No. 1, School of Education, Essex Institute of Higher Education, reprinted in P. Holly and D. Whitehead: Action-Research in Schools - Getting It Into Perspective, Institute of Education, 1984, Cambridge.

Winter, R., (1982a), 'Picking up the cues', in The Times Educational Supplement, March 19th.

Winter, R., (1982b), 'Dilemma Analysis - a contribution to methodology for action-research', in Cambridge Journal of Education, Vol. 12, No. 3.

Winter, R., (1986), 'Fictional-critical writing: an approach to case study research by practitioners', in Cambridge Journal of Education, Vol. 16, No. 3.

Young, M.F.D., (ed.), (1971), Knowledge and Control, Collier-MacMillan, London.

Zetterberg, H., (1962), Social Theory and Social Practice, The Bedminster Press, New York.

Author index